On the Way

The Teaching Church

Edited by Frederick R. Trost

Kirk House Publishers
Minneapolis, Minnesota

On the Way

The Teaching Church

Edited by Frederick R. Trost

Library of Congress Cataloging-in-Publication data

.On the way : the teaching church / edited by Frederick R. Trost.
    p. cm.

Includes bibliographic references
    ISBN-10: 1-886513-58-9 (trade paper : alk. paper)
    ISBN-13: 1-886513-58-9
  1. United Church of Christ—Teaching office. I. Trost, Frederick R.

BX9886.O5 2005

268 /. 85834 22

2005049296

CIP

Kirk House Publishers, PO Box 390759, Minneapolis, MN 55439

Manufactured in the United States of America

Table of Contents

Preface

In 1913, shortly before the outbreak of the First World War, Igor Stravinsky's famous "Rite of Spring" received its premier performance in Paris. The ballet attracted people from all over Europe and beyond. From the outset, the audience reacted to the music with excitement and dismay. The initial musical notes, sounded by solo bassoon, were greeted by angry shouts and ridicule. Amidst the passionate voices that arose from the audience were some who defended the music. The dissonance of the notes composed by Stravinsky, it is said, caused one listener to pound his fists upon the heads of those seated in front of him. Others began punching each other in the aisles. A duel was arranged between two complete strangers who were appalled and enchanted by the music. The well-known composer, Camille Saint-Saens, described Stravinsky as crazy while Maurice Ravel described him as a genius. Claude Debussy is reported to have urged everyone to calm down so that the music might be heard above the cacophonous stir. Meanwhile, Stravinsky was present backstage as the orchestra and the dancers nobly performed despite the clamor that had erupted in the concert hall. And so, the "Rite of Spring" was presented publiclyfor the first time and has since been judged by some to have been a crucial "turning point" in the art of the western world. (1)

Theology as the teaching of the Christian Church, with its many variations on the themes of the Incarnation and the life, death and resurrection of Jesus Christ, likewise takes place amidst the noise, fury and passions of its times. There are all kinds of responses to the gospel. The biblical story elicits reactions that can be knowledgeable, informed and courageous, but also foolish, mindless and without substance. Theology, if it is faithfully done in the shadow of the cross, takes place not solely in the tranquility of a seminary library or in a pastor's quiet study, but amidst the wounds and heartaches of these times. It occurs in a world in which the report of Jesus' birth breeds fear in the shepherds and causes Herod to mobilize his troops. Teaching the faith is accompanied by the fury of what takes place in the world around us; the tears of all the ages, and often the derision of those who feel compelled to dismiss truth claims about God and humanity as the wild imagining of those who allow themselves to be deceived. In such an environment, it is imperative that those who would perform the music of faith not lose sight of the score, even if it seems offbeat to the sensibilities of the times. Reflecting on Scripture sometimes finds the Church on its knees, both struggling with and compelled by the call to discipleship. Archbishop Oscar Romero, the "pastor of the poor," insisted that those who wish to teach and serve the gospel ought always have the Bible in front of them and their hands folded in prayer.

The great Swiss theologian Karl Barth never tired of emphasizing the intimate relationship in the teaching church between the biblical text, the prayers of the people, and the soundness of that which Christians proclaim. "Prayer without study would be empty. Study without prayer would be blind." Martin Luther held that the indispensable teachers of the Church are not the famous theologians whose books line the shelves of our libraries, but rather those who teach their children to say their prayers.

In autumn of 1982, in an attempt to enhance the teaching ministry of the Church and to encourage theological study and reflection, particularly among pastors and teachers serving in the life of the Wisconsin Conference of the United Church of Christ, the Conference began publishing a theological journal we called *On The Way*. The title of the journal reflects a belief that the Church has been, from the Day of Pentecost to the present, a community of pilgrims sent into the world as witnesses to the truth of God with us in Christ. The journal was conceived in the conviction that witnessing to God's truth is both astonishing and humbling and that it is the commission not only of the ordained, but of all who have been baptized into the death and resurrection of Jesus Christ.

The Church's pastors and teachers, we believed, have a critical task, to "equip the saints" for their life together and for public testimony in the world. As servants of the Word, called into communities of faith scattered across the earth, pastors and teachers are to go about their work in the sure and certain belief that, as Saint Paul put it, "in Christ God was reconciling the world to himself." (2 Corinthians 5:19, NRSV). We turned to both academic and pastoral theologians to help us with the journal and thus to challenge and encourage the thinking of those who were engaged in ordained service in our congregations. We published several companions to *On The Way*. One of these, *No Other Foundation*, was a booklet of exegesis and homiletics that appeared several times annually for nearly twenty years. It contained Bible studies crafted by seminary professors as well as sermons of working pastors, all based on the lectionary texts for the Church Year. Furthermore, in its commitment to "the teaching Church," the Conference created opportunities for theological dialogue in forums and discussions in which joyful and sincere theological work was practiced by the clergy. All of our efforts at the time emerged from a belief that word and deed are interdependent. Where the Church is authentically present in this world, the proclamation of the gospel and the grateful acts of faith belong together as a hand fits a glove.

The French writer and theologian, Pasquier Quesnel (1634-1719) wrote:

> To do nothing but study is to forget the ministry; not to read or study at all is to tempt God. To study only to glory in one's knowledge is a shameful vanity... But to store one's mind with the knowledge proper to the saints by study and by prayer, and to diffuse that knowledge in solid instructions and practical exhortations... is to be a prudent and laborious minister.

This book is composed, in part, of some of the original essays that appeared in our journal *On The Way*. Those essays appear here, along with several previously unpublished pieces, in affirmation of the vocation of the pastors and teachers of the Church and in order to encourage the effort of the one who would seek, by the grace of God, to be both a dedicated servant of the Word and "a prudent and laborious minister."

Luther's advice remains as contemporary today as it was when first given in the sixteenth century: Pastors and teachers ought not imagine they know everything there is to know but rather, guarding against all presumption, arrogance and carelessness, "daily exercise themselves in their studies and constantly apply them to practice,... persevering in reading, teaching, learning, thinking, meditating,..." remaining "hungry and thirsty" all their days, remembering that the Church of Jesus Christ is not built on our reason or strength but rather upon the grace of God that abounds above and beyond all we might think or imagine. In such manner, may the "teaching church" accept its vocation and go about its task as the saints have sought to do in the immediate past and throughout the ages.

Frederick R. Trost, Pastor
The Festival of Pentecost, 2005

(1) An account of this memorable performance of Stravinsky's "Rite of Spring" is given in a beautiful book by Patrick Kavanaugh entitled *The Spiritual Lives of Great Composers*, published by Sparrow Press, 1992.

Acknowledgments

I wish to express my deep thanks to the many faithful friends whose contributions to the theological integrity of the communion of saints sustained our journal and continue to stand as testimony not only to a vibrant faith, but just as importantly to the vitality of the teaching ministry, without which the Church is tempted to lose its way:

Walter Brueggemann, Professor of Old Testament and Academic Dean at Eden Theological Seminary in Webster Groves, Missouri, and William Marcellus McPheeters Professor of Old Testament at Columbia Theological Seminary in Decatur, Georgia.

+ Eugene Wehrli, Professor of New Testament and President of Eden Theological Seminary, Webster Groves, Missouri.

Paul L. Hammer, Professor of New Testament Interpretation at Colgate Rochester Divinity School, Rochester, New York.

Barbara Brown Zikmund, Professor of Church History at Chicago Theological Seminary, President of the Pacific School of Religion, Berkeley, California, and at Hartford Theological Seminary in Connecticut.

+ Reuben A. Sheares, II, pastor in the United Church of Christ and Executive Director of the United Church of Christ Office for Church Life and Leadership.

+ Louis H. Gunnemann, Professor of Practical Theology and Dean at Mission House Theological Seminary, Plymouth, Wisconsin, and Professor of Ministry Studies and Dean at United Theological Seminary, New Brighton, Minnesota.

Martha Ann Baumer, pastor in the United Church of Christ and Visiting Professor of Pastoral Studies at Eden Theological Seminary, Webster Groves, Missouri.

Ansley Coe Throckmorton, pastor in the United Church of Christ, Executive Vice President of the United Church of Christ Board for Homeland Ministries, and President of Bangor Theological Seminary, Bangor, Maine.

Susan Brooks Thistlethwaite, pastor in the United Church of Christ, theological professor and President of Chicago Theological Seminary, Chicago, Illinois.

M. Douglas Meeks, ordained minister in the United Methodist Church, Professor of Systematic Theology and Philosophy at Eden Theological Seminary, Webster Groves, Missouri, Professor and Academic Dean at Wesley Theological Seminary, Washington, DC, and Cal Turner Chancellor Professor of Theology and Wesleyan Studies at the Divinity School of Vanderbilt University in Nashville, Tennessee.

+ Frederick Herzog, Professor of Theology at Mission House Theological Seminary, Plymouth, Wisconsin, and at Duke University Divinity School, Durham, North Carolina.

Susanne Hein, a member of the Evangelical Church of the Union (Union of Evangelical Churches) in Germany, and an administrator in city government, Moers, Rhineland.

Hans Berthold, Professor and Dean of the *Pastoralkolleg*, (the Institute for Continuing Education and Pastoral Studies) of the Evangelical Church of Westphalia, Iserlohn/Schwerte, Germany.

Reinhard Ulrich, Professor of Religion and Philosophy at Lakeland College and in the Mission House Center for Theological Study at Plymouth, Wisconsin.

Hans-Juergen Abromeit, a member of the theological faculty at the *Pastoralkolleg,* (the Institute for Continuing Education and Pastoral Studies) of the Evangelical Church of Westphalia, Iserlohn/Schwerte, Germany, and Bishop of the Evangelical Church in Pomerania, Germany.

Dorothy C. Bass, church historian, author, and Professor at Chicago Theological Seminary, Chicago, Illinois; a member of the Evangelical Lutheran Church in America teaching at Valparaiso University in Indiana.

Lee C. Barrett, Professor of Theology at Lancaster Theological Seminary, Lancaster, Pennsylvania.

Richard L. Christensen, former missionary in Africa, Assistant Professor of Church History at Phillips Theological Seminary, Tulsa, Oklahoma, and Director of the Mission House Center for Theological Study at Lakeland College, Plymouth, Wisconsin.

Richard Stuckey Williams, pastor of the United Church of Christ serving in the Wisconsin Conference of the United Church of Christ.

Mark S. Burrows, Professor of Church History at Wesley Theological Seminary in Washington, DC, and Professor of the History of Christianity at Andover Newton Theological School, Newton Centre, Massachusetts.

Carl J. Rasmussen, member of the United Church of Christ; theologian, attorney, and managing partner with the Boardman Law Firm, Madison, Wisconsin.

Gabriel Fackre, Professor at Lancaster Theological Seminary, Lancaster, Pennsylvania, and Abbot Professor of Christian Theology Emeritus, Andover Newton Theological School, Newton Centre, Massachusetts.

Walter Brueggemann

Authority in the Church (Part I)

The Authority of Jesus

The theme of authority is a vexed one in our contemporary social setting. And our church participates fully in that vexation. Indeed, one can guess that it is *the* key question, both for a frightened world and for a weary church. We discover that as believers we are not immune to the problematic.

I

All around us, we are experiencing the collapse of conventional authority. We do not understand all of the reasons for this, but we need not doubt that it is happening. For good reason it makes us nervous. In my own setting, two simple examples suffice. On the one hand, within our local congregation, we are having some (heated) discussions over the prospect of an American flag in the sanctuary. It is perhaps a sign of the times that the question should even surface, for it bespeaks a mixing of authority systems. But even worse is the ground on which the issue is argued. It is hardly adequate ground to drive around churches in St. Louis and take a poll to see which churches do what.

Or on the other hand, in the civil community, our metropolitan community is under a court order about racial segregation, and the court order bites deep because it includes the suburban school districts. Now of course the issue of busing is inflammatory and disputed. But perhaps the most curious aspect is the public officials in the county and in the state—the ones who champion "law and order"—doing everything they can to erode the authority of the court to make such a decision. Of course it is not lost on such public officials that one can make a lot of political gain out of resistance to the court on this particular issue, but what an oddity that "law and order" folks should resist the court. It symbolizes the crisis of authority we are in.

So in the believing community and outside of it, we must decide how we shall respond to this crisis. In place of validated authority among us, civil or theological, we are tempted in two directions. On the one hand, we are tempted to substitute power (force) for authority. This is our temptation in the secular community. On large scale, more arms. Closer home, more police, but power is not a trade off for authority. And power is not easily translated into authority, because authority concerns legitimated power. And illegitimate power can never finally have authority. Lenski (*Power and Prestige*). comments on this problem and the ways of working at it. He quotes Edmund Burke:

> The use of force alone is but temporary. It may subdue for a moment; but it does not remove the necessity of subduing again: and a nation is not governed which is perpetually to be con-quered.

And then Lenski comments:

> Those who seize power by force find it advantageous to legiti-mize their rule once effective organized opposition is eliminated. Force can no longer continue to play the role it did. It can no longer function as the private resource of a special segment of the population.(51-52)

The recent events in Poland raise the question if brute force can be so readily legitimated as Lenski suggests.

Or we try to live unauthorized lives, lives that are not called, not summoned by anyone, not submitted to anyone. My judgment is that in our church tradition it is not the imposition of *false authority* as much as it is the seduction of *non-authority* that besets us. Through an ideological kind of psychology, the self is made into the ultimate authority that is no authority at all. And we do discern about ourselves as well as others, that lives that are not "missional", i.e., authorized beyond self, are lives without full and free identity. (See my comments, "Covenanting as Human Vocation," Interpretation 33, [1979], 115-129).

Examples of this abound and could be cited by any of us. A seminary student spends the summer in field education in the affluence of Aspen and Snowmass. The folks who come there come in keen expectation that this is the garden of paradise. Well, it may or may not be. But many come there and find it all an empty burden; just like the place they left. Lives that are not missional are lives without full and free identity. A middle judicatory of a church has an elaborate and intense planning process. While the world around us disintegrates, the planning process yields as a major goal "increased fellowship." The settlement is for a community turned in on itself. And the end result is a community without vitality or power.

We have lost our way. We have believed the ideology of self-fulfillment and self-actualization. And it makes the church tired, because we use up our energy on ourselves, posturing or dabbling in a host of things that remain un-assessed by our proper mission.

The problem of authority is a deep problem. It touches everyone. We are all seduced and domesticated by our modern world; a world that does not want to be serious about authority. It has been so long culturally since we have experienced real authority that we run either to false authority, and we find ourselves in the presence of *authoritarianism;* or we fear every authority, false and true, and we flee from it all and we end with *autonomy.* Most of us in more liberal traditions have our antennae out for every hint of authoritarianism. But we are less attentive to the alternative temptation to autonomy. (The twin seductions of authoritarianism and autonomy are well explored by Richard Sennett, *Authority* (New York: Knopf, 1980). In the latter mode we are de-legitimated, or, if you will, illegitimate. We cannot give a reason for our life, or for our faith, or for our hope.

II.

Now how we respond to that reality matters greatly. I make a response you would expect me to make. But I want to spend some time on that expected response in the church that may contain some unexpectedness within it.

We will not become clear about *authority* until we face the *author.* Our ministry, our common life in the church, our personal lives, cannot be sorted out until we ask about *the authority of Jesus.* We are agreed, are we not, that we have no authority of our own. We are not self-authorized. We have no ministry of our own except the ministry of Jesus. Indeed, we have no life of our own except the one daily given, for our daily comfort is that "we belong to our faithful Savior Jesus Christ."

But that is not a conclusion to the issue. It is rather a beginning of the consideration. We are engaged in a great argument now about the authority of Jesus. We are tempted to take a mechanical, scholastic, magical view of the authority of Jesus. By that I mean there are false teachers in the church, both liberal and conservative, who want to settle the question of the authority of Jesus on the terms of the world. And the outcome is authority *from above,* i.e., authority "like a God," who can make everything right, as though Jesus were the "Almighty Shell Answer Man." And if Jesus were like that, then we really can claim the whole game as Christians. We can claim a monopoly in our society and decide everything and judge every one and have it our way. Such a view of Jesus is very poor theology, but it is marvelous for establishing social monopoly and social control.

But that is idolatry, for the Jesus of biblical faith is not like that. We cannot presume Jesus. This is obvious from the very nature of the question we are asking. He will not be pigeon-holed, either with those who hold him high by the modes of the world, or by those who melt him away to some standard pattern of savior-hood.

So consider the authority of Jesus. My purpose is not to say something new, but to remind us of what we know best and tend to forget. To recall what we know about the authority of Jesus is important in its implications for our ministry and for our common life. The authority of Jesus is an abiding dispute in the church. The Gospel of Mark is essentially a dispute about the authority of Jesus. On the whole it is clear that throughout Mark, either

a) the authority of Jesus is *rejected,* or

b) the authority of Jesus is *accepted and wrongly understood.*

So I review with you now three texts concerning Jesus' authority.

III

The first text is Mark 1:21-28. Jesus has just called the first four disciples. He is in a hurry. He goes to the synagogue and teaches. We are not told in Mark, as in the other synoptics, what he teaches. But whatever it is, it disturbs and staggers. His listeners are astonished. It is because he has *authority.* And there is this marvelously revealing statement:

He taught as one who has authority, not as the scribes.

Scribes are not bad people. They are careful, clear, calculating, clear-headed. They have good memories. What they do well is to summarize and reiterate, again and again, what has been said and believed and practiced in the past. They speak what is known among us. They hold the world as a place closed and fixed and settled. Last week I talked on the phone to a student who had transferred to an eastern theological school. Nobody doubted it is a good school. He does not doubt it is a good school. That is why he transferred. And he is not sorry that he did. He said the folks are bright, work hard, teach well, think well, write well, are articulate. But they are *boring,* at least the ones he had met. Because for the scribes, all that remains to be done is to move the pieces around. Undoubtedly the world needs scribes. But scribes have never changed anything important; have never healed anybody. Above all, scribes have never made anything new. Because they believe everything is given that will be given.

And Jesus is an utter contrast. He is not a scribe. He does not reiterate or summarize. Nor does he speak in weariness or in anger. He does not castigate. But he speaks a new word that evokes a new reality that did not exist until he spoke it (cf. Romans 4:17). Jesus' authority is that he moves out of God's gift of newness that refuses to honor the old regularities of life. Beyond that, we cannot go. But this is enough for us. Our ministry, our lives, if we have a false Jesus, are likely to be scribal, and life becomes a tired, quarrelsome holding action.

The authority of Jesus is for shattering and for making new. We who are genuine evangelicals are not strident folk who believe that Jesus easily solves it all. Nor are we tired liberals who believe there is only us. But we are folks who touch close to the fountain of God where newness is given. That is what the church sees clearly and distinctively in Jesus of Nazareth. We scarcely know how to speak about it, as Mark did not know how to speak about it, but it dismisses all our usual categories for assessing authority.

IV

Mark 11:27-33 is our second text. One would think the folks in this chapter had not read chapter 1. Jesus just told his disciples about the power of faith to move mountains, i.e., to reshape the world. And the chief priests and scribes and elders who do not want the world reshaped ask him, "By what authority?" They ask. But it is clear they do not want an answer. That is how it is with us when we stand before the authority of Jesus. We want to ask, but we do not want an answer. We would rather dispute, to keep the game going. They only mean to trap Jesus. But Jesus is no fool. So he responds in kind. He will play their silly game with them. He asks them a question that they dare not answer. And so they shrewdly shut their mouths. And the conclusion comes easily to Jesus. "I won't tell you either." Jesus does not tell us about his authority.

The authority of Jesus is *inscrutable*. It must not be talked about too much. It will not be explained. It is pornographic to know too much about the sources of Jesus' power. The church loves to reflect on and dispute about his authority. On occasion we make a public spectacle of our dispute over that question. But here it is clear. His authority is not to be understood in conventional categories. It will not do to recite a creed, though creeds serve other purposes. They do not settle for us the authority question. They only announce a resolution that we have reached for the time. We should be suspicious of people who shout it too loudly and know too much.

I have a fellow pastor and friend in Missouri who regularly corresponds with me. In his heart, I suspect, he conducts heresy trials of me, though he has always treated me courteously. But I worry, because I think he knows too much about Jesus' authority. The problem for us is that Jesus' authority is not like that of the Pentagon or even a bureaucracy. It will not be quantified. He partakes of *holy hiddenness.*

Well, if it is not to be loudly asserted, what then?

First, the authority of Jesus is to be *discerned,* not proclaimed. (cf. Luke 7:22). John the Baptist asks the question of authority. And Jesus will not answer. He only points to the newness among the blind, the lame, the dead, the poor. His authority is discerned wherever there are inexplicable breaks toward humanness. The authority of Jesus is not abstract or theoretical. It is concrete and specific. So the church does not speculate. We tell stories. That is how the gospel first functions, as stories of Jesus' authority.

And the other way in which the authority of Jesus is known is that it is *practiced.* It is in the doing of his will of newness that we come to know his identity as the *author* of life. And those who do not practice in obedience do not know.

V

The third text we consider is Mark 15:36-39. Here the term authority is not used. But it is the agenda. It is a scene at the cross, in the solemn stillness after the failure. Jesus uttered a loud cry and died. The curtain of the temple is torn. The others are gone. Here is left only the Roman guard. And he says: "Truly this man was a son of God." How did he decide that? On what evidence? Mark mocks the church. In Mark, the disciples, i.e., the church, never rightly understand. And after the disciples had abandoned him in his death, this outsider of a soldier knows. The contrast is sharp. The disclosure of authority is not given where we would expect it. I submit Jesus' authority is known by the soldier because of Jesus' self-giving love. It is his self-giving that tears apart the old world and makes a new one possible. It is the embrace of death in a missional way. He does not save himself. It is this that discloses his real humanity, his profound divinity, his utter authority. The soldier sees clearly that his authority is not marked by his fullness, but by his emptiness (cf. Phil. 2:5-6).

So consider these three texts:

a) Jesus' authority is not given to maintain the old world, but to bring in a really new one.

b) Jesus' authority is not to be explained or disputed, but only discerned in the specific and practiced concreteness of caring. All the rest is inscrutable and we must leave it so.

c) Jesus' authority is discerned in his emptiness and not in his fullness. And that contradicts all our other categories of authority.

As I reflect on these claims, these observations seem important:

1) This notion of authority is against all our cultural notions. Authority in our culture wants to *maintain* the world like the scribes, not speak a new one; wants to *explain* the truth, like the Pharasees, not practice it.

2) This Jesus (who is newness, inscrutable and emptied) one would not expect to make a difference. And yet we make the confession that he is finally the only one who makes a difference.

3) It becomes clear that the Jesus question is urgent. We have to reopen the agenda among us, not about Jesus, but about our relation to this newness-giving, inscrutable, empty one. Do we really belong to this one? Do we really mean to shape our life and our ministry after him? Easy answers should not be offered.

(On The Way, Vol. 1, No. 2, Autumn 1982)

Walter Brueggemann

Authority in the Church (Part II)

The church has never much liked the authority of Jesus. It has always wished Jesus had some other kind of authority. We have preferred that Jesus be more like all the other Messiahs who prate about.

I

Very often the church has been busy fashioning an alternative, "*Ersatz Jesus*," more in keeping with the estimate we have of our own authority. The church has wished Jesus were more like the scribes; a little less newness, a little more moving of the pieces around. Less hoping, more managing. The church has wished that Jesus' authority were not so hidden in human concreteness. It is hidden there because that is the last place we expect to find it. If only that authority were a little clearer, a little more spectacular, a little more explainable, so that we could replicate it! The church has wished that Jesus' authority had more to do with fullness and less with emptiness. We would wish, in the words of Professor Higgins, that he "should be a little more like me."

It is written, right there in the center of Mark. Peter, who plays the role of the church in the Gospel of Mark, says that marvelous thing: "You are the Christ." You are the authorized, authorizing Messiah. And then Jesus punctures the whole thing by telling him what it means:

"You know it means I have to die."
"You know life comes through death."
"You know to be with me is to be vulnerable."

And right away Peter, i.e., the church, rejects the whole program. Embracing the authority of Jesus is rather like eating tomato aspic. It looks so good, so smooth, so red. And when you bite into it, it turns your teeth. And it tastes like nothing as much as tomato aspic. Well, we are like that in the church. We have got a whole plate full of the stuff in the person of Jesus. And it turns out not to be what it had seemed, or what we had hoped. And now, we have this topic before us, because we are deciding, re-deciding what to do about him.

The church has always flinched from the authority of Jesus, not because of what would happen to *him,* but because of the clear implication of what would happen to *us.* Because we are not stupid. Our struggle with the authority of Jesus is because we are aware of our destiny with him. The peculiar authority of Jesus bespeaks a peculiar future for the church.

It would be a little encouraging to be able to say that somewhere along the way the church went astray. Then we could hope for a recovery or a restoration. But Mark insists otherwise. The church did not at some late point in the process lose its way. It resisted and wrangled and quarreled from the beginning, from the moment of being formed as church and called as disciples. Because this Jesus, this tomato aspic set before us, is a fundamental affront in the world, even that part of the world that is the church. The conflict over the authority of Jesus is not because of a misunderstanding, but because of an understanding. It is a conflict in *principle.*

Now I say this for this reason: it is important for us to recognize that the crisis of authority we presently experience is not due to our peculiar cultural setting. It may be exacerbated by our circumstance. It may take a special form of problem because of that. But the problem is not *the oddity of culture.* It is because of *the scandal of Jesus.* And the problem for us as congregations, as pastors and bishops, as believing persons is that the scandal of Jesus sets our teeth on edge and our lives at risk. And we are confronted with a way of being authorized that feels to us like we are dangerously unauthorized. We would rather have a safer badge that the world will honor. So we push and pervert and accommodate. But nothing gives. Even in the very act of accommodating and wishing for something better, we know better.

We have this call to newness that requires us to act against all the scribal yearnings we have. We have his call to concrete acts of humaneness that requires us to resist all grandiose theoretical claims. We have this call to emptiness so that even centurians will take note, against all our lusting for fullness. The truth is, because of Jesus, the authority of the church is an insoluable crisis, and we make only provisional arrangements. So I remind you of some texts which you know very well.

II

The first text is Mark 6:7-13. Jesus sends out the twelve. This is the great missional assertion of the church in Mark. Jesus gives the church authority over unclean spirits. Now our eyes and ears have grown so conventional that we do not notice the staggering claim of this text:

1) The church is fully authorized by Jesus. There is no qualification, no explanation, no sharing with anyone else. This is it. The disciples leave with a massive and powerful mandate. They are given an unambiguous mission, to deal with *unclean spirits.* Now that leaves everything open for us, for we would all have our notions about what this means. But whatever it means, it is clear that this mission is not conventional, routine or trivial. For what scribe among us has battled an unclean spirit? Scribes do not take on unclean spirits, but at the most moths and cockroaches. Scribes have a way of organizing the world to pretend that there is no such category as unclean spirits. And we do not notice.

The church is Jesus' mode of assaulting the principalities and powers that beset the creation, that talk us out of our identity, that seduce us into alternative modes of living. Now I will not carry that very far, because the shape of that is different for each of us. But if any of you are defeated about the Christian life, take note. We are sponsored in the world to square off against the primordial powers of evil that beset us. Of course there is no agreement among us. But when we ask what it is that keeps us and folks like us from faithful, joyous, caring humanness, this may hint at the answer.

2) Note the mandated church is *to travel light,* without visible resources. Take nothing except a staff, sign of authority. That's all. Take no bread. Do not say what shall we eat or what shall we wear? No bag, no purse, no extra clothes. The power to cope with the *unclean spirits* depends on *being empty-handed.* The power to move against the rulers of this age depends on not playing by their rules.

I had a psychiatrist once tell me: "You only have so much energy. And all the energy one uses to defend self leaves that much less for the real action." Now I suspect that the matter of traveling light is difficult because we have not much faced the issue of unclean spirits. If we are to do lesser things, then this instruction is not so urgent. But we are called to do greater things. And so the instruction about traveling light looms large.

So I put the question to you, even as I myself do not want to think about it. Have you brought too much "stuff" along? And how could we as church be more resource-less? A writer in the "Christian Century" recently wrote that in main-line churches, most decisions are informed by what it would do to our pension plans. Of course. Did you bring a purse? A doctrine, a morality, a fear, an anger, a catechism, a liturgy? They render us powerless.

3) The text ends on a high note: *They did it!* They cast out the demons... perhaps militarism, consumerism, sexism, racism, ageism, rage that

has a death grip. Demons are cast out by people who are clear about their authority and who are therefore able to travel light. They anoint the sick. And they heal them. That is, they restore them to full functioning creatureliness. I almost didn't expect this verse in Mark, because the disciples are such a blundering, incompetent lot. And aren't we yet! But here, for an instant, even in Mark, they did it. They took the mandate. They went resource-less. And the gospel had its transforming way in the world through them. We might well hold close to that text for the tough days to come.

III

Our second text is Mark 10:35-45. Jesus has just told the disciples for the third time that he must go die. It is as though he kept repeating that point because he did not think they had caught on. And of course he was right. So they were on their way to Jerusalem, to the big show-down. They were so unsuspecting. They still did not see the shape of the confrontation. They did not see how scandalous Jesus is, how much opposition he evokes, how dangerous he is, and how risky it is to be with him. They seemed to think, as we always do, that somehow, we can make Jesus fit in so there won't be so much hostility.

They are on the way. Jesus hears this noise. And he asks, "What's the problem?" The response must have shattered Jesus. He became aware at this crucial moment. His closest friends had not a clue about his authority or theirs. They were discussing thrones! We were speculating about places for us in the new age. In yet another dispute, we were disputing in the categories of the old age, as though thrones had anything to do with evangelical authority in the new age. We were engaged in doing charades about the new age according to the hopes and fears of the old categories. The church tends to think of itself as succeeding by the old norms.

Jesus winces. He says, "You have missed the point. Our agenda on this journey is not thrones. It is cups to be drunk and baptisms to be faced. It is decisions about living and dying and martyrdom and risk and not setting out." And they say, "Well, we will do that." And Jesus, (tough, authorizing Jesus) says, "Okay, you get the cup, but I still won't guarantee a throne. Because a throne is not mine to give." I don't know about you, but I would only eat tomato aspic in order to get dessert. And Jesus assures his disciples, "I am not the one who gives dessert. I only administer the aspic."

And then Jesus makes his lordly announcement about authority. Finally he gets to the subject; the thing that most interests them (and us). It is as pertinent to us as if he had announced it this morning. The world thinks authority is to be in charge, to wheel and deal. And we are all seduced into that. But we are the ones who know another way of authority; to be a servant, slave of all. It's so simple, and so obvious and yet we find ways and ways to convolute. Jesus holds out to his church a way of authority that feels to us and to the world like being unauthorized. We are authorized to be servants in the world where servants never seem to have authority.

Now I think you are like me. You live in the tricky exchange of Mark 6:7-13 and 10:35-45. On the one hand we are clear that we are mandated against unclean spirits, ready to travel light, with visions of success. But that text is eroded in our common life by this other reality about thrones that override cups and baptisms. And our sense of authority is to be double-minded; to be empty-handed and yet to be like one of the great ones who lord it over. And so we struggle and put off deciding.

Well, of course we do. There will be no resolve of that issue in this world. But I would urge that we make this struggle a public agenda in the church. We need to be clear about the real issues. Because the real issue is not strategy or lack of resources. Our strategies and resources all wait for us to face the authority of Jesus that entrusts us with an odd authority. There is a waiting to see if there will be a time when the Roman centurion, the hard ruler of this age, will observe the feeble body of the church and say, "Truly this community is the body of Christ."

IV

A third text is Acts 3:1-10. You will observe that here I cheat. I had hoped to stay in Mark. But I have stepped outside Mark for the third text on the authority of the church. You know this text well, like the others. Peter and John (who together here are the church) see a lame beggar; a waiting, desperate world. The scribes are forever flipping dimes to them, because they only want to maintain the beggar, not transform the world. And Peter the bishop, the voice of the church says: "I don't have any silver or gold. I didn't bring my purse. We didn't make our budget. I am without resources, as I was commanded to be."

"But I did bring my authority." It is the authority for newness. It is the authority for a concrete act of humanness. It is authority that comes from emptiness, of being without silver and gold, without purse, without all the ways of power that this world credits. It is an authority in touch with the deep evangelical power that has been entrusted among us. It is the authority to evoke people to a new life that violates all old definitions of reality.

Peter's authorizing speech is an imperative that dares the beggar to enter the new age of well-being. And it is a verb (*peripatei*) uttered on behalf of the one who is not a scribe: "In the name of Jesus, walk." Now who could utter such a lordly word? Only the one who has no silver and gold. And all were amazed that the new age had come. (v. 10).

Now that story refutes much popular religion. The "electronic church" tends to suggest that people with more silver and gold will raise more beggars to new life. Don't believe it. The power of the new age is not grounded in our fullness, but in the emptiness of Jesus.

I do not speak an easy word to you about our authority. I do not myself find it an easy word. But it is a possibility. It is a promise given to us. It requires we quit trying to talk Jesus out of his vocation of suffering, as did Peter. It is remarkable that after Peter tried to talk Jesus out of his vocation of suffering (Mark 8:32-33), Peter nonetheless joins the vocation that heals in its emptiness. And we are called to that in a world that seduces us always into fullness. I cite these texts not that we beat ourselves in guilt. But rather that together we penetrate the issues and problems and possibilities that float around in our common life. We are the ones, the very ones, the urgent ones, who could give our life in ransom (Mark 10:45). It requires we leave off our endless chatter about thrones in the next age.

(*On The Way*, Vol. 1, No. 2, Autumn 1982)

Walter Brueggemann

Authority of the Pastoral Office

This third presentation was given for the installation of Robert Mutton as an Association Minister in the Wisconsin Conference. It is therefore articulated in terms of the office of bishop. I have left it so, because I believe the office of bishop is a crucial question in our church. But beyond that, some may find the comments more pertinent, if one thinks in terms of the pastoral office, i.e., the calling of every pastor of the church. In any case, I am glad to offer these comments in celebration of Robert Mutton, whose calling as a bishop I highly prize.

Everything has pointed to this moment today, the moment of installation. And I am glad to share in it, because I have been able to stay fairly close to Bob Mutton's pilgrimage. I have known him first as a rather spacy seminarian, and then as a swashbuckling youth minister. And this now is rather like "coming of age."

So the question I put today is this: what is it like to "make a bishop?" I hope you are not offended by that term, for that is what we are doing here. We avoid the term in our church, because of the ideology of freedom and autonomy in our culture. We avoid the term. But we do not escape the reality. And I am glad we do not, for the latter part of the New Testament affirms that the health of the church depends on the right kind of bishop. Now what I have to say in this moment is not unrelated to the discussions we have had earlier:

> The *authority of Christ,* authorized to newness, authorized to emptiness.

> The *authority of the church,* authorized to heal, authorized to travel light.

And only after we have talked about Christ and the whole church can we speak of the bishop, for the bishop receives his/her authority only from *Christ,* only by *way of the church.* All that we have said about the church is true of the bishop, called to travel light for the sake of newness, tempted as we all are to want a throne, to lord it over others.

So at the most I can pose a number of questions that are important, but should not be answered lightly or quickly:

What kind of bishop do you call Bob to be?

What kind of bishop are you able to be, Bob?

What kind of church is possible here that requires and permits a certain kind of bishop?

Because the bishop exists for the sake of the church's mission.

I think there is a growing awareness in our beloved church that bishops (i.e., especially ministers of Conferences and Associations) may necessarily be skillful managers, but they must do more than manage. Bishops must be caring pastors, but they must be more than pastors. I suggest that bishops have always been needed and authorized in the church in times of stress to guide the church to a faithful confession, to keep the church from selling out. My judgment is that we are in such a time in the church, much seduced by the world around us, seduced by a successful Jesus, by consumerism, by legalism, by permissiveness, by liberalism of an ideological kind. We join up with various parties. But none of that lets us be the church. It is the bishops' task to articulate the church's identity, to locate the mission, to reassert the calling, to draw lines and make distinctions, to identify resources and locate the ways of power and energy for our common ministry.

I have fixed on Ezekiel 34, which is a remarkable statement. I got to that text by the discovery that in v. 11—which we render, "I will search out my sheep" —the Greek has, "I will *episcopisonai*," i.e., "I will be a bishop among my people."

The text moves in two parts. First there is a sorry recital about the way this community has been exploited by false shepherds-kings-bishops:

You eat the fat.
You clothe yourselves with wool. You slaughter the fatlings, but you
don't feed the sheep.
The weak you have not strengthened.
The crippled you have not bound up.
The lost you have not sought.

You don't value the flock. You use the flock for your own well-being, for your own agenda. It is always a temptation, for all of us. But the church does not exist for us, for the leaders, for the bureaucrats, for the managers. It exists for the faithful flock, for the sake of the mission.

Ezekiel presents a sorry picture. It is a mess. The leadership has failed. So Ezekiel finds God saying:

I myself will search them out.
I will rescue.
I will bring them out.
I will gather them.
I will feed them.

It takes very little imagination to see the church is like *a scattered flock,* all over the map, no common shepherd, no single vision, no overriding purpose. And that has to do with the void of legitimate authority in a community too impressed with autonomy and authoritarianism.

But it need not be so. "I," God says, "I will be the bishop of Israel." And this is what a bishop, in the image of God, does:

I will make them lie down in safety.
I will seek the lost.
I will bring back the stray.
I will bind up the crippled.
I will strengthen the weak.
I will feed them in justice.

This awesome bishop will risk his life that the community may prosper. Now the caring of the bishop does not have to do with psychological strokes or even money. It first has to do with *nurture in evangelical faith of a radical kind.* That is how the flock is gathered, around the promises of God which matter in the ordering of our common life. Now Bob Mutton is not God. But today he is installed to continue the great tradition of "caring for the flock."

So Bob must be thinking about caring for the flock, not overwhelmed by too much program, but to focus on being a flock under the mandate of the Great Shepherd. So today let this church and this bishop consider what they are up to. Consider what kind of church it is called to be, and what kind of bishop it must have to be such a church. Certain kinds of bishops go with certain kinds of churches.

In Ezekiel 34, there is a *slovenly exploitative shepherd.* And that goes with a *scattered, hopeless flock.* Understand, I do not for a moment suggest bishops who have personally cheated the church. Rather it is when the bishop fails, the flock becomes encultureated and cannot be identified as the special flock.

But also in Ezekiel 34, it is promised that a caring bishop who exists for the sake of the flock can result in a community that is rescued, freed, strengthened and capable of justice.

Now this new bishop, envisioned by Ezekiel, is promised to be a new David. And a new David is known by us to be Jesus Christ, the new bishop of the church, a new shepherd of the flock. So we propose today to make a bishop whose eye is fixed on the one who loves the flock and who resolves to do what must be done, to lay down his life for the flock. The well-being and faithfulness and effectiveness of the flock depends on bishops who lay down their lives for the sake of the mission.

Now I observe three things about this possibility:

1) Bob is not asked today to be utterly used up, ragged, consumed by the church. We are not talking about a bishop whose life is laid down for all the daily agendas within the flock. Bob needs space for his own humanness and his own Christianity. But we are talking about the mode and substance of his leadership. His mode has to do with the emptiness that gives him power. His substance is to be fixed on Jesus who is our shepherd.

2) We do not propose something here for the bishop that is not proposed for the whole church. It is not only the bishop but the whole church which is to practice the laying down of life for the others. All of us have become strident and full and grasping in the church. We get so removed from the realities, as the Lord of the church never does. So this new bishop might permit this church to look freshly and dangerously at our common life. It is my judgment that the time comes soon for the faithful flock to be engaged in the laying down of life, a call which will not be screened out by either our ideological conservatism or our ideological liberalism.

3) I am not speaking about a facet of life to be added to everything else, but a fundamental refocus of the church. We have perhaps been too fascinated with the ways of the world, too lustful of power, too yearning for fullness. It has come to characterize us even across the great spectrum of our church.

And now. . . beginning again. Beginning in exile? Beginning at the null point? Beginning in reliance on the gospel? Beginning with some evangelical resolves that we do not fully trust. Beginning again as we always must, less encumbered, more resolved.

My hunch is that for our church, the times will grow more fearful. Scattered sheep and indulgent flocks will quit early. But ours is another possibility. And what we do in this service, this celebration of broken body and poured out blood, aims at that possibility—to visit in justice, seek out, find, rescue, gather. We could together be who we are not yet, by the mercy of God. A gathered church likely will be found only where there are lean bishops.

(*On The Way*. Vol. 1, No. 2. Autumn, 1982)

Eugene S. Wehrli

Scripture Alone: the Bible and the Church

The place of the Bible in the life of the Church has become a matter of concern and discussion. I assume that if the place of the Bible was self-evident to all, it would not occur to us to discuss it. Further, the authority in which the Bible is held by the Church is difficult to assess. It depends on commitments and values that have been shaped by culture, knowledge, understanding, faith, and the activity of the Holy Spirit. The contemporary area of questionings of the Bible's place are enumerated by James Barr (*The Bible and the Modern World*) as: relevance, communicability over a broad cultural gap, the limitation of a segment of history, and using Bible study as an evasion from dealing with what we believe and live for today.

"Scripture alone" has been the heart and focus of classic Protestantism. However, when that position was first affirmed there was little thought about the origin of biblical material or the process by which the materials had been transmitted. Today we are much aware of how the life, worship, teaching and needs of the early community shaped the materials of the Bible. No longer can its origin be thought of simply in terms of inspired individuals or content. Traditions of the past were continually reworked in new ways. The Bible is shaped by a process in the Church; it is the community's book.

I would like to begin then by developing two propositions: 1) The Bible has come out of the life of the Church—the Church creates the Bible and 2) the Bible alone can renew or transform the Church—the Bible creates the Church. These paradoxical statements raise the issue: if the Church produced the Bible in an historical process, how does the Bible gain authority over the Church and its history?

I. The Bible Has Come Out of the Life of the Church

Does the Church have authority to control the interpretation of the Bible because the Bible came out of its life? We need to examine first what lies behind this statement before we reach any conclusions.

The revelation of God focused in the person of Jesus and the result was a community of disciples gathered around his risen presence and under his lordship. Through the resurrection God created a new people. The resurrection created a church, not the Bible in any immediate way. The gift of the Holy Spirit was the empowering of that community to new life and mission either at Pentecost (Luke-Acts) or the resurrection (the rest of the New Testament). The authority of the Church, then, is focused in the resurrection of Jesus Christ and in the gift of the Spirit. This divine authority was experienced historically.

The canon of the New Testament did not exist formally for another 150-300 years and even the individual books were 20-60 years away from composition. Meanwhile the Church transmitted, shaped, and used the words and stories of Jesus and so in a profound way the Church was the human authorizing agent of the Bible.

Yet—just because the Bible was born out of the life of the Church as it sought to be faithful to the traditions of Jesus—it is not alien to the witness of the Church or the issues of life in the world. Before anything was recorded, preachers and teachers were relating the traditions to a changing world and to different cultures. We cannot speak of individual authors for much of the material, therefore. It was shaped and reshaped by the community as it sought to hear God's Word on the human scene. The Bible reflects the struggle of the community of faith as it sought to live by the light that had been given it.

A number of the traditions can be traced before they received written form. For example, the parable of the talents, according to Luke, explains why the *parousia* is delayed. The nobleman had to go into the far country to receive his kingdom. Then he would return for an accounting. In Matthew, at the climax of Jesus' eschatological speech, it is announced that the master is coming and that the accounting will be held soon. This is a parable of last judgment. Earlier in the oral tradition the parable had been given a general moral interpretation as its original specific focus had been lost. The moral was, "For to everyone who has, will more be given..." We can only guess at its original historic use when Jesus spoke it: he probably addressed public officials who safeguarded the purity of religion at the expense of failing to risk themselves in mission in the world. They took economic risks but failed to share the faith.

Here we see an example of how the tradition was preached to speak to the changing concerns and questions of the community over a span of sixty years. Early preachers were relevant and the tradition spoke to them in a lively way. The Church has carried the tradition and would seem to have authority and priority over it. The Church was continually interpreting and shaping the oral traditions in the light of its own proclamation of the gospel.

On the one hand, the present understanding of the Church's role in reshaping the tradition that issues in the Bible creates a problem for the authority of scripture; on the other hand, some tragic consequences occur when this living relationship between the Bible and the Church is lost or neglected. When this occurs:

a) Faith becomes conformity to a document. The Bible becomes a law book rather than a call to life under God. The Church suffers at the expense of the Bible.

b) Destructive consequences of individualism occur. The Bible is seen as the purveyor of the spiritual life of individuals. The Church loses its central place and even becomes unnecessary. The institution of the Church is considered a concession for those who like to organize, but ultimately it is religiously unessential.

c) The Bible becomes a book of practicality. It gives answers to life's problems. It can be used by conservative or liberal as a club to push their agendas. It is manipulated by special interests.

d) The Bible is read as a history book, giving us information about early times. It is accorded the same status and subject to the same investigation that is given all historical materials. It gives objective happenings of the past or even objective predictions of future events.

e) Where intimate relations between the Bible and the Church are lost, modern cultural values tend to predominate. Socially, that is likely to be individualism and practicality; intellectually—reason. Reason is the norm to which the Bible must conform. Rationalism dominates the glasses through which the life of the Church is viewed. Commitment in history is understood to violate the universal canons of reason and openness to all truth.

Impartial justice (blind justice) is affirmed rather than passionate justice. In enlightenment congregations it is embarrassing to have persons believe too much. The living relation to God is subsumed in impartiality, detachment, and objectivity.

II. The Bible Creates the Church

The question now is: if the Bible has come out of the life of the Church, does not the Church have the authority to say what the Bible means? The question is somewhat comparable to the ancient one: If Jesus was baptized by John the Baptist, is not John the Baptist greater than Jesus?

a) It is a fundamental fact, however, that the closer we understand the Bible to be to the earliest Church, shaped through an historical process that involves the whole community, the more we can affirm and understand that every period of rediscovery of the Bible is a revitalization and reforming of the Church. To rediscover biblical faith is to rediscover the heart of that which is life-creating for the community. Coming from the Church, in every subsequent age the Bible calls the Church back to that which is its heart and life.

The Bible provides at least two things for the Church. It points to that which is central in the Church's coming into being. It gives both the call and the claim that is laid on the Church by God. Secondly, it stands in critical distance from the Church of every other age. It is not captive to or a product of the culture of that age. It is not institutionalized or accommodated to social values. Consequently, it can communicate the Word of God in ways that call the Church to be renewed in accord with its roots and central identity. It can give a perspective that identifies the presence of God in history and calls for faith as a new and contemporary experience. Resurrection faith also enables the Bible to stand at some distance from its own age, judging both it and the Church. No book is harder, for example, upon the disciples; thus it clarifies its own misconceptions as they were early known.

Since the culture of the Bible is not the contemporary one, this creates a problem as well as a possibility. The problem is how we can hear the witness that is couched in cultural forms that are different from our own. In interpretation we may give false authority to a cultural setting in which the message is historically experienced, reflecting the Church's involvement in its own setting (like accepting the earth as historically flat or creation in seven days); or we may hear the words in the context of our own cultural usage, so that the real intent of their communication is obscured (as words like subordination, or resurrection of the body).

Historical biblical study helps us focus so that we can better hear the communication of the original author or the community's witness as it was intended. The most helpful exegesis is that done by persons who share the faith of the Church as their story, so they can fully hear and enter into the faith witness that the text is making, as people informed. Passion, not detachment, is most likely to catch what is really intended in the word of proclamation.

While historical criticism in the service of faith has been most helpful, it has also created the dilemma of expertise which tends to lessen the confidence of the laity in their ability to read and hear the Word. Further, historical criticism has also been tempted to declare its independence from faith in the name of scientific objectivity, the modern form of rationalism, and in doing such has been both manipulative of the text and unable fully to hear its faith affirmation. Instead of the text speaking to and shaping the interpreter, the interpreter has maintained mastery over the text. The shift has been from listening to control.

Rebellion on the part of the Church and the laity at this removal of the Bible from their hands is evident in the springing up of many biblically oriented groups outside of the main-line or established Church. While these groups may be acculturated in their own way because of lack of historical and critical orientation, nevertheless they are a legitimate protest against the loss of ability to hear the authoritative word of God through the biblical text.

b) A new literary approach to the Bible offers a possible new direction in the face of this dilemma. It treats the present state of the text as a whole, regardless of its history, and seeks to respond to it through its images, structure, movement, and verbal patterns and echoes. It seeks to allow the interpreter to be mastered by the passage, or the Word of God speaking through the reading, rather than to engage primarily in the analysis of the strands of the present state of the text. More authority is given to the present state of the canon, rather than the commonly implied assumption that the earliest form of the text is best. This takes the role and the work of the community in hearing the tradition seriously. Rather than scientific effort with its analysis, objectivity, facts and data subdividing the material into original pieces, it seeks to listen to the whole where the hearer is addressed. The key postures are now synthesis, pulling together, integration, opening up possibilities of seeing, and the communication of meaning. The fundamental question is not either, "What happened?" or "How was this transmitted?" but "What does it mean?" The canon as it stands is affirmed. Having been shaped by the history of the Church, it has the power now to recreate the Church by focusing it on the center of the faith.

Such a procedure allows Bible stories to work like cultural stories seeking to communicate meaning. For example, the story of the virgin birth has meaning before the historical question is asked, whether it is asked or not; whether it is answered or not.

c) There is another helpful contribution to the problem aspect of biblical interpretation due to the critical distance between the Bible and us—a distance that we have maintained and that gives it its creative, life shaping power for the Church in our age. It is the increasing stress on the liturgical mode as it relates to the Bible. More and more we are aware that many biblical materials have been shaped in the worship of the faith community. Baptism, for example, shapes not only large blocks of material in the New Testament but also gives the images by which the Christian life is formed ethically, as "put off" and "put on" the new person, "born anew," being "sealed," and "dying and rising with Christ." Or the confession, "Jesus is Lord," when every knee bows and tongue confesses, becomes the grounding and foundation for the new ethical life "in the Lord" and for the courage to deny lordship to Caesar. The New Testament has not only come out of the life of the Church, but out of the life of the Church at worship, gathered before God in praise and thanksgiving. The ethical catechisms are all rooted in worship and contain faith affirmations of baptism and thanksgiving.

Oppositely, the Bible provides the Church, in its liturgy, a unique language of its own. The liturgy functions as a mythic and symbolic integrating reality, giving meaning and shape to life. The biblical language and symbols give the liturgy, not just preaching, its unique life-giving power. A new reality, the kingdom is come, means a new language. In fundamental ways the new language shocks cultural language. The use of cultural language alone reduces all to what is humanly intelligible and nothing is said beyond the cultural perspective. Powerful liturgy is shaping because it uses the unique and symbolic language of the biblical faith. For example, the parables of Jesus weren't understood, yet they broke open the disciples' world.

This working of the liturgy parallels and even embodies what I was describing as the new literary approach of the Bible. What the scholars are discovering has been present to the Church and its laity always, though it must be confessed that our worship, too, has been overlaid with reason and intellectualism and has been short on story, drama, symbolic meaning, and therefore wholeness, the power to integrate life around meaning, and the opening of sight for new ways of seeing and ethical empowerment.

d) One additional concern may be in order here. Willi Marxsen observes that the New Testament reveals that there was more than one symbolic theology in the Early Church, more than one set of images; yet such differences never led the Church to question its unity. The tendency of the present Church to schism is also a sign of our moralism and rationalism that expresses itself in dogmatism and doctrinaire hardness. Such hardness defines Christianity intellectually and becomes schismatic from those who do not share the same doctrinal position.

The biblical community had both theological diversity and unquestioned unity because the heart of the faith was best pointed to symbolically by its theology. Its faith statement synthesized life and made it whole; its symbols (even as our cross on the altar) were essential minimums that opened up broad possibilities of meaning rather than closed off debate.

This is not to say that there were no limits to faithful thinking, but those limits were not defined as a fence that surrounded the faithful and shut people either in or out. The limits were those of centering, knowing where the center is and pointing to that. Instead of the fence, the image is that of the pole star. If you know where the pole star is you are not lost, no matter where you may be on the wide and fenceless sea. Or again, a circle is defined by the center, not by a tightly bounded circumference.

The Bible is confessional, affirming God's presence in history as it is shared in a community. It can only be understood from within, by persons seeking to live out from its center. Like prophets the scripture is from the community's life; it seeks to nurture the faithful community and ultimately to build it up. Its dynamic lies in its center, not in using it to draw boundaries!

I return to the theme of this section anew. Because the Bible came out of the Church's life—including that of dramatic liturgy, symbolic theology, literary wholeness, and the use of story and narrative—to relate the mighty acts of God in cross and resurrection, its witness has been able to call forth new life and power in the Church because it does communicate God in Christ, the center, in synthesizing, meaningful ways. It enables us to see anew, to see who's who and what's what in our distraught, alienated, and mistrusting world.

To be comparable in treatment of these two propositions, we finally need to ask, "what happens to the Church when the Bible is lost to the Church?"

1) The Church loses its life-giving center of power though it might still have the correct labels. It becomes both institutionalized and schismatic as, for example, the electronic church now demonstrates. Structures are maintained or even magnificently built up but they do not communicate the whole-making divine presence that transforms society. The language of faith is lost to the language of culture, of psychology, business, and sociology. Likewise, the clergy lose focus on their central vocation as pastors, liturgists, and teachers of the faith and think of themselves now primarily as counselors, managers, process leaders, and enablers.

2) The loss of center in our enlightenment or rationalistic culture means that we get dogmatic closures rather than life-giving theology. The result is alienation from one another in the community of faith. Faith becomes conformity to a doctrine, or a social ethical position to which one is loyal and all who do not maintain a similar stance are suspect in their Christianity. In the midst of our positions, the Bible may still be honored and its data known, but it is not expected to stand critically over and against us, calling us to change and be renewed by life-giving faith. Paul Minear observes that never has

Jesus Christ had a better press than today and never have his commands been taken less seriously.

3) When the Bible is lost to the Church, then the study of the Bible moves from faith thinking (the service of the community of faith) into the hands of the school and the university. Historical criticism, for example, became the work of the rational university, divorced from the life of the community of faith. The Bible was studied diligently but it was no longer understood as a witness to the faith of a living community. Phyllis Bird comments:

> America's first experience with critical biblical interpretation was over by the middle of the nineteenth century, dying without issue, it appeared, and without original contribution. The new study had been confined to a small circle, and it had been a German import into a domestic battle field, a weapon for theological combat rather than a root-stick for planting. Liberals, who had pioneered the study, had no use for it in the end, for it was easier to seek the single truth of reason and revelation through reasoned intuition and textual study. (*The Bible as the Church's Book*, 61)

As a rational discipline, historical criticism failed to deal with the Bible as the Church's book, and to the degree that the Church was enamored with the university model and its intellectual authority, the Church was led away from its own life-creating center.

As in much else, so in scripture, the whole is greater than the sum of its parts. So the Bible—communicated through the liturgy; through a literary approach that hears repetitions, themes, imagery, climaxes and movement like a symphony; through the narrative—helps to balance our own rational commitment. God cannot be expelled from history and nature by scientific objectivity or cause and effect. Our own commitment to knowledge will be inevitably enhanced, rather than a deceptive side path, when it is in the context of the community of faith and worship that we learn to think and study together.

III. Additional Issues

There are some additional issues that we will address briefly:

a) In our discussion of the relation of the Bible and the Church, where does God "fit in"? While I hope that the answer to this has been evident, nevertheless, I would like to focus on it for a moment. It is God who gives this relationship of Bible and Church its creative reality. The renewing power never belongs to the Bible but to the God whose presence and will is communicated through the witness of the Bible and who is the source of the life-giving character of scripture. The Bible communicates the life-giving power because it witnesses to that which created the life of the Church in the first place. The Bible witnesses to the faith that called the Church into being by the resurrection. Only God in Christ at the center gives the Church its being and its identity. The Bible is the fundamental expression of God's way with the Church. Its ultimate authority is that God authorized the Church and its witness. The "no people" have been made "God's people."

On the other hand, the Church's self witness is the Bible. God uses this witness to confront persons with the divine presence in the midst of the flow of history, giving it life and a meaning that is not inherent within the natural process itself. The Bible is the witness to the foundational events of salvation and new community, and this witness is necessary for the continuing reformation of the people born in that event. The Bible is the story of the Church's being born and has become the norm and the authority by which the calling and the life of the Church is continually judged, shaped, and focused.

Further, the Bible can only speak in this way when it is heard in openness to the Holy Spirit, God's own presence. The Holy Spirit enables the words to be heard and the images apprehended as the calling of God. Since the Holy Spirit is active in the new community, Bible study, if it is Spirit filled, is best done in the context of the community of faith. It is the community that can hear the Word through the Spirit and through which our private hearing is judged (1 Thessalonians. 5:20; 1 Corinthians 14:25ff) and also made possible. For this reason, I am a strong believer in group Bible study within the community of faith. The Spirit can be heard in the communion where the Holy Spirit is present and attended to. The Spirit in the community is the possibility of hearing.

Objective study in the school alone can never hear the word of the Lord. The Spirit, tested in the faith community, enables the scriptures to be heard in the spirit in which they were written. Individual and intellectual hearing is always tempted to be subjective, privatistic. So Paul wrote to the Thessalonian church, "do not quench the Spirit, do not despise prophecy, but test everything."

b) If the Spirit is still speaking in the Church today, why is the canon closed? The canon focuses on those realities that gave birth to the Church. It is not foreign or alien to the contemporary Church. The Church does need contemporary witness to the empowering presence of God. However, this witness is always called forth and tested by the primary testimony that the creative, birthing stage of the Church experienced. Root (foundational) events help us to distinguish the Holy Spirit from other spirits today. Therefore, the canon will always be the witness to the central creative event and continue to be God's means of renewing and recreating the event in other times and places. Every sermon takes the scripture and seeks to let it speak today. The sermon may be the life-creating reality where God chooses to use it. Nevertheless, the sermon is secondary to the scripture that it discloses, and next time in a new environment and situation, the new sermon will not reinterpret the old sermon, but will seek to hear and share the same text that speaks so powerfully. Each sermon and each person ultimately seeks to witness to the One who is encountered in the primary witness.

c) I understand the canon to be essential in the Church's history, not in order to fight heresy, but because it is the positive communicator of God's love affair with the Church in history. An historical faith needs an historical focus. The incarnation necessitates not only a community of faith but also from the first moment that community has a structure, an explicated faith— a creed; so a faith that finds God in life and community, inevitably from the first moment is bound to shape a witness that communicates the faith and to identify the witness that sustains the communication of God's Word. That is the canon. Only rationalism can assume that there was an original time when there was no structure, no credo, no defined leadership, no incipient testimony of faith that is the canonical process.

A mystical religion that is either abstractly intellectual or otherworldly demands movement from the structures of historical life and society into deep inwardness where all that is called "external" vanishes. Such a religion has no need for, indeed no ultimate use for, a canon at all. At best holy writings have to be abandoned and left behind in order to encounter the deity in inwardness. At worst, too many writings or too much love for them become an additional enslavement and a hindrance to spiritual inwardness.

The Church needs a canon, not only for its witness to God in history where things always have body and shape and are never formless, but also for the sharing of the faith with each new generation in Christian education and for testing the cultural values that might enslave. Because the Church must be involved in society, it is always tempted to get enmeshed in the culture of the society.

The same can be said about the selection of the canon that we have said about the Bible. The canon, too, comes out of the life of the Church; it was not externally chosen or arbitrarily set. Those individual works made the canon that nourished the Church and communicated the living God. Those books made it that were more than edifying; they were life giving. The heart of the earliest canon was the four gospels and the letters of Paul. The new scholarly discovery that a gospel, like John, not only discusses the faith, but communicates it and calls it forth is presented as a breakthrough.

The Church has known that all along. That is why the book is in the canon; that is why it is read!

Canonical books were so productive in the life and faith of the community that there was never even any real debate about the core books. They were so well established in the community's use that they were the Church's book before the Church became self-conscious enough to have its canonical discussion. Out of that confidence the Church today can recover its heritage of faith and hear God's Word in the contemporary setting. These are the witnesses that serve the community of faith in its worship language, in its education, and give it identity in a world of alien systems of faith and alien ways of creating contact and interaction among persons and society.

(*On The Way*, Vol. 2, No. 2, Winter 1984)

Paul L. Hammer

Biblical Authority:
the Cross and Resurrection in Scripture

How shall we understand the authority of the Bible? With these writings from a thousand years of Hebrew and Christian history as the scriptural canon or "measuring stick," how do they serve as canon in the actual life of the church? In what ways are they canon or norm or standard?

I would like to suggest that they serve as canon in at least three ways. First, they serve as canon in terms of their *content.* These witnesses of the multiple writers point to the richness of what God has been doing, is doing, and will do, as well as to the faithfulness and faithlessness of human response to God, especially in Israel and the church.

Second, they serve as canon in terms of *process.* This points to the living God at work in new ways as history unfolds. The biblical writings witness to an ongoing interpretive work of God's Holy Spirit. Though rooted in the past, that interpretive work does not simply repeat the past nor get locked into it. The biblical writings themselves are powerful witnesses of that process and of the God who is doing new things.

Third, they serve as canon in terms of *scripture reshaping scripture.* Later writings reshape earlier ones, even challenge them, to meet the needs of new situations in an unfolding history. Jesus himself did this in Matthew's witness: "You have heard that it was said to those of ancient times,... But I say to you..." (Matthew 5:21-22)

Any serious study of the four gospels clearly indicates that in their witness to the story of Jesus (though they have some elements in common), Matthew is not Mark, and Luke is not Matthew, and John is not Luke. Each arises out of the needs of their particular audiences and they shape and reshape the story to meet those needs. Any lumping of them mars the unique witness of each gospel and the continuing work of God's Holy Spirit.

I have just completed a five-Sunday Evening Lenten Series on "The Cross and Resurrection in Paul's Letters and the Four Gospels." We spent the first evening on Paul's "undisputed" letters (those seven which many scholars see as written during Paul's life, largely after 50 C.E. Others, written in Paul's name to meet new situations, came later). We then devoted one evening each to Mark, Matthew, Luke, and John.

A handout included, first, two pages of some major texts from Paul on the Cross and Resurrection, and then twenty pages copied from Aland's *Synopsis of the Four Gospels* for comparative study. We started with "Jesus Mocked by the Soldiers" and continued through "The Resurrection" texts. For many in the group it was the first time they had experienced such a synopsis. Some wondered why they had not been exposed to this earlier in their churches.

Obviously we cannot include here all that happened over those five weeks, but let me point to a few highlights. In Paul's letters there are no stories of Jesus' suffering and crucifixion, but Paul writes to the Corinthians, "For I decided to know nothing among you except Jesus Christ, and him crucified." (1 Corinthians 2:2) Later he writes, "and if Christ has not been raised, then our proclamation has been in vain and your faith has been in vain. But in fact Christ has been raised from the dead." (1 Corinthians 15:19-20) For Paul, the risen body of Jesus is no longer flesh and blood (1 Corinthians 15:50): "It is sown a physical body, it is raised a spiritual body." (1 Corinthians 15:44)

For Paul, the heart of the gospel is the love of God in the cross and the power of God for new life in the resurrection. To listen to this is to experience the authority of the Bible.

There are so many significant differences among the four gospels, as well as of course some common elements. This demonstrates that there can be no simplistic understanding of authority. Each gospel needs to be allowed to make its own proclamation without trying to harmonize it with the others. There are rough edges that do not fit into a single neat package. But for me, it is precisely those rough edges that ring with authenticity and authority. They reflect the rough edges of human life itself. If everything fit into a single neat package, for me it would be a highly suspect, "put up job."

Here we can look only at a few examples. We shall explore the seven words of Jesus from the cross. Mark and Matthew, following Mark, have only one, "My God, my God, why hast thou forsaken me?" (Mark15:34; Matthew 27:46), though Matthew changes the Aramaic *Eloi* to the Hebrew *Eli,* given his more focused concern for the Hebrew scriptures, in this instance, Psalm 22.

Why this word of Jesus from the cross in Mark? It may be that the suffering and persecuted situation of Mark's audience, around 70 C.E., caused them to utter similar cries. For them to hear this cry of Jesus in

Mark, let them know that Jesus himself had known the feeling of being forsaken also, and he was with them in their despair.

When we turn to Luke, we find three different words of Jesus from the cross. One is his prayer for his Roman crucifiers, "Father, forgive them; for they know not what they do." (Luke 23:34) The second is his word to one of the robbers, "Truly, I say to you, today you will be with me in Paradise." (Luke 23:43) The third is his final word, "Father, into thy hands I commit my spirit." (Luke 23:46) All of these are unique to Luke's Gospel.

Given Luke's proclamation of Jesus' coming as "good news of great joy for all people," (Luke. 2:10) Jesus' prayer of forgiveness, even for the Romans who killed him, was part of that good news. Luke wants to create a climate in the Empire toward the end of the first century, not of enmity toward the Romans, but of good news for them, too.

Luke's overwhelming concern for those excluded by society and by the religious establishment throughout his Gospel comes through here on the cross as well. Jesus promises a guilty robber inclusion in God's Paradise.

Most scholars think that Luke knew Mark's Gospel. Why did he not include "My God, my God, why hast thou forsaken me?" Perhaps that word was too much for Luke. Jesus, forsaken by God? No! And instead of quoting Mark's word from Psalm 22, Luke brings a word from Psalm 31, "Father, into thy hands I commit my spirit."

Which is it? Both are it! Both are authoritative, each *in its own context,* the one in Mark, the other in Luke. We do not have to try to harmonize them. We simply have to listen to the message that comes through each one.

When we turn to John, we have still three different words from the cross. The first is the word pertaining to Jesus' mother, "Woman, behold your son!" and to the beloved disciple, "Behold, your mother!" (John 19:26-27) Among the gospels, only in John are Jesus' mother and a disciple at the cross. Neither Jesus' mother nor the beloved disciple is ever named (i.e. nowhere in this gospel is the beloved disciple called John nor is Jesus' mother called Mary).

Given the highly symbolic character of so much in this Gospel, some have suggested that Jesus' mother may be a symbol for the community (as is Lady Zion in the Old Testament) and the beloved disciple a symbol for the individual Christian. Of course, the text can point also to Jesus' care for his mother as he is about to die.

The second word is, "I thirst." (John 19:28) Such a word ties into an Old Testament text (Psalm 69:21) and links Jesus with the thirst of those who had suffered in Israel's history. It also points to the real humanity of

Jesus in the face of those who said that he only "seemed" to suffer. They were called Docetists ("Seemers"), but this Gospel affirms fully that "the word became flesh and lived among us." (John 1:14) Yet, the very one who thirsts is the one who gives living water. (John 4:10)

The third word from the cross in John is, "It is finished." (John 19:30) What is it that is finished? It is the love of God that now has gone all the way, even into death. The word, "God so loved the world that he gave his only Son," (John. 3:16) has reached its climax. This Gospel can speak of the cross as a "lifting up" (John 3:14; 8:28; 12:34), but it points to more than simply the physical lifting up. It points also to his being lifted up to reign over the world. What is it ultimately that reigns over this world? It is the self-giving love of God, expressed in all its depths in the cross of Christ. Only John's Gospel brings us the piercing of Jesus. (John 19:31-37) There we find that blood and water flow from Jesus' side. For this Gospel, blood points to the flowing love of God in Jesus' death, and water points to the new life that flows with that love. Biblical authority works authentically when we let each writer's witness to the cross engage, nourish, guide, and challenge us in our lives and in the church.

When we turn to the section on "The Resurrection" in the four gospels, again we note significant differences, as well as common elements. Unlike Paul's letters in the first generation of Christians (who make no reference to it), all four of the gospels have empty tomb narratives, though the details differ and reveal again an interpretive process at work. In these second generation Christian writings, there appears to be a greater need to point to the continuity between the person of the earthly Jesus and the person of the risen Lord. The empty tomb stories are powerful witnesses that the One whom God raised from the dead is indeed Jesus of Nazareth, however one may understand the form of the risen Lord (which, as we saw, Paul defined as a "spiritual body").

In terms of the resurrection appearances of Jesus, each gospel is unique. There are none in Mark (Mark 16:9-20 clearly is a later addition to Mark), two different ones each in Matthew and Luke, and three in John (plus one in the John 21 appendix). It is significant to note how, as the interpretive process continues, the witness to Jesus keeps expanding on both ends.

Mark goes back only as far as Jesus' baptism, Matthew and Luke to his birth (each in his own way), and John to "In the beginning." On the other end, the resurrection appearances expand from none in Mark to four in John. Again, there can be no simplistic understanding of biblical authority. It is an authority that demands a listening to each of the gospels and letting each of their messages engage us.

We cannot pursue here all of the distinctive differences among the gospels in their witness to Jesus' resurrection, but let us explore a few examples. All of the gospels point to the witness of women (though the names differ in part). The one name that occurs in all of them is Mary Magdalene. In a most moving story, unique to John's Gospel, she is the only woman in the resurrection stories (John 20:1-18) and she becomes the person whom the risen Jesus commissions to go and tell his disciples. In a patriarchal society, it is striking that in this gospel Jesus sends forth two women as the first "apostles" (ones "sent with a commission"): the Samaritan woman in John 4 and Mary Magdalene here.

In all of the gospels the women are told by either a young man (Mark) or an angel (Matthew) or two men (Luke) to go and tell the disciples, but note the differences. In Mark, "they went out and fled from the tomb; for trembling and astonishment had come upon them; and they said nothing to any one, for they were afraid." (Mark 16:8) Is this any way to end a gospel? Some early Christians did not think so and later added Mark 16:9-20. Yet, we may ask whether a first and appropriate reaction to the astonishing resurrection of Jesus might not be silence, especially for Mark's suffering and persecuted hearers. The resurrection of Jesus did not immediately turn their lives into joy.

But for Matthew, Mark's ending did not fit his message for his hearers. He wrote instead, "So they departed quickly from the tomb with fear and great joy, and ran to tell his disciples." (Matthew 28:8) In Luke, the women "told this to the apostles (for Luke, only the twelve are "apostles"); but these words seemed to them an idle tale and they did not believe them." (Luke 24:11) Jesus' male disciples did not believe the witness of the women in a society where it had no credibility. Yet for Luke the witness of women finally prevailed. (see Luke 24:22-24)

There is so much more in the various and unique stories of Jesus' resurrection appearances, but perhaps this is enough to show the variety of the four gospels. To let each of them speak their messages, without any attempt at harmonizing them, is to let the Bible be authoritative canon in terms of content, of process, and of scripture reshaping scripture, for the sake of different audiences in the ongoing interpretative work of the Holy Spirit. And may the work of interpreting scripture lead finally, as it did for the Emmaus Road disciples, to heartburn. (Luke 24:32)

(This essay originally appeared as a monograph. Undated, it was projected for On The Way *in an issue planned for 1997-98. This issue of the journal, however, remained unpublished.)*

Barbara Brown Zikmund

Entrusted to Us: The Ministry of Reconciliation

When I was growing up I was sure that I would never be a historian. For you see, my father was a historian. Whenever we went on a trip we learned about those who had traveled that way before. When there was a roadside sign that said, "historical marker," we stopped. We visited reconstructed forts, restored mansions, historical dramas, cemeteries and many, many museums. We followed the Oregon Trail west and the Underground Railway south. We were always researching place names. I remember my delight when I discovered that Novi, Michigan was really stop number six on the inter-urban line heading north out of Detroit. My father was a museum director and he was fond of saying, "Good history is never flat."

We are gathered here to celebrate the history of the United Church of Christ, in this part of the world known as Wisconsin, and in the wider national context. A quotable UCC writer, Oliver Powell, has called the United Church of Christ "a beautiful, heady, exasperating mix." He wrote, some ten years ago, "The United Church tradition is an especially rich slice of Protestant history. It is the story of risky adventures of faith. It is mission. It is a particular style of church life and government." (A.D., September, 1975).

Powell, and many others, have pointed out that we understand ourselves as "God's people." A people is a body of persons "who share a distinct and common style of living, thinking, and acting that sets them apart from others. At times it may even alienate them from others. They own a common history. They share common memories. They have a collection of familiar stories to tell, songs to sing, precious symbols to gather around, defeats to mourn, and victories to celebrate." (A.D., September, 1975, 40).

What is our common history? How can we share our memories? On anniversaries, such as this one, it is appropriate to try to answer these questions. I propose to move quickly through our history to share some of my own memories. After all, the history of the Church is only vital when it becomes someone's history. As long as the memories stay locked up in documents and events of the past they are unable to bind us together as a people. When they are shared, the stories released give character to our common life.

The United Church of Christ was officially constituted the year I graduated from a large urban high school in Detroit. I knew about the *Basis of Union* and the various controversies that had swirled around its birth, but I had no idea that I would come to find its history so fascinating.

In this address I have decided to tell you about my pilgrimage through "UCC land." These are some of the things that I have discovered about our church. In one sense, what I am about to do is superficial. Scholarly historians will wince at some of the generalizations that follow. But, for most of you this presentation will do two things: First, you will learn some things about UCC history. Second, I hope that you will be inspired to name some of the important things about the United Church of Christ that you have discovered.

Let me go back to Detroit, Michigan. As I was growing up my parents were Presbyterians. During my high school years, however, the church in the neighborhood where all of the teenagers went was Mayflower Congregational Church. It was a big congregation, about 1500 members in the 1950's. Its youth choirs, youth camp and Pilgrim Fellowship drew teenagers from a wide area. My parents wanted me involved in church and my historian father believed that the Congregationalists were practically cousins of the Presbyterians and so my parents changed their church membership. Eventually I joined Mayflower Congregational Church.

So it was that I began my life in the United Church of Christ with a strong dose of Congregationalism. Some very fundamental principles in the UCC come from that tradition. Here, as with all of the other traditions I want to explore, I will name five important insights. What are the legacies we draw from Congregationalism?

1) The Church is the Gathered Community of Believers.

This principle is fundamental to Congregationalism. The church is not a building. The church is not an organization; it is not a Synod or a Conference. The church is not its leadership; the pastor, the clergy in general, or the pope. The church is first and foremost the gathered community of believers. It exists when believing Christians come together to be God's people. It does not require state establishment, or even ordained leaders in order to be the church.

2) The Church is Bound Together in Covenant.

Congregationalism embraces the covenant theology of the 16th century Reformation in special ways. Covenant theology speaks of God's covenant with God's people. And the covenant is the means whereby believers are united in the church. The covenant is like the twine that binds together a bundle of arrows. One arrow can be broken. But when bound together each strengthens the other. The *Salem Covenant* of 1629 captures the essence of covenant ecclesiology:

> We covenant with the Lord and with an other and doe bynd our selves in the presence of God, to walke together in all his waies, according as he is pleased to reveale himself unto us in his blessed word of truth.

Every Congregational church is constituted by some form of church covenant.

3) The Church is Under the Headship of Christ.

This understanding of Congregationalism is sometimes forgotten in its zeal to uphold the principle that the church is a covenanted people. But, the government of the church is not a democracy. It is not free to do what the majority wills. That would be "mob rule." As early Congregationalists put it, "The church needs to respect the crown rights of the redeemer." The people are called to gather, act and decide under Christ. This is why in Congregationalism there is no such thing as a "proxy vote," or an "absentee ballot." When the church gathers, the Holy Spirit informs its life. As one Puritan writer put it, "It chooses not those it wants, but those whom Christ has fitted." Decisions cannot be made until Christ is in our midst. This is why we do not instruct our delegates to General Synod how they should vote. Rather, we trust that they will be the Church of Jesus Christ in that place.

One other thing needs to be said about this Congregational view of the church as the gathered community of believers in covenant with each other under the headship of Christ. That is, the church lives in its worship in its meetings. In fact, in Congregational thinking there is no division between worship and congregational meetings. One flows into the other, each builds the common life. With our management mentality we may want to shorten and even cancel "congregational meetings" because there is no business, or we may think that the agenda is complete. In Congregationalism, however, there is always the business of meeting to strengthen the life of the church. It is no accident that those churches that dot the landscape of New England were called "meetinghouses."

4) The Church should be Free of Political Control.

Congregationalism made an important contribution to the history of the world. In much of history people have assumed that religious commitment and political loyalty had to be combined. Even early Congregationalism, as

it sought freedom from the state Church of England, assumed the intercon-
nection. New England Congregationalists shaped a "church-state" in their
efforts to escape from a "state-church." But eventually Congregationalists
realized that the only way to keep the church free from political control was
to guarantee separation of church and state. Out of Congregational zeal for
ecclesiastical freedom came political protection for voluntary church bodies.
For Congregationalism, political forces were always important and the church
needed to be free to support and to critique the powers and principalities.

5) Churches Have Obligations to Other Churches.

Congregationalists like to celebrate the unique independence of local
churches, but the reality of our history is that Congregationalism knows that
isolated churches perish. From the earliest years Congregational churches
came together in councils, consociations, and synods. They regulated and
disciplined leadership. They shared mission projects. They clarified their
thinking about faith and practice. They were always careful to protect local
autonomy against what some called *Presbyterianizing* tendencies, but they
felt strong moral obligations to the wider church. Congregationalism has
been very connectional throughout its history; but it has always been
especially reluctant to formalize those connections.

Here then are five contributions to my understanding of the United
Church of Christ drawn from my Congregational roots. I left Detroit and
went off to Beloit College, here in Wisconsin, a school grounded in Congregational values and history. I decided after college to go to seminary, and
because I was married at the end of my Beloit education, my husband and
I looked for graduate schools where he could do an advanced degree work
in political science, and I could go to seminary. We also thought that it would
be good to go to school in another part of the country.

To make a long story short, we ended up at Duke University in Durham,
North Carolina. When we looked around to see where we might go to
church there were few options. So it was that in 1961 we joined the
Congregational-Christian Church of Durham, North Carolina. We soon
discovered that this congregation had originally been part of the Christian
denomination.

Remember the Christians? They were a small group of churches that
merged with the Congregationalists in the 1930's to form the National Council
of Congregational Christian Churches. Most of us know very little about
these Christian churches, yet they are a very important corner of our UCC
history. They grew up in the revivalism and religious enthusiasm of nineteenth
century America. It is easy to choose five important principles from the

Christian legacy, because quite early in their history the "Christians" formally agreed on certain principles fundamental to their understanding of the Church:

1) Christ is the only head of the Church. The important word here is "only." These Christians were independent folk. They were enamored and energized by the new democratic spirit in America. They resolved not to get caught in the old hierarchical habits of church history. In the 1790's James O'Kelly was a leader of a group known as "Republican Methodists." They were the product of the Wesleyan revivals, which swept Virginia and North Carolina in the mid-eighteenth century. However, when Francis Asbury began organizing American Methodism and made the decision to consecrate bishops, O'Kelly and his friends had enough. They were for "republican" principles and they had no patience with hierarchy. Christ was the only head of the church.

2) Churches should look to Holy Scripture as the only rule of faith and practice. All of the historical traditions that inform our history are biblically serious. It was the Christian group, however, that carried this commitment out, almost to a fault. On the North American frontier, the assumptions and definitions of theology and ecclesiology that had flourished in Europe for years seemed absurd to them. Patriotic Americans wanted to get back to basics, to pare down all the trappings of church life to essentials. They wanted to restore the church to its original purity and build a new church in the new nation. In many ways they were not unlike the Chinese Christians today who refuse to let the weight of Church history shape their contemporary commitment to the gospel. This devotion to the Bible degenerated to Biblical literalism at points, but our Christian heritage reminds the United Church of Christ that we must keep the Bible central.

3) Church membership is dependent upon Christian character. The Christians were very practical people. They were unimpressed with dogmatic theological formulations and they were very suspicious of creeds. They looked with skepticism at the trappings of established religion in England and in New England. William T. Scott, Sr., historian of the southern Christian churches points out how they believed with common sense that the community could tell when persons ought to be admitted to church membership by the way they lived their lives, not by what they confessed. A radical understanding of church emerged - - "a spiritual democracy, a religious brotherhood, a Christian fellowship." This concern with how we live our lives, and not just what we believe, is an important legacy from the Christians.

4) Churches must preserve the right of private judgment and liberty of conscience. The fourth principle follows easily from the others. The Christians held an optimistic view of human nature. Early Christians took an aggressive stand against slavery, long before the abolition movement gained public support. Afro-Christian churches were organized in the South and the movement refused to make cultural distinctions between blacks and whites, men and women, or clergy and laity.

5) Churches need no other name than Christian. Religious liberty could most easily be protected, argued the leaders of the various "Christian" groups, if churches stopped arguing about irrelevant matters. The principles of Presbyterianism and episcopacy, the distinctions between doctrines that do nothing but divide Christians pale beside our unity in Christ. We must stop all of our petty arguments and distinctions and celebrate our union in Jesus Christ.

In 1874 when the General Convention of the Christian Church adopted a *Manifesto*, setting forth these principles of unity, they stated, "We are ready to form a corporate union with any body of Christians upon the basis of those great doctrines which underlie the religion of Christ… We are ready to submit all minor matters… (including what we are called) to individual conscience." In some listings of the "Christian principles" the commitment to unity is set forth as a separate principle, making a total of "Six Principles." It is not surprising that most of us know little about this movement in North American Church history. Their success is, in some measure, shown by their obscurity.

But let me continue with my story. After three years of seminary and some additional study in the doctoral program, my husband and I left North Carolina and moved to Philadelphia. He began teaching at Temple University and I began to discover another part of UCC history: the German Reformed story. Obviously some of the principles I have already mentioned are important to the Reformed perspective, but let me lift up five special insights from German Reformed history that I grew to appreciate of during my years in Pennsylvania.

1) A well-ordered church connects us with the Church universal. German Reformed contributions to UCC life come from the state church environment of Switzerland and Germany. At the beginning, German Reformed colonists were not eager to change their church experience in the New World. They valued the connectional and constitutional patterns of representative or presbyterial polity. They found the structures of church life helpful, providing ethnic solidarity in an

Anglo environment and stability on the unpredictable frontier. Through the careful leadership of consistories (made up of congregational elders and their pastor) they saw themselves as members of the Church universal, larger than any local parish.

2) The Church is grounded in a shared faith. The German Reformed Church had a special tool to define itself and to sustain its life: the *Heidelberg Catechism*. Being raised in a church that looked with skepticism at catechisms, I was initially cautious about those UCC congregations that found this catechism so important. In my experience, however, I have come to value its influence. There is a devotional power in its emphasis upon the spiritual comfort found in Christian discipleship. I understand how it gave those colonial Germans a sense of security, as well as responsibility towards their new American homeland. It continues to nourish a covenant theology and confessionalism that values disciplined living as a sign of participation in the covenant.

3) The Church lives in its sacramental actions. In my earliest experience with Presbyterian and Congregational churches, Holy Communion, or the Lord's Supper, was an important but infrequent part of worship. We were low church—confused by rituals and skeptical about their worth. In my Pennsylvania years I learned about the contributions of John Nevin and Philip Schaff to UCC life. These two men, who taught at the German Reformed seminary (Mercersberg) in Pennsylvania during the mid-nineteenth century, introduced progressive ecumenical thinking into the German Reformed Church. They offered a balanced corrective to the popular individualistic and subjective attitudes of many Americans. They also helped the German Reformed Church see its faith and practice as part of a legacy stretching back through the sixteenth century and drawing upon the strengths of medieval Christendom. They invited German Reformed people to find the promises of God in the regular churchly rhythms of Word and Sacrament, through pulpit and altar liturgies, rather than the intensive excitement of revivalism. Today, the insights of Mercersberg Theology strengthen UCC approaches to worship and liturgy.

4) The Church has a commitment to education. Every part of UCC history is serious about education. Although the Congregationalists actually founded more schools and colleges, I am impressed with the German Reformed stance. When those earliest German Reformed colonists gathered to establish churches, they turned to the school teachers in their midst for leadership. It was through contacts with the great universities of Germany that the German Reformed leaders

stretched the intellectual horizons of the entire Church. They insisted that their churches be led by educated clergy and laity. Even their internal battles over the German language (dividing them into "German Synods" and "English Synods") speaks of their concern for education.

5) The Church is theologically one. In the very earliest years, when Lutheran and Reformed people found themselves in the mix of Anabaptists and Quakers on the Pennsylvania frontier, they began something called "The Union Church." It was a practical arrangement whereby two different congregations (usually one Lutheran and one Reformed) shared the same building. Sometimes the church literally had two doors; Lutheran and Reformed services were held on alternating Sundays. Later they sponsored a common Sunday School. Lutheran and Reformed pastors served each other's people. Some of these "Union Church" arrangements exist to this day in parts of Pennsylvania. It is important to realize that behind this practice was the theological assumption that the Church of Jesus Christ could not be divided by human habits. There were "union church" fights, and the "union" did not always succeed, but the fact that it existed at all was, and is, amazing.

After several years of living near Philadelphia, I found myself on the faculty at Ursinus College. This small liberal arts college was founded in opposition to the Mercersberg movement. It was named after one of the authors of the *Heidelberg Catechism*, a school teacher named Zacharius Ursinus. Teaching at this small liberal arts college was very satisfying.

It was not long, however, before my husband and I began to think about returning to the Midwest. We remembered our good years at Beloit and we believed in the small liberal arts college. Eventually we found a place very similar, Albion College. This Methodist-related college was located in Albion, Michigan, a town of 12,000 people about 100 miles west of Detroit. The year was 1969. The move nearer to family was very satisfying. The move to Albion, however, also further stretched my knowledge about the United Church of Christ. For you see, the only United Church of Christ congregation in town was Salem Evangelical UCC.

There are many German Evangelical churches scattered across the Midwest. Many people do not realize, however, that these historically German Evangelical churches are quite different from our UCC German Reformed congregations in Pennsylvania. The German Evangelical Synod of North America grew out of a second wave of German immigration that flooded into the Mississippi valley (and elsewhere) in the mid-nineteenth century; over one hundred years after the arrival of the Pennsylvania Germans. (1) Midwestern German immigrants tended to come from northern German states. Some of them had experience in the Evangelical Union Church of Prussia. They appreciated Lutheran theology and practice. They shared their faith with a balanced pietism.

There are five legacies I celebrate from this tradition:

1) Healthy church life is grounded in personal piety. German Evangelicals developed a style of pietism that walked a middle road between the rigid orthodoxy of some of the Lutherans and the godless rationalism of radical freethinkers. They combined a practical appreciation of the "unionist" church movements of Prussia with the fervent pietism of the Barmen and Basel Missionary societies.

Walter Brueggemann has noted that both the orthodox and the free-thinking rationalists were unacceptable to Evangelical piety. The orthodox response to the challenges of the Enlightenment and the freedom of the American frontier, was "to draw the wagons into a circle and assume a fortress mentality." The rationalist approach to the same realities so dissipated the gospel by cultural accommodation that there was no energy or vitality left. (see "Our Heritage and Our Commitment" in *Festival of the Church*, 1978, 5-6).

The Evangelical tradition took another approach. It accepted the best intellectual work of its times, especially historical critical Biblical scholarship. Although members of the Evangelical Synod approached the Bible as seriously as orthodox Lutherans, they felt no need to build a creedal or confessional defense of its purity. At the same time, they also rejected the reductionist humanism of the rationalists. They believed that "the practice of faith was primarily a matter of the heart; that good will, passion and nearly a naivete about the gospel were the guards against taking ourselves too seriously or imagining too grandiosely about how we were in charge of all of God's reality..." (Brueggemann, 5-6)

2) The Church is embodied in the pastor. Although the Evangelical tradition was never characterized by excessive individualism, the importance of the pastor among these frontier German farmers pushed beyond the pietism of the individual, as important as that might be. Why? Because, Evangelicals believed with Luther, that "where the pastor is, there is the church."

In the frontier situation this understanding of the Church was very effective. It did not require a building, it did not require a critical mass of people, it did not demand much authorization from wider church authorities. Local German Evangelical pastors literally embodied the Church.

Such authority and clericalism can be criticized, but it has its value. After all, the central affirmation of the Christian faith has to do with incarnation. The pastoral office gave Evangelical congregations clarity about the faith, and confidence in shared witness. The leadership of the pastor was always more than that of a "learned scholar." It focused upon faithfulness and integrity rather than being overly concerned about effectiveness and competence. It continues to provide a model for equipping and empowering Christian people.

3) Church people support the weak and the homeless. There is a special pastoral character within the German Evangelical tradition. The pastor has a special shepherding role among the people and the church has an important ministry to the weak and the homeless. One of the most impressive records of outreach and care in the United Church of Christ is found in the health and welfare ministries founded by our congregations of the Evangelical tradition. This outreach not only served the needs of orphans, aging people and all who needed adequate medical care: it also provided special opportunities for women's ministries as Evangelical deaconesses.

4) Wider church meetings are important.. The identifying mark of the German Evangelical tradition was the annual conference. Indeed, the establishing of the "Verein," the "society," was one of the earliest expressions of this tradition. Brueggemann writes that the annual conference was a tricky creature to characterize; it was easier to say what it was not.

It was not like the Methodists who conduct real business and receive sealed instructions at the door. Nor was it like a free church tradition in which droves stayed away because it didn't matter. It mattered! Not for the business nor for the education nor for the inspiration. It mattered because it was the main visible act of belonging to the fellowship. It was not much worried about whether it was connectional or non-connectional, or about who spoke for whom. It was rather the practice of face-to-faceness, which kept the "Verein" functioning... Evangelicals let their identity come from within the fellowship.

In short, it had to do with what might be called "corporate interiority." (Brueggemann, 17-18). Although some of this fellowship was held together by ethnic identity, the importance of the wider church in Evangelical history cannot be denied.

5) The church belongs to Jesus Christ. Finally, I cannot forget the ecumenical flavor of Evangelical theology and practice. It is no

accident that the conversations that started the long journey towards the United Church of Christ uniting General Synod of 1957 began in St. Louis (close to the heart of the former Evangelical Synod of North America).

The Evangelical tradition picked up that marvelous trilogy—"In essentials unity, in non-essentials liberty, in all things charity." Some things are essential and some things are non-essential. The genius of the Evangelical legacy, as I see it, is the compassion and charity it has sustained while everyone else argued over essentials and non-essentials. The word that surfaces again and again is "irenic."

Behind it all there is an Evangelical assumption that the unity of the Church in Jesus Christ cannot be denied. I have always been impressed with the power of this conviction. I am grateful for its ability to overcome congregational fears about losing local autonomy during the "merger talks" of the 1940's. For I firmly believe that the United Church of Christ would never have come into being without what I want to call an "Evangelical Christocentric patience."

In 1975 the Zikmunds left Albion, Salem UCC and a number of other Evangelical churches in those Michigan farmlands so that I could join the faculty of The Chicago Theological Seminary, a school grounded in Congregationalism and serving as one of the seven "closely related seminaries" of the United Church of Christ. Five years later I moved to California and Pacific School of Religion. It turned out that I was a historian. My father had died, but I carried on the family tradition. I had learned the history of my church in the way my father believed history should be taught. I had been there. I understood it when a long time member of a UCC congregation rooted in Congregationalism joked that he'd been a Congregationalist all his life and no one was going to make a Christian out of him now. I appreciated the need to teach the Sunday School kids some German songs to share with the older members at the Salem UCC all-church picnic.

In this journey I had also learned that these four streams of UCC history are not as simple as our literature sometimes tries to make them. When you come to know the United Church of Christ well, there are hidden histories, developments and scenarios that break down stereotypes and stretch assumptions. In the last ten years I have spent my energies exploring these "hidden histories in the United Church of Christ." (see two edited volumes, *Hidden Histories in the United Church of Christ*, vols. I and II, United Church Press, 1984 and 1987).

Let me close this presentation with five insights about the United Church of Christ which are grounded in my work with our classic and hidden histories:

1) The United Church of Christ is more than its historical orthodoxy. In all historical work we develop habits of interpretation. When a "historical orthodoxy" dominates, parts of the story are simply overlooked. They do not fit our preconceived expectation that "four streams became one," and so we deny their validity. Eventually, certain histories literally get lost.

Historical orthodoxy draws upon traditional historical resources: congregational records, letters, official resolutions, biographies and autobiographies of visible leaders. This history of the Church is only partially known through these sources. Furthermore, not only do more inclusive sources need to be pursued, the perspectives of those telling the stories need to be more diverse. Only as we look at the histories of many racial and ethnic groups of theologically marginal movements and of the experiences of women in UCC history will we really be able to understand our church's past and prepare adequately for the future.

2) The United Church of Christ is an ecumenical church. We have said in our history and printed on our symbol, the prayer of Christ "that they may all be one." If we really believe that, and I find a deep commitment to our unity in Christ embodied in all of our histories, what does it mean in our times? The word "ecumenical" refers to the "whole inhabited earth." If we are truly ecumenical, we are called to incarnate the diversity and pluralism of the world.

In the 1940's and 1950's our churches responded to this calling through "church merger." They formed a "united" and "uniting" church. Today, we approach the ecumenical agenda with new concepts and words. We speak of "partnership" and "consensus." We also wonder how the Christian witness can move beyond its western European habits to honor persons of cultural traditions and other living faiths, while remaining true to Jesus Christ.

3) The United Church of Christ is a justice church. All of the people who have become part of the United Church of Christ were seeking more than personal gain. They believed the church could not be just a safe harbor for individual members. They were driven by the assumption that "to believe is to care and to care is to do."

What do we do? We attempt to follow the words of Micah, "to do justice, to love kindness, and to walk humbly with your God." In the late 1980's, how to be a justice church is a struggle. There are many agendas pressing our congregations, our Associations, our Conferences and our General Synod. When we fail to agree we get nervous that the church or our faith is too weak. But God does not require us to "agree." God calls us to be "faithful." I pray that our commitment to justice does not waiver in our search for UCC identity or community. Perhaps we need to remember those words of Jesus about losing our life in order to find it.

4) The United Church of Christ is open to women and men of all ages. It seems so obvious to say this, and yet in the history of the Church it has not always been so. There have been churches of rulers and bishops; there have been churches of monks and mystics; there have been churches of preachers and priests, manipulating the laity; there have been churches of men, ignoring the gifts of women; there have been churches of whites, excluding peoples of color; there have been churches of families, denying patterns of singleness and homosexuality; and there have been churches of adults, ignoring children.

I am especially proud of the UCC commitment to women and to the opportunities within our church for women to serve and share their discipleship. We must continue to insist that the Church of Jesus Christ is a fully inclusive community of faith and witness.

5) The United Church of Christ is a case study of North American mainline Protestantism. From time to time we all make jokes about the UCC. What is it? Our theology seems fuzzy. Our polity is confusing. Our history seems too complex. Our identity is vague.

We know that we are not the "Church of Christ." We are no longer just "Congregational" or "Evangelical," or "Reformed" or "Christian." We have Black congregations and Hispanic congregations. We have Hungarian congregations, Armenian congregations, and Samoan congregations. Some of our churches focus upon confessional matters. Others define themselves as liberal community churches. In our worship services we may use highly liturgical forms or settle with a scripture reading followed by a sermon. You cannot always predict what you will find when you visit a United Church of Christ congregation.

Yet, as I finish sharing this rather personal journey through "UCC land" I hope that you feel at home. Without denying our need to be self-critical and to keep our church faithful to the gospel of Jesus Christ, I want to affirm the authenticity of our unity in diversity.

In my introduction to *Hidden Histories in the United Church of Christ,* I closed with words which seem appropriate here:

> If it is possible to sustain denominational integrity in a pluralistic world, the United Church of Christ provides an interesting case study. Its diverse history contains examples and resources that promote church unity. At the same time, its diversity highlights issues that forever divide the Christian community: theology, ecclesiology, gender and ethnicity (including race). Only time will tell if Paul's words about seeing in part but someday seeing face to face will be fulfilled in the United Church of Christ.

Endnote

1. The Evangelical Synod of North America was also composed of congregations in the East, especially in Ohio and in New York State, and in the South, particularly in New Orleans and in portions of Texas. Editor).

(*On The Way*, Vol. 5, No. 2, Winter 1987-88. This address was originally presented to the Annual Meeting of the Wisconsin Conference, UCC, in June, 1987.)

Reuben A. Sheares, II

The Marks of the Ministry

This presentation will certainly reflect my own personal and intellectual limitations, beyond which I am not able to rise. It will also be influenced by the fact that this is the last presentation in this Convocation and therefore *seems* to want to address the question, "So what?" What does all of this mean, or imply, for me, for you, for us, now, tomorrow? What difference will all of this make for our understanding and our performance "back at the ranch"? These questions are deeply personal.

This presentation also flows out of the profound appreciation I have for all of the other lectures and the lecturers from whom I have learned a lot. I am grateful to each of them.

Particularly, this presentation will appropriate the three presuppositions stated by Barbara Brown Zikmund yesterday, and will add a fourth and a fifth. Those three presuppositions as I paraphrase them are: (1) Ministry is the calling and the task of the whole people of God, (2) The Christian community needs leaders for the care and the uplifting or up-building of the church, and (3) There are persons graced and gifted by God for leadership in the church. The fourth presupposition that I will add is that we here are among those who are so called, graced and gifted for leadership and for ministry in the church. And then the fifth presupposition is that ministry by the whole church, or by those so-called, graced and gifted, must ever be rooted in the good news of God in Jesus Christ. That, it seems to me, is the essential mark of ministry in all times and in all places.

With that assertion, you already have the essence of what this presentation is all about. What follows is simply an explication of that in highly subjective terms, with some excursions into biblical analogies.

I. Jesus Christ: Questions and Challenges

The ministry of the church, or of us as persons, must ever bear the mark of Jesus Christ. Ministry is always in His Spirit, in His Name, and out of His Reality. For He is the Vine, always. We are, at best, branches. *And,* because that is so, we always face the need to abide in Him, both in life and in ministry.

Now, some challenges fall out of that for us and for the whole church. The challenge can be stated in the question, "What think ye of Jesus?" There are at least two critical places in the Bible where dimensions of this question get raised. One is from John the Baptist who, through his disciples, raised the question with Jesus, "Are you the One who is to come, or shall we look for another?" The other is from Jesus, Himself, and was addressed to His disciples at Caesarea Philippi. That question was really two questions — essentially, "Who do the people say that I am?" and "Who do you say that I am?" So that, even if we agree that Jesus is the Vine, the nature of that Vine becomes critical. In a way, the biblical questions are questions that come to us as a challenge: "Is He the One, or are we looking for another?" and again, "Who do you, or who do we, say that Jesus is?"

Without elaborating in great detail, we can acknowledge the various ways in which people make affirmations about Jesus of Nazareth. There are terms like "Brother" and "Example," or "Teacher" or "Prophet." And alongside of these there are ways in which we understand Jesus to be one in a line of religious personalities who might even be the best of them all. Persons can testify out of their own life and experience the difference it makes when Jesus is taken seriously in any of these understandings.

Yet, there is affirmation out of the life of the church that Jesus is not for us just one in a series, but is unique. Some of that, I believe, is captured in the affirmation, "Jesus Christ is Lord and Savior." It is a word that says that what God was about in Jesus the Christ is unique. In the language of the UCC "Statement of Faith," it is there in Jesus the Christ that there is a conquering of sin and of death.

Well, the question before us is, "What do you think of Jesus?" The answer is critical for both authority and power in the church and in ministry. The answer is critical for the clarity and the boldness of our ministries and the ministry of the church.

II. What Does the Church Offer?

Inherent in all of this is an implicit, if not explicit, answer to another question, namely, "What does the church have to offer?" Or, "What makes the church different from other benevolent, self-improvement associations?" and further, "What does the ministry of the church, or the ministry of the ordained, have to do with ultimate questions? What gives our life and work a sense of urgency?"

I have intentionally sought to raise this question as a Christological concern, because I believe that the way in which we perceive and understand Jesus Christ has much to do with the way in which ministry is understood and performed and the mission of the church is defined. Well, the questions are before us.

III. John the Baptist as Model

If Jesus Christ is Lord and Savior, or to put it differently, if God has acted signally, uniquely and pivotally in Jesus of Nazareth, the Christ, so that you and I are no longer looking for another, then it might well be that John the Baptist is an example or model, if not a mark of ministry for us. That is so in the sense of his role as a "pointer" and one who prepares the way by which persons may come to the One who first came to us, and for us. This notes and asserts that we are not the one. The church is not the one. But in our life and work, in ministry, we point to Him who is the One. And that relates to what we think about Jesus.

IV. The Ministry of Apostles as Examples

A mark of ministry might also be exemplified for us in the ministry of the apostles. Selectively, I have chosen a few elements or components for comment. It could be said that the ministry of the apostles was one of testifying and witnessing to what they had seen, or heard, and experienced as the Word of God intersecting with their lives and the human condition. There are these two constants: 1) the Word of God in Jesus Christ and 2) the human condition.

Yet there are variables, one of which is suggested by the question, "Is there anyone who has seen, heard or experienced anything out of which they can testify and bear witness today?" It is as if the question to Jeremiah arises for us out of the human condition: "Is there any word from the Lord today, or for today?" That question is also deeply personal. How would you answer it?

Ministry as testifying and witnessing is a model for us. It suggests that the church is a preacher, even as the clergy, the pastor, is a preacher. And yet, that preaching is informed by the question, "What think ye of Christ?" What do we, what does the church, preach?

V. The Gospel for Everyone

I am struck by the fact that the apostles believed the gospel was for everyone, even though they had to work their way through some hurdles to get to that clarity. Sequentially, this perception was probably not based on the Great Commission, though for us the Great Commission has its own validity and force. Nevertheless, they believed that the gospel was for the Gentiles, as well as for the Jews. And if we were to update that language for our time, it would be a way of saying that the gospel is for others, as well as for ourselves. The apostles apparently believed in a universal application and proclamation of the gospel. That is clearly in their behavior. They proclaimed that gospel unashamedly, whether it was perceived as a stumbling block to the Jews, or folly to the Greeks. This is instructive for us. For in ministry today, centered in the gospel, we are having to deal with the fact that the gospel may be perceived as either a stumbling block or as folly. In such a situation, what does one do? Does one seek to remove the offense of the gospel? Will one attempt to find something else to preach that is more acceptable?

The apostolic belief that the gospel is for everyone formed the basis for the evangelistic task in which they engaged, and the urgency was fed by their sense of the uniqueness of what God had done and was about in Jesus Christ. And the footnote reads, "... thousands were added to the life of the church."

VI A Minority Church

Clearly, the early church was a minority church. But, we might ask, was that by choice, the result of circumstances? Or what? It does not seem that they chose to be a minority, and it does not seem as if they acted to remain a minority. For the gospel was for everyone! They sought to claim the whole world and the whole creation for God in Jesus Christ. It was not within their power to ensure the results, but it was within their capacity to be faithful witnesses to the gospel.

There are many ways to be a minority church, some of which are acceptable and some of which are unacceptable. In my judgment, an unacceptable way is to be smug, or elitist, in our minority status so that we do not even make the effort to share the gospel with others. It would be a way of asserting that the gospel is for us, but not for others.

VII Above or Against Culture?

The apostles also appeared to take their culture with a grain of salt. One needs to exercise care in explicating this point, and not remake them in our image. But they understood the lordship of Jesus Christ, and therefore the contingent, or non-ultimate, nature of their culture and of the world. Therefore, there might well have been a radical dimension to the exhortation to be in, but not of, this world — to be in, but not of, the prevailing culture and the conventional wisdom thereof.

Perhaps they understood themselves to be in a transforming relationship with the culture, the wisdom, the world of their time. Certainly, they sought not to be conformist. Key symbols of this are the prisons, or the martyrdoms, or the beatings, or the persecutions they experienced. This may be suggestive of a mark of ministry.

VIII.   Peter as Model: Foibles

It may well be that Simon Peter is a model of ministry for us. He appears to have been impetuous, erratic. This may serve as a model of ministry.   I chose Peter not because of any notions of the keys to the kingdom, but because of his foibles.   He is a person with which I and, I suppose, we all can identify because he is clearly most like us.   In many ways he is most like the church. In life and in ministry: the foibles!

Yet, I am always impressed from the scriptures with what God was able to do with Peter and through Peter — either in spite of, or because of, his foibles. That's a partial reminder to us and may even carry the force of some good news for us.   Both individually and collectively, are we not aware of our own foibles and the foibles of the church? We are all indeed earthen vessels.   We are inconsistent; we are sinful. There is always the possibility of faintheartedness, or denial, or betrayal. We are aware of our inadequacies, of our limitations, of our infinitude. And yet, alongside of all that, there is good news of what God can do with and through us, with all of our foibles.

IX.   Conclusion

I do not know where all of this leads, but an affirmation is central to it all. The ministry of the church, or the ministry of each of us as persons, must ever bear the mark of Jesus Christ. A question that is always before us remains: "What do you think of Jesus?"

Ministry, then, is a struggle for faithfulness in the midst of which we offer up unto the Lord the works of our hands, so that the Lord of the church and the Lord of history might sift and redeem that work.

*(Unpublished, undated monograph from a theological colloquy con-
vened in the United Church of Christ)*

Louis H. Gunnemann

The United Church of Christ and Its Ministry

The title of this paper, "The United Church of Christ and Its Ministry," identifies my effort to respond to concerns expressed when I was invited to speak to you at this meeting. I am grateful for the invitation to speak on this subject, for it is a topic of great urgency throughout the Church.

Some focus can be given to the subject by posing a question: For what kind of ministry must the Church prepare its ordained leadership in this time? Three sub-topics will serve as a framework for the discussion, each put in the form of a question:

1) What is the significance of the socio-religious reality of our time that calls for critical consideration of the nature of the ministry?

2) What formulation or re-formulation of the doctrine of the ministry is required to address that reality in faithfulness to God's mission?

3) What are the implications for the seminaries and the governance/program structures of the Church?

I

To the first question, then: What is the critical significance of the socio-religious reality of this age? Our judgments about that are bound to be quite diverse. The sociologist has become the "guru" to whom many people turn in this day for understanding socio-religious trends, while historians, theologians and philosophers often seem to be left scrambling to find a credible diagnostic principle. Now, as mainline religious institutional change has generated concern and anxiety in the "establishment", sociological analyses are in. This is seen as a time of crisis.

Inevitably, in a time of crisis, the issue of survival for the institutional church is the focus of attention. As pressing as that concern may be, it is not the focal point of my attention in considering the mind of ministerial leadership needed today. I prefer to cast the question of the ministry not in the context of denominational survival but in the context of the new socio-religious reality that characterizes what many call the "post-modern era."

"Post-modern" clearly suggests that an era has come to an end; that we in fact are living in an end-time. Almost fifty years have passed since Reinhold Niebuhr, in his Gifford Lectures of 1939, gave a characterization of the modern era which is at the same time a clue to the meaning of the "post-modern." Niebuhr claimed that "it is the autonomous individual who really ushers in the modern civilization" (Reinhold Niebuhr, *The Nature and Destiny of Man,* Vol. I, 59). Few would challenge Niebuhr's contention that the autonomous individual is the distinguishing mark of the modern era. Can it be said with equal confidence that we are now in that end-time when the autonomous individual is being annihilated? Has John Locke's seventeenth century vision of the autonomous self run its course?

Autonomous individualism has been well observed in the past three centuries. From de Tocqueville's acute insights concerning its fulfillment in American democracy, to Philip Rieff's identification of the "turned-in-upon-itself individualism" that feeds our therapeutic society, to the most recent assessment by Robert Bellah and colleagues, the role and condition of autonomous individualism in our society has been documented and analyzed. (See Robert Bellah, et al, in *Habits of the Heart,* 6ff.) The ambiguities of autonomous individualism have posed the critical question of our time, claims Bellah, as he says: ". . . the question is whether an individualism in which the self has become the main form of reality can be really sustained?" (Bellah, 143). Bellah's judgment carries an implicit warning: "Modern individualism seems to be producing a way of life that is neither individually nor socially viable." (144)

The dilemma of the modern individual has been characterized by Peter Berger as the loss of the "plausibility structures" by which autonomous individuals find social confirmation of their reality. (See *The Heretical Imperative,* 17-18). In the absence of plausibility structures the autonomous individual is not only cast adrift but is alienated and alone, and, as Bellah puts it, "just a step away from despair." (146) Alienation, loneliness and despair are the marks of the end-of-an-age time in human history.

In tracing the experience of the autonomous individual in this manner I am seeking to expose the socio-religious conditions within which the Church must carry on its ministry. Post-modern humankind's self-understanding has become so distorted in its perception of reality that it has been rendered incapable of transcending the limits of its self-defined universe. An autonomy that has turned in upon itself because of the loss of objective plausibility structures essential to its meaning has produced an illusory freedom which is pursued not so much with passionate commitment as with desperate hunger. This characterizes the post-modern individual. It constitutes the socio-religious reality in which the Church is being tested in ways not experienced since the time of St. Augustine in the fourth century.

It is worth noting that the impact of these features of the post-modern condition of humanity is borne out in striking ways in the most recent sociological study, *American Mainline Religion*, by Wade Clark Roof and William McKinney. These researchers have traced the decline of American mainline churches in terms of both numbers and influence. They see both liberal and moderate Protestant churches suffering, thus pointing to what they call the "collapse of America's religious center". Those denominations whose teachings, values, and practices were framed by the "ascriptive loyalties" that Peter Berger identifies as plausibility structures are fast losing their traditional role in post-modern society.

At the root of this threatening development in North American church life is the growth of what the authors call the "new voluntarism". The new voluntarism, claiming absolute and private freedom of choice in forming any loyalty, has no use for the ascriptive loyalties that have been shaped in a deeply rooted Christian tradition. The strength of the denominational system for more than 150 years has been its ability to hold forth these loyalties that in a voluntary society were able to energize the autonomous individual's "will-to-belong". But when ascriptive loyalties are subordinated to the choice of the absolute autonomous individual, the voluntary religious organization we call the "church" is suddenly irrelevant. Thus the rejection of ascriptive loyalties results in a growing number of persons who are non-affiliated and non-churched. Roof and McKinney conclude that this is the chief threat to both liberal and moderate Protestant churches which see a growing number of "not-so-committed members" moving with the secular drift. (184)

II

This brings us to our second concern: What formulation or re-formulation of the doctrine of the ministry is required if the Church is to address this reality with faithfulness? This, of course, raises fundamental ecclesiological questions, for the ministerial leadership we cultivate today is meant for a model of church organization that seems increasingly irrelevant and impotent. In making such a judgment I am not overlooking the unique record of influence and accomplishment of the denominational system in both North American society and its church life. Of all the voluntary associations in which American Christians participate - and there are thousands of them - the denomination has contributed immensely to social stability, to structures of moral values, and to religious faith. It is certainly fair to say that the autonomous individualism of the nineteenth and early twentieth centuries gave fullest expression to the religious energies released on this continent in the denominational system. The denomination, the primary organizational vehicle for the mission of the Church in a voluntary society, proved its worth throughout what Kenneth Scott Latourette has called "The Great Century of the Expansion of Christianity".

The accomplishments of the denominational form of church life are not to be disregarded, but they should not be permitted to interfere with a critical assessment of its limitations. Nearly sixty years have passed since the publication of H. Richard Niebuhr's indictment of the denominational system. His charge that denominations represent "the moral failure of Christianity" was grounded in his study of the "institutionalization" of social division and discrimination by that system. (See his *The Social Sources of Denominationalism.*) In the past six decades similar charges have been leveled frequently at the denominational system; still it perseveres as the warp and woof of the fabric of North American religious life. Only in recent decades has that model of church life come under significant theological critique as a result of ecclesiological studies in the ecumenical movement. Lesslie Newbigin, for example, reminds us that:

"...denominationalism is the religious aspect of secularization. It is the form that religion takes in a culture controlled by the ideology of the Enlightenment. It is the social form in which the privatization of religion is expressed. ..(Denominations) are themselves the outward and visible signs of an inward and spiritual surrender to the ideology of our culture." (*Foolishness to the Greeks*, 145-146).

Newbigin's indictment reflects also, of course, the critique of autonomous individualism made by Bellah and others in *Habits of the Heart*. The question posed, therefore, is whether the denominational mode of church life has also reached the end of its time. Is it viable in the light of the new socio-religious reality we have identified? Should it be maintained, no matter what the cost? If the answer to these questions is negative, what is the alternative? In a voluntary society, what are the options for the Church?

These questions become even more critical in relation to the growing racial, cultural, and social pluralism that presses upon all of western Christianity today. How can the denominational model overcome the "radical egalitarianism of our individualist society" which succeeds only in "drawing together middle-class individuals who find it difficult to attract or meld with those of different class, race, and economic levels" (Bellah, 206)? These words reflect Niebuhr's contention that the denomination is Christianity's moral failure in relation to racial and class divisions.

Again, what are the options? A blueprint of the future design of the visible church has yet to appear. In the fourth century crisis of the Church St. Augustine offered no blueprint, but he did identify the foundational elements that carried the Christian movement through many centuries of social and moral upheaval. What are such foundational elements for a new comprehension of the visible form of the Church? To identify them in ways that relate to the socio-religious reality of this time is the task facing the Christian community today. A call to look at foundational elements is not a call to a new traditionalism, but to a recognition of the place of tradition in a community of faith that lives by images and truth that transcend the time boundaries of this world. That involves, as Peter Berger has said, not a concern "with a return to tradition, but with a return to a *struggle with tradition*" (*Heretical Imperative*, xiv).

We have come to a time when a struggle with tradition in the context of present-day religious realities is a priority matter for the whole church. It is a matter of responsibility to the historical reality of both individual and corporate existence. For the UCC, which stands largely though not solely within the Reformed tradition and shares much with the wider Reformation faith, that will mean a reconsideration of such traditional concepts as call, election, free grace, sanctification, and so on, in the context of a religious culture that, on the one hand, has completely subjectivized all of these traditional doctrines of the church universal and, on the other hand, has become pluralistic, reflecting incredibly diverse perceptions of reality and religious belief. Quite specifically, however, with reference to the nature of the Church it will require a readiness to be disabused of the images of the Church that have been formed in the milieu of autonomous individualism and a secularized version of voluntarism. In that milieu, which has prevailed for more than three hundred years in much of Western Christianity, the visible form of the church has come to be regarded as the creation of human religious purpose and devotion. As such it contradicts all of the biblical witness about the nature of the community of faith. For it is clear from the biblical record that the ecclesial character of the community of faith is not derived from the religious interests of its members but from God's call in Christ. To be called is to be the Church.

To struggle with the biblical tradition concerning the nature of the Church is to utilize what Walter Brueggemann has called the "subversive ecclesiology" of the covenant community - subversive in the sense that it undercuts prevailing images of the church as our community of choice and convenience. To be called is to become God's people, chosen and claimed for purposes that transcend our human aspirations and goals. To be the church, then, the community of faith can live only by the self-consciousness of being possessed for God's purposes.

Modern church life avoids a struggle with that tradition by accommodating its style of religious life to the diverse needs and wants of the autonomous individual, who, no matter how interested in religious matters and/or spiritual development, is basically a parasite on the community of faith.

Given this reality—that culture accommodation is bankrupting the organized church and calling into question its self-understanding as a community of faith—the immediate and pressing task is to explore anew the implications of being an ecclesial community, the called people of God. That task, I believe, is the focal point of the question: what kind of leadership does the Church need for a renewal of its self-image and the shaping of its life? The words "ecclesial community" as the way to speak of the "called people of God" must be taken with ultimate seriousness. Those words denote the singular characteristic of the community of faith that differentiates it from all other communities where human religiosity is the reason for their existence. Of course, by reason of its human condition the Church is always both an ecclesial community and a religious community at the same time. It is at the intersection of the claims of the ecclesial community and the religious community that the matter of ordained leadership is most critical.

To underline the distinction between the ecclesial community and the religious community is to expose in a radical way the need to rethink the question of leadership. For the models of leadership in voluntary religious communities have their source in the world of human religiosity, whereas the model for leadership in the ecclesial community comes from the One who calls the community into being - Christ the head of the Church. As anyone knows who has served in leadership roles in the Church, especially as ordained persons, the contradictions between these two models of leadership create almost intolerable tension. In the ecclesial community authority to function in leadership roles is given by the one who calls - the Christ. In the religious community authority is given by the community of faith itself. In this connection see Barbara Brown Zikmund's distinction between "embodiment" and "empowerment" with reference to the ordained minister's authority (see "Minister and Ministry in a Covenant System," *New Conversations*, vol. 4, no. 2, Fall 1979).

It is at this point that our articulation of the doctrine of the ministry requires not only clarity but honesty as well. While the UCC shares with other denominations similar confusion about the ministry it is urgent, in view of our particular history, that the matter be addressed with vigor and candor. We are reluctant to admit that our model for ministerial leadership has become, over the past two decades, a clear example of the religious model in which there is no transcendent referent and where secular organizational models prevail. Thus, ordained ministers are professionals who have chosen a career of religious leadership and are employed by non-profit organizations such as local churches, service groups and ecclesiastical agencies. The ordination given by the religious organization they serve is considered to be their professional license, providing them with recognition, privilege, and a certain amount of power. This model is clearly in contradiction to the model that derives from the faith proclaimed by the ecclesial community. This contradiction, which we seem to be unable or unwilling to face, is surely one of the major reasons that the UCC has no theology of ordination.

The situation is complicated, of course, by our difficulties in coming to grips with the diverse traditions represented among us. Perhaps our greatest problem with these diverse traditions is that they are little understood in their historical context. Moreover, in a time that accentuates the "calling of the whole people of God" we have much difficulty in defining the role, responsibility and authority of those whom we ordain. We seem always to be unclear whether the ordination is for leadership in the ecclesial community or the religious community. We share that lack of clarity with other church bodies, of course. In most North American churches the concept of the "calling of the people of God" has been interpreted to accentuate the "ministerial role" of the autonomous individual under the egalitarian ideology prevailing from Enlightenment times. The result is a persistent and uninformed anti-hierarchicalism that resists assignment of authority to the ordained ministry. The Church, then, is left simply with a functional view of ministry that draws its standards, style and form from the needs of a religious organization in a voluntary society. The ideal of a democratized ministry has been uncritically accepted.

In this connection, failure to struggle with the tradition has been very costly. That cost has been the loss of a theology of ordained ministry. Under the banner of the "free church" model an egalitarian ideology has eliminated two critically important roles from the office of the ordained ministry: a) the representative role, that is, responsibility for representing the authority of Christ in matters of faith; and b) the instrumental role, that is, serving as the instrument by which the life of the church is ordered around Word and Sacrament for its ministry in the world.

My use of the words "representative" and "instrumental" probably sends shock waves through many who hear them. But, bear with me, please. We tend to hear those words in the language of an age that gave emphasis to ministry as an "order" which constitutes the Church. What is forgotten, however, is that the Reformation tradition accentuated the representative and instrumental roles in relation to the well-being of the church, that is, so that the life of the church be so ordered that the gospel can be spread and the community built up in love. This is the reason for the Reformation emphasis upon the office (duty) of ministry rather than an order of ministry. Calvin put the matter in words that carry immense significance even though our modern ears do not hear them:

"Christ ascended... (so) that he might fill all things. The mode of filling is this: by the ministers to whom he has committed this office and given grace to discharge it, he dispenses and distributes his grace to the Church, and thus exhibits himself as in a manner actually present by exerting the energy of the Spirit in this his institution, so as to prevent it from being vain or fruitless. In this way the renewal of the saints is accomplished and the body of Christ is edified, in this way we grow..." (*Institutes of the Christian Religion*, Book. IV, chapter 3, section 3).

To the modern autonomous individual the terms "representative" and "instrumental" have sacerdotal overtones. The historical evidence is not to be denied. But we are living in an end-time in which old images and categories must be stripped of their crustaceous covering and be allowed to convey the important truths they represent. In this kind of struggle with tradition, the terms "representative" and "instrumental" will emerge as designating ministerial roles essential to the life of the church as the body of Christ, as the people of God, as the called community. In an end-time era, the ecclesial community must test every institutional structure to see in what ways they may be impeding the movement of the people of God.

To characterize the ecclesial community as a movement is to underline its form as a dynamic organism which exudes energy and power. The fluidity of a movement, its constant pushing beyond the barriers and walls of social custom and injustice, its challenging of the status quo—all of that may generate anxiety among those more comfortable in institutional solidness. That very fluidity places a premium on the representative and instrumental roles of those who have been assigned to the office of ministry. Has it not always been so in the history of the Church? For the ecclesial community, understood as the called people of God - a people exemplifying the dynamism of an organic entity rather than an institution - the critical need is for order, that is, order that keeps the movement responsive to the course set in God's call. That order, however, is derived not from command but from example and symbol. Order comes from the acknowledged presence of Christ, particularly in the Eucharist, but also from the community's fulfillment of the priesthood mandate to be unto others as Christ is to them. It is in and through the office of ministry of Word and Sacrament that this order is made clear.

Ordination, historically, has its roots in recognition of this need for order. From the beginning, ordination had no sacerdotal implications. It was the ecclesial community's assignment of the critical duty by which its apostolic mission could be fulfilled. The subsequent expansion of the office of ministry reflects the influence of social and cultural conditions in which Christians found themselves in the first two centuries. The excesses of that development moved the principle of order for mission to a principle of ecclesiastical rule and sovereignty. Reaction to that excess has moved to other excesses so that the concept of order finds minimal support in a culture dominated by autonomous individualism.

In the post-modern era, when autonomous individualism has run its course, order in the ecclesial community is even more critically important. The increasing malaise of aimlessness in modern life, the confusing choices offered in a pluralistic culture, and a rampant gluttony of materialism - all of this requires the ordering of life that only Christ can accomplish through the power of the Spirit working through Word and Sacrament. I am deeply convinced that any reconsideration and reformulation of the doctrine of the ministry, if it is to be faithful to the One who has called, must be grounded in this understanding of the ministry of order. The temptation faced always in the ecclesial community is to fall into the trap of "religionizing" the gospel, that is, accommodating it to the religious impulses of the human spirit. Unless those impulses are brought under the discipline of the gospel of free grace, the office of ministry will be forced back into a sacerdotal mode. I repeat a point made earlier: the office of ministry is always set at the critical intersection of the gospel of grace and human religiosity. Clarity about the purpose and nature of the representative and instrumental roles of the office of ministry requires constant examination and reiteration. Only then will the ecclesial community be nurtured, edified, and kept in the unity of the apostolic mission.

III

Such a restatement and reformulation of the doctrine of the ministry within the context of current theologies of ministry raises the final question to be addressed: What are the implications of this for the seminaries and for the governance/program structures of the Church? For the sake of giving focus to the discussion that is to follow, I prefer to address the question of implications in a series of affirmations and propositions:

1) In this end-time of Western culture the visible form of the Church will, and, I believe, must show itself as an ecclesial movement, a dynamic organism, thus calling into question its institutional forms. Only then can it make Christ's claim clear, unencumbered by institutional aims. Only then will it be able to open doors to the alienated autonomous individual of this time.

2) In this period of questioning of its institutional expression the Church is required to struggle with the tradition as an expression of its historical consciousness and as recognition of its reality as a community of memory. (In this connection see H. Richard Niebuhr's pertinent discussion of the nature of community in his *The Meaning of Revelation* (1941), 84, 1960 ed.). A critical component of this time of questioning is a reconsideration of the doctrine of the ministry with the intention to free it from its current secular and cultural accommodating mode.

3) This reconsideration of the doctrine of the ministry requires a redefinition of ordination, returning it to its original significance as the means for providing the ministry of order in the community of faith. How the ministry is conceived determines whether or not we take seriously the meaning of the headship of Christ in the Church. The representative and instrumental roles exhibit the Christ; the functional role tends to be responsive only to the expressed needs of the religious community.

4) The Church, as the ecclesial community, must recover ordination for the sake of the apostolic mission. By recovery, I mean the guarding of it as the Church's possession and rejecting its use as professional license or certification. This effort will entail much struggle and conflict, for it threatens the persistent residue of autonomous individualism in the life of the Church, now institutionalized by current practices of ordination. Present generations of clergy may not be persuaded by this claim, but the Church dares not equivocate any longer about ordination. The focus upon the ordained ministry as the ministry of order through Word and Sacrament does not imply rank, but it does identify by symbol and function the source of authority for the journey and for all other forms of ministry that belong to the vocation of all baptized persons. It must be acknowledged that this concept runs head on with the democratized understanding of the ordained ministry that prevails today. (See Williston Walker, *The Creeds*

and Platforms of Congregationalism, and H. Richard Niebuhr and Daniel D. Williams, *The Ministry in Historical Perspectives*, for a record of the democratization process in the nineteenth century.)

5) The qualities of leadership required for the ministry of order have two foundational elements: a) a faith commitment to Christ that renounces self-advancement and career accomplishment in favor of the graces divinely granted; and b) an intellectual commitment to the disciplines necessary for direct confrontation with the challenges to the faith that continually emerge in this fallen world. On these foundational elements the God-given gifts for ministry can be finely honed and tempered for the critical tasks of proclamation and teaching. I am emphasizing here what Robert Bellah has called a "creative intellectual focus," which is essential to counter the "quasi-therapeutic blindness" that has afflicted the churches for over a century, and which cannot "withstand the vigorous forms of radical individualism with their claims of dramatic self-realization or the resurgent conservatism that spells out clear, if simple, answers to an increasingly bewildered world." (238) Bellah's point touches the critical intersection of the gospel and human religiosity where the office of the ordained ministry is tested to the fullest.

6) The recovery of a doctrine of ministry which can serve the leadership requirements of the ecclesial community in this end-time will involve a vigorous examination of the adequacy of ordination standards. That examination requires intensive joint effort between the Church's governance, program structures, and the seminaries. Continuous attention to the quality of leadership for the ecclesial community requires a covenant of mutual responsibility. Only in this way can all baptized persons, whose vocation is to share Christ's ministry, be equipped for service in this time. The task and responsibility for such leadership development belongs to the whole Church and its institutions, and if taken with the seriousness I have sought to underscore it will mean a pact of ownership and support on denominational as well as Conference levels. In all of this let the United Church of Christ be truly the Church.

Bibliography

Bellah, Robert, et al, *Habits of the Heart: Individualism and Commitment in American Life*, Berkeley: (University of California Press, 1985).

Berger, Peter, *The Heretical Imperative: Contemporary Possibilities of Religious Affirmation*, Garden City: (Doubleday, 1979).

Calvin, John, *Institutes of the Christian Religion*, Philadelphia: (Presbyterian Board of Publication, 1930).

Newbigin, J. Lesslie, *Foolishness to the Greeks: The Gospel and Western Culture*, Grand Rapids: (Eerdmanns, 1986).

Niebuhr, H. Richard, *The Social Sources of Denominationalism*, New York: (Henry Holt and Co., 1929).

Niebuhr, H. Richard, *The Meaning of Revelation*, New York: (Macmillan, 1960).

Niebuhr, Reinhold, *The Nature and Destiny of Man*, Vol. I, New York: (Scribners, 1943).

Roof, Wade Clark and McKinney, William, *American Mainline Religion: Its Changing Shape and Future*, New Brunswick: (U of Rutgers Press, 1987).

Walker, Williston, *The Creeds and Platforms of Congregationalism*, Boston: (Pilgrim Press, 1960).

Williams, Daniel D., *The Ministry in Historical Perspectives*, New York: (Harper and Row, 1956).

(*On The Way*, Vol. 6, No.1, Spring 1989)

Louis H. Gunnemann

The Pastoral Office in the Twenty-first Century

The title I have given to this paper calls for a brief word of explanation. My assumption is that to speak about the pastoral office in the life of the Church today requires us to take into account trends and developments that already point to a new shaping of that office as we move into the twenty-first century. In a paradoxical way the future is being shaped in current developments in all aspects of life.

I

There is, then, a double focus in this discussion of the pastoral office: present realities and future possibilities. That double focus requires: first, candor and critical honesty about current conditions, and, second, the willingness and courage to face the trends, now discernible but not always understood, that will shape the context of the Church's ministry in the early decades of the next century.

As daunting as such an effort may be, we must acknowledge, of course, that it has been undertaken in other transition times. When such transitions underline critical issues in the Church's life the question of adequate religious leadership comes to the fore. That concern is clearly present in all of Judaeo-Christian history. The community of faith continually lives in the tension stemming from the awareness of being a people called by grace and at the same time obligated to faithful and responsible living in alienating situations. To live in that tension the Church requires leadership that knows both the power of divine grace and the demands of faithfulness.

It was Richard Baxter, in the seventeenth century, who reflected so well the concern for responsible leadership in the Church when he wrote these words in his classic book, *The Reformed Pastor*:

> Alas! it is the common danger and calamity of the church, to have unregenerate and inexperienced pastors, and to have so many become preachers before they are Christians; who are sanctified by dedication to the altar as priests of God before they are sanctified by hearts dedicated as disciples of Christ; and so

to worship an unknown God, and to preach an unknown Christ, and to pray through an unknown Spirit. . . (21)

Although Baxter's lament was directed at the priests of the Church of England, he wrote it as part of an effort to generate greater spiritual discipline among his Puritan colleagues in the ministry. He saw the authenticity of the Church resting upon the authenticity of the faith and calling of the pastors of the Church. Baxter's lament is echoed throughout history, from the Old Testament prophets who railed against false prophets, to the Apostle Paul's concern for the churches in his care, to Irenaeus and Chrysostom in the early centuries, to St. Francis, to Luther and Calvin, and to Bonhoeffer in our tragic twentieth century. The quality of leadership in the community of faith is critical at all times but never more so than in times of crisis.

In the thirty-five years of my own involvement in theological education and the training of ministers the issue of quality leadership in the Church has been paramount. That concern was heightened by the social and cultural revolution of the Sixties and Seventies. In those decades it was common to speak of the "crisis of the ministry" while we witnessed a steady decline in regard for the pastoral office. Ironically, more attention was given to the welfare of those demitting than to critical reflection upon the effect of the loss of the pastoral office in the Church. Slowly, in the ensuing years, attention was directed to the question: What kind of leadership is needed for the Church in these times?

In the years between 1960 and 1985 three approaches to the question of adequate and appropriate leadership emerged. In some degree their differences reflect the confusion in the churches concerning ministry. Nevertheless, each one contributed important insights that are being integrated into current re-conceptualization of the pastoral office.

The first approach, rooted in the socio-moral ecumenism of mid-century, looked to the emergence of a new emphasis upon the ministry of the laity for the kind of leadership needed in the churches. For some this seemed to be simply a dismissal of the office of the ordained ministry; a final and terminal thrust at clerical hierarchicalism. But a more balanced picture emerged in that movement, as depicted by Hanns-Ruedi Weber:

> A high doctrine of the laity *includes* rather than *excludes* a high doctrine of the ordained ministry. The important thing is that the nature and task of the laity is no more defined by comparing them with a special group within the Church: the ordained clergy, the theologian, the professional church worker, but by a new appreciation of the Church in the world (*The Layman in Chris-*

tian History, Stephen C. Neill and Hanns-Ruedi Weber, Phila-delphia: Westminster, 1963, 388).

The second approach to the question of adequate leadership for the Church was exhibited in H. Richard Niebuhr's book of the previous decade, *The Purpose of the Church and Its Ministry* (New York: Harper and Row, 1956). For Niebuhr the issue of adequate and authentic leadership could not be addressed apart from the prior question: "What is the purpose of the Church and its ministry?" Niebuhr's approach marked a significant shift in focus from the question of how to secure and train qualified leadership to the substantial question of the nature of the Church and its ministry. A plethora of books marking this shift appeared since Niebuhr's in 1956. The question Niebuhr identified, of course, is the corollary of the question at the heart of the twentieth century ecumenical movement.

A third approach, ironically, underlined the confusion over this question in the churches. That confusion is illustrated in the mammoth study undertaken in the late seventies by the Association of Theological Schools, the results of which were published in *Ministry in America* in 1980, (David Schuller, Merton Strommen and Mil Brekke, eds., New York: Harpers). Based on the premise that the expectations about the ministry on the part of both clergy and laity would identify qualities needed for church leadership, a survey of five thousand persons was made and analyzed. The hope of distilling from those expectations a series of standards and goals to be applied in the education of clergy was doomed from the start. Most efforts to reshape seminary curricula to those expectations have been abandoned.

The fundamental question posed by Niebuhr has resurfaced in the past five years, but with a greater critical awareness of the difficulties involved in defining the Church and its ministry in times like these. Books by Edward Farley, John de Gruchy, Joseph Hough and John B. Cobb, Jr., are examples from among a dozen or more.

This shift of attention to the question of the very nature of the Church and its ministry is the context of my discussion of the pastoral office. For the pastoral office is a particular form of the ministry, with a critical place in the life of the Church. In the remaining sections of this paper I want to clarify the distinction and the relationship.

II

The pastoral office of the Church's ministry is grounded in the New Testament understanding of the Church as the embodiment of Christ's ministry in and to the world. The prepositions "in" and "to" are critically important to our understanding of the pastoral office. "In" the world emphasizes that the embodiment of Christ's ministry under the power of the Spirit takes place in the context of the realities of the human situation. That is, the pastoral office does not gather a flock from out of the world to enjoy a private relationship with God. Rather, it nurtures and guides those whose existence in the world continually demonstrates the new reality of God's redemptive activity. The preposition "to" underlines the purpose of the pastoral office "to equip the saints for the work of the ministry" to the world which awaits the dawn of the new age of God. This characterization of the two poles of activity or foci of purpose, although little acknowledged in much of the Church's life, is, I think, a faithful interpretation of the New Testament teaching. Its significance is critical to understanding the nature of the pastoral office. Acknowledging that the community of faith is Christ's body, then Christ is the Head of that body, and all human leadership in that community is by definition both *representative* and *instrumental*.

The use of the terms "representative" and "instrumental" will help us clarify the development of the "offices" of ministry as they appear in the New Testament record. The term "office" is being used in its generic sense as "duty assigned and recognized." In the New Testament, "offices" were assigned by the gifts of the Spirit. Persons equipped with these gifts provided the essential leadership for the community of faith. That leadership was seen as representative of the Christ who is Head of the Church. In exhibiting and sharing the gifts of the Spirit that leadership is also instrumental. And, as the Apostle made clear many times, the criteria for the testing of that leadership was always its impact upon the welfare of the Body. From the beginning, then, the pastoral office referred not to position or status but to representative and instrumental functions.

From the apostolic roles assigned by Christ himself and from the offices identified in the Ephesian letter as essential to the Church's life and ministry, we can draw two conclusions. First, in all leadership roles Christ is the model. That model underlines the primacy of manner or style in the performance of assigned duties. "Do as I have done unto you" is the imperative for all disciples of the Christ, but doubly so for those entrusted with the pastoral office. Commanded of the disciples in that powerful thirteenth chapter of John's Gospel, and demonstrated in ultimate fashion on the Cross, that style has always been understood by the Church as the only style appropriate for those who represent Christ. That, of course, was the concern of Richard Baxter when he wrote *The Reformed Pastor*.

The second conclusion to be drawn from New Testament sources is that the shaping of leadership roles reflects the special needs of the Christian community as it faces its responsibility for Christ's ministry in and to the world. That shaping represents always the influence of the socio-cultural context within which the ministry is carried out. Such contexts have both particular and universal connotations. An example is seen in the Ephesian letter where the writer's perception is that the Church is the sign and seal of God's purpose of unity for all humanity. From that vision of the divine purpose the writer deduces the particular kinds of leadership needed by the Church - needs that are met by the gifts of Christ himself "to equip the saints for the work of ministry and for building up the Body of Christ" (Ephesians. 4:11-12).

St. Paul's perception of the offices of leadership was clearly his response, under the guidance of the Spirit, to his vision of the purpose of God "to unite all things in Christ" - a vision that grasped the desperate reality of a humanity alienated from God and utterly fragmented and lost. He saw the new community of the Spirit, the new order of creation from Christ, as God's answer to the human condition. For this reason, Paul could identify those leadership roles that were assigned through Christ's gifts as the "offices" that would enable the Church to be the Church. Those offices were considered to be both representative and instrumental, ensuring the ongoing ministry of Christ in the world.

We have here, then, an ordering of the Church's life that is consonant with the universal purpose of God in Christ as well as consonant with the particular needs of the world at that time. The ministry, that is, the leadership offices of the Church, is always shaped by particular and universal contexts. Acknowledging the gifts of the Spirit and assigning responsibilities to those who exhibited those gifts became the Church's way of ordaining a leadership that was both representative and instrumental. In that ministry Christ is present and his power is at work. That is why the Church has been able to say, "this is a high and holy calling," referring not to status or position but to function.

Ordination, therefore, is to the pastoral office, not to ministry in its generic sense. As David Steinmetz has said: "Ordination is not a general commissioning for the service of God; that is the purpose of baptism" ("The Protestant Minister and the Teaching Office of the Church" in *Theological Education*, Spring, 1983, 45-54). The pastoral office is for the sake of the Church's ministry to the world, and that is the purpose of ordination. That office is entrusted with the integrity of the church's ministry.

III

It is important that we take a few minutes to refer to the special problems relating to the shaping of the pastoral office by the particular socio-cultural context of the Church's ministry. This touches upon some of the most sensitive issues facing the Church, for it has produced images of the ordained ministry that continually distort the pastoral office and inhibit the growth of the community into its fullness in Christ. The pastoral office, translated "pastoral duty or responsibility," assigned through the Spirit's work in the Church, faces always the special burdens of the particular contexts of the Church's ministry. Two of these are especially demanding: that which derives from the relationship of the institution or organization to the socio-cultural ethos of the time, and that which arises from the ambiguities and tensions facing individual members of the community in their wide-ranging circumstances and opportunities for ministry. The Apostle Paul felt the burden of "being all things to all people" - a burden every pastor knows. In addition, beset by the demands of the particular context of the Church's ministry the pastor must also carry the fundamental responsibility of representing the universality of Christ's ministry. That responsibility creates tensions that are often avoided. Particularistic contextualism almost wins out over the universal.

The tension between particularistic and contextual universalism (the Church that is in but not of the world) is really the story of the Church throughout history. Although not as pronounced in the first three centuries, that tension was heightened immeasurably by the legalization of the Christian faith. The Church was thrust into civil roles and responsibilities that soon diminished the servant style of the pastoral office and made it magisterial. Inevitably, the magisterial role was fixed on the Church's ordained leadership by the break-up of the Roman Empire and the subsequent social and political turmoil and fragmentation. Among an increasingly illiterate people the pastoral office became the locus of both civil and religious authority. The consequent shaping of the pastoral office and the interpretation of the Christian faith in ecclesial/political terms became the major burden of the Church for more than one thousand years. The identification of the universality/catholicity of the Church with the papal office was inevitable. Rome won out; at the same time Rome lost, for its shaping of the Church in a monolithic style of catholicity neglected the importance of particularistic contextuality. Rome's monistic universalism and its magisterial construction of the pastoral offices became its Achilles' heel as a restless world began to awaken.

Protestant churches have not escaped the distortion of the pastoral office by the magisterial model. The dominance of the magisterial character of the pastoral office, despite the vigorous counter-influence of monasticism in the early and late Middle Ages, has left an indelible imprint on the Church.

The image of the pastoral office today suffers from the distortion. This is evident in popular prejudices about clerical hierachicalism in which many lay persons view the very concept of the pastoral office as a threat to the ministry they have through baptism. And, of course, some clergy either consciously or unconsciously see themselves as having a magisterial role. At the same time there is the possibility that the continued acceptance of the magisterial style of the pastoral office by many persons is a reflection of the passive/dependency syndrome of much of today's privatized Christianity.

Images of the pastoral office in North American Protestantism reflect an ongoing acculturation process. It is more than a matter of passing interest that the seventeenth and eighteenth century dominant image was that of the "Master." This was, in part, a carry-over from pre-Reformation times of the magisterial image, but it was given a particular twist by Calvin's situation in Geneva and by the Puritan situation in New England. The "Master" had authority in both religious and civil matters. The nineteenth century produced radically different images of the ministry, although elements of the magisterial remained. Those images reflect the role of the Church in a time when it could serve the culture as a major force in the dissemination of public information and the shaping of values, morals, education and politics. As a consequence, evangelists, revivalists, pulpiteers and builders shaped the pastoral office to the needs of an expanding nation and growing national consciousness. The clergy generally were perceived as essential instruments for the building of a "Christian America." Churches as voluntary organizations par excellence demonstrated ways for citizens to organize for any cause. (See Robert Handy, *A Christian America*, and Martin E. Marty, *Righteous Empire*.)

Twentieth century images of the ministry have distorted the pastoral office in quite different directions, reflecting major socio-cultural changes in a maturing nation. The pastoral director model suggested by H. Richard Niebuhr never gained widespread influence except as it was caught up in a new image that reflects the impact of the technological revolution of our time, that is, the image of the minister as the manager. Enabling the voluntary organization called the church to function effectively and productively was the goal of the manager and the churches found it expedient to buy that model of leadership. At the same time, as we know, the technological revolution produced stresses and strains that took a heavy toll on the human psyche. The result was the emergence of the therapist who, in clerical collar, fit very well into the expectations of a therapeutic society.

The appearance of all these images of the ministry has engendered confusion and resulted in the loss of a definitive understanding of the pastoral office. It is clear that for much of the ordained ministry the contextual particularities of the age, unchecked by a sense of the universal or catholic shape of the ministry, simply model, with a bit of religious overlay, the social class and secular mores of the age.

IV

What is clearly at stake as the twenty-first century looms nearer is the credibility of the Church and its ordained ministry. Can a reconsideration and recovery of the pastoral office restore that credibility? The skeptic may reply: "So, what's new? The Church is always looking backward in its efforts to legitimate its existence." My response is that, while reconsideration and recovery are intimately related in what I propose, they are essentially two different things. I have sought to make that point by emphasizing the importance of each of the two contexts in which the Church's ministry is shaped: the particular and the universal. And I have sought to show that it is the failure of the Church to maintain the tension between these poles that has resulted in damaging acculturation.

Can the acculturation process ever be avoided? History clearly shows that whenever that has been attempted the Church has become irrelevant to all except the privatized faith of religious people. That is obviously a major concern as the Church faces the unknown elements of the new age. What, then, is of chief importance in the reconsideration and recovery of the pastoral office for the twenty-first century?

I propose two facets of endeavor. First, the maintenance of the tension between the particular and universal contexts of the Church's ministry. We have already discussed this, but it is important to emphasize that the maintenance of tension requires far more intentionality in the several tasks of the pastoral office than is usually given to it. I will return to that matter in my concluding section. The second facet of endeavor is equally critical, but calls for a revival of the meaning of vocation in the life of the Church. Is it possible to do that as long as we are captives of the Enlightenment's vision of the autonomous individual? I have argued in another paper that the age of the autonomous individual is passing. Into the consequent vacuum all sorts of claims have rushed. In such a time is it not the responsibility of the Church to represent and to exhibit again the meaning of the call God gives to a life that is free of self-serving?

To maintain the tension between the universal and particular requires, as I have indicated at the beginning of this paper, candor and honesty as well as a willingness to face trends toward the future that are not discernible. In bringing this paper to a close I want simply to point to things to be considered, thus to suggest a kind of agenda for the coming days as we seek to recover the pastoral office.

One is tempted to back away from the awesome task of assessing the significance of trends now already shaping the future of human life. There are "developing crises" underlined daily in the media: ecological and environmental, economic and social, diminishing resources and runaway population growth, technological discoveries and developments that baffle the mind and imagination. The list grows daily. Three examples can show the threat to human existence as we know it.

First, technological developments in the media of communication and in travel threaten the face-to-face experience in human relationships. At stake is the very existence of the human community: ways of knowing, of hearing, and of learning.

Second, bio-chemical discoveries and developments that pose never-imagined questions about the future of physical life. From these have issued ethical questions of boundless dimension for which the human mind and spirit are ill-equipped.

Third, the emergence of a two-tiered society in which the haves and the have-nots have ceased to communicate, with indifference leading to callousness among the haves and despairing frustration feeding hopelessness among the have-nots.

All three examples exhibit the extremities of the human condition that are bound to increase in the coming decades. With what understanding of its ministry can the Church in faithfulness to its Lord face these conditions? To suggest that the recovery of the pastoral office is the critical element in the Church's response may seem to some simply an exercise in futility. The justification of that suggestion, however, lies in the universality of the context of the Church's ministry: the alienation of the creation from the Creator, the continual human cry for a new creation, a new heaven and a new earth. It is to that universal context that the traditional functions of the pastoral office have immediate relevance - functions that exhibit and convey the reality of the God whose love for the world in Christ is truly good news.

But does the particular context of the Church's ministry, framed by the crises we have identified above, call for radical changes in the functions of the pastoral office? The answer is surely, yes. Adaptation has been required in every new situation throughout the Church's history. Nevertheless, the traditional functions, grounded in the universal context, continue to provide the shape of the pastoral office even as the execution of those functions is adapted to new circumstances. As the embodiment of

Christ's ministry, the pastoral office takes its cues from his ministry; proclamation by word and sacrament, prophecy, teaching, etc.

My confidence in the role of the pastoral office for the Church's ministry in the twenty-first century has been reinforced by the signs of significant adaptation of the functions of that office to the requirements of the new age. Radically altered forms of proclamation are direct responses to the way messages are heard, known and learned in this technological time. In an essay in the November, 1988 issue of *Prism*, Professor Edwina Hunter of the Pacific School of Religion identified changes that have taken place, and others being advocated in recent books. A widespread revival of interest and concern for the sacraments is evidence of the recognition of their place in these times. With that interest has come a concern to illuminate long-neglected or ill-perceived meanings. Perhaps least understood and most often neglected, the prophetic ministry of the pastoral office will most certainly show its importance in the new age. Recovery of the prophetic office flies against the pervasive forces of acculturation in every age. But there is growing awareness today that if the pastoral office embodies the essential elements of Christ's ministry it will also embody his own fulfillment of the prophetic tradition.

Renewed accent on the prophetic function of the pastoral office underlines the crucial importance of the teaching function. The teaching function, as we know, was paramount in the early centuries of the Church's history. Gradually restricted to the bishops, since presbyters were often not qualified, the teaching function became magisterial in character, gaining its authority from status and power. The consequent authoritarian character of the Church's teaching has prevailed to the present. It is, therefore, providential that recent new ways of carrying out the theological task and interpreting the faith offer an open door for the teaching responsibility of the pastoral office. Credit belongs to creative theological scholarship, and to liberation and feminist theologians, as well as to many others, for moving the theological task from its sole location in academia into the highways and byways, the homes and the classrooms of the church. The new mode of theological work depends upon the practice of the faith. In the context of the practice, teaching and learning take place. Enabling that process is the task of the pastoral office.

The interweaving of the wide-ranging demands of these three functions is confusing without their centering in the ministry of Christ. It is the distinctive character of the pastoral office as a Spirit-given vocation in the community of faith that makes such centering possible. The Church as the embodiment of Christ's ministry depends upon both the representative and the instrumental roles that characterize the pastoral office. "Let the Church be the Church" was a call from an important time in the modern ecumenical movement - a time when the credibility of the Church was also at stake. Now, in the time of the dawning of a new century, filled with both promise and foreboding, the recovery of the pastoral office will be a critical factor in enabling the Church to be the Church.

(*On The Way*, Vol. 6, No. 1, Spring 1989)

Martha Ann Baumer

The Continuing Formation of Pastors

Recently, I sat in the Abbey on the island of Iona, part of an assorted congregation gathered for an informal celebration of the Eucharist. Presiding and preaching was the current Warden of the Abbey, Brian Woodcock. He spoke directly to those who had been there for the week's conferences. At the Abbey the focus had been Celtic Christianity and at the nearby MacLeod Center, peace in Northern Ireland. He told us that the week had not been about Northern Ireland, or about Celtic Christianity, but "about you." He described how in the study and conversation surrounding these two topics, what was really happening was some sort of involving and changing of the participants themselves. To learn information, to think together about implications, to be in relationships with others, whether new friends or old, compatible or not, to care about faith and peace and justice is to discover one's self in new ways; it is to be affected and changed in the process. It is " about you." I was not among either of the groups, but I heard a clear message. When I try to distance myself in the learning process, when I think the sermon is interesting but not aimed at me, when I think I'm just an impartial observer, I'm really kidding myself. It is about me!

Pastoring, I am sure, is like that. It is about you and about me. It is about pastors and about lay folk and about all whom their lives touch. The pastor is called to be a servant of Christ, to represent the church to itself and to the world. There are various images, roles, tasks, titles and responsibilities for the pastor. The descriptions and prescriptions are helpful, but, finally, it is about the person. It is about you!

For a year now, I have been at work developing ways in which my seminary can support its recent graduates as they begin their ministries. The program comes from observations of the needs of the church and its clergy. Many new pastors have had little experience of the church and those with significant experience often find themselves in very different circumstances from what they had known. Many came to seminary without prior academic training in disciplines easily related to theology, its content and methods. Most are in a role which they may have observed or otherwise understood, but which they are discovering in new ways as they live it. Whatever their preparation and prior experience, the first pastorate or chaplaincy is the crucible in which the various pieces become blended and molded and the pastor emerges in the form which is likely to provide the basic shape of that person's ministry from then on. Those first years seem crucial and the resources available to the new pastor vary greatly from one situation to the next.

It is not only new pastors who are being formed. Though the process may be less noticeable, all are continually changing, hopefully growing, as they experience their lives and work. Pastoring is a continuing, personal process. The person of the pastor cannot be masked, put aside or ignored. The pastor does not adopt her pastoral persona for certain functions as a suit of armor in which to do battle. She will move from task to task and the particulars will change accordingly. Pastoring is "about you," and each of us is constantly being affected and molded as we go through life. We're never finished learning and growing and we need to take responsibility for our continued development as we seek to be faithful to the Christ, to the church, and to those who are particularly affected by our lives. It is easy to ignore this, or even to try to reject it as being true, and we often do so. I believe a far healthier and more faithful way is to embrace personal change and growth as an essential element of being a pastor.

Perhaps the first step is to recognize and welcome the fact that pastoring is personal and is a continuing process. Theological education, particularly in church-related seminaries, attempts to engage persons in the process of developing foundations and criteria for ministry. Such requires participants to look hard at their personal faith, their relationships in every direction, their understandings of basics of life such as who is God and who or what authors our life and work. It quickly becomes "about me," even as we strive to maintain some sort of objectivity and to gain even larger and more varied perspectives about life and faith. Virginia Samuel Cetuk of The Theological School of Drew University notes, "theological education is not about learning, it is about change." She goes on to add, "it is precisely about changing students' worldviews and receptivity to others; it is about changing their self-understandings in relation to God and others; it is perhaps even about changing their dreams." (1) Though I would argue that learning itself is about change, I strongly agree with her point.

Change is the nature of life and certainly of ministry. It never stops. As the pastor enters ordained ministry, faces new situations, moves to a new community, engages different persons, change happens. Every time she reads a book, prays seriously, listens to a complaint, becomes a parent or grandparent, loses a spouse, change happens. The pastor approaches every new day with his particular set of experiences and his particular identity. That contributes to the shape of what he sees and hears and the ways in which he understands. The experiences of the day in turn shape the pastor and she will approach tomorrow a different person. Sometimes the change is minuscule; often the individual resists any change and may even try to deny it. But I suggest that we both acknowledge the personal nature of pastoring and also seek to grow positively as persons of faith and as pastors as we welcome and engage life and ministry.

Surely this is a way of life for every faithful Christian, not to be taken lightly. God claims to be making all things new and is not only doing so but is inviting us to join in the process. What a privilege! The Ephesians and we are admonished that "speaking the truth in love, we must grow up in every way into him who is the head, into Christ, from whom the whole body, joined and knit together by every ligament with which it is equipped, as each part is working properly, promotes the body's growth in building itself up in love." (Ephesians 4:15-16). Not only are we invited to grow, we are reminded we do not do so alone.

The pastor is called by Christ and the church to represent the church to itself and to the world. The pastor does not function, ever, in isolation anymore than the baptized live in isolation. We are always part of the body of Christ. For the pastor, the claims may be more intense because pastoring itself belongs not to the individual but to the Church of Jesus Christ. Representing the church, as the pastor does, requires carrying the church's faith and heritage within one's self and being aware of how and when to share that appropriately. The pastor has agreed to be a teacher and a leader of the community of faith. The interaction is virtually continuous with the players always changing. Sometimes the pastor is intersecting with the world on behalf of the church, sometimes she is functioning primarily within the faith community, sometimes both. Basic to it all, of course, is our relationship to Christ. Pastoring is relating and relating is always personal. It is about you, about me, about us!

There are risks in all of this, some of them obvious. To welcome and engage personal change is to risk one's life. We do so with confidence because of the constancy, the will, and the compassion of the triune God. In pastoring, this means learning with and from one's people and the communities of which the pastor is a member. It means intentional biblical and theological study to examine and develop anew in each context the basic understandings and criteria which shape preaching, judgments, counseling, understanding of and participation in the whole Church of Jesus

Christ, reaching out to proclaim the Gospel in mission. It means welcoming insights from other disciplines, knowing and caring about discoveries and inventions and new understandings that shift the realities of life. It means tending to relationships with care, taking the time and giving the attention to listen carefully to the other. It means reaching out to others for companionship and support. Most new understandings and insights require shaping and practice before they are honed to appropriate use. Such happens in continual conversation as ideas and understandings are tried, remolded, tried again, given rest, applied in other contexts, seen from different vantage points.

Engaging the pastoral office as a growing, developing way of life requires letting go of that which no longer fits or serves faithfully. One key to such is being able to accept the forgiveness of God and to forgive one's self. Some things need to be let go; forgiveness says we are given new life in Christ. Churches often fail to give the pastor the time and space for healing and renewal; pastors are often unable or unwilling to claim such or do so inappropriately. Yet, without receiving forgiveness and letting go, growth and, therefore, life are endangered. It is not possible to grow without change. Change often includes pain. And pain requires healing.

Along the way, the pastor must also acknowledge and give attention to what we've come to call "boundaries." If pastoring is about the person, then the person needs to know where he starts and stops, what is appropriate in various relationships with various persons, when to say "yes" and when to say "no." To accept responsibility for the life God has given to me, I must live it and not someone else's. To accept the love God has given to me and to all, I must care for others with respect for each and for all. Those boundaries are always in danger of being hidden or being eroded. Like all fences, they require tending. This, too, is part of the reality of pastor as person.

While pastoring is "about you," it is not *all* about you! As members of the community of faith, the body of Christ, we do none of this alone. The pastor's living and growing is done among those who can and generally do offer the support, love, correction, guidance, counsel and care required. Most of us could more intentionally and carefully seek such support and welcome it when it's available than we now do. We are not left to our own devices though we may think or act as though we are. We claim the company of the triune God who has promised to be with us, who keeps promises, and who often comes to us in human forms. While pastoring means personal growth and change, it is not an individual self-improvement program. It is not for the sake of the pastor, except as the pastor is a beloved child of God and a member of the body of Christ. Pastoring is for the sake of the body and its members; it is for the Christ. It is growing and maturing as a child of God among and with all the children of God, as a member of the body whose particular vocation is that of pastor. It is living and growing with and for the Church of Jesus Christ.

That sermon I heard at Iona didn't end with comments about the week's study. The Warden continued, talking of the Eucharistic meal we were about to share. He recalled for us that as we receive the body and blood of Christ, so we become the body of Christ in the world, called to live accordingly. The Supper, he told us, is not only about God, it is "about you." Thus we are fed, called, made new, empowered. Thus we belong to the Christ and in him to one another. Thus we know who we are and what we do. Pastoring is personal; pastor/person belongs to Christ. Whatever the risks, whatever the losses, whatever the outcome, we are in the hands of the One who is love and life. That, and only that, makes it all possible.

Note

1. See Virginia Samuel Cetuk, *What to Expect in Seminary*, Nashville: (Abingdon Press, 1998), 45.

(An address given at the Annual Meeting of the Wisconsin Conference in 2000, and originally projected in 2000 for the Pentecost-Trinity Season issue of *On The Way*. This issue, however, remained unpublished.)

Ansley Coe Throckmorton

To Live the Faith

From my vantage point, both as a believer and as a "professional" in a church agency, there is no more important issue for the Church than the preparation of its future leaders. But it is an issue that calls for patient reflection, not quick fixes. There is current now a view of the nature and style of Church leadership (lay and clergy) that is partly the consequence of widespread confusion about the nature of the Church, and therefore of the proper character of its leadership in the late twentieth century. In a lecture on Church leadership, Robert Wood Lynn said this:

> The generation that is now coming into responsibility for leading the 'oldline' Protestant institution into the 21st century faces an unusually difficult thicket of perplexities; challenges so demanding, in fact, that we can rightfully speak of a leadership crisis in the 1990's (1).

The fact of that crisis can hardly be disputed. It has to do with both extraordinary new challenges and also too often with leaders in every setting who, for whatever reason, are concerned with turning the clock backwards, with maintaining and reviving ailing institutions and who fail to see that new life and new forms are emerging, the shape of which we dimly see, if at all. Furthermore there is now, too often, an excessive preoccupation among Church leaders with management, products, programs and services, all the proper primary province of business, but not of the Church. The consequence is that there is little openness to the activity of the Spirit, little attention to living the faith at any cost, and a blindness and unresponsiveness to the great hunger in the human heart and among the peoples of the world for meaning and truth. The gospel lies fallow, waiting for witnesses.

I believe that the purpose of Church leadership is to help the community of faith function as a redemptive community. If that is its true purpose, then the character and functions of leadership and the style and content of preparation for that leadership are radically affected. Walter Brueggemann, speaking of the Church and its needs, has said:

> What must survive is not simply the physical community; what must survive is an alternative community with alternative memory

and an alternative social perception rooted in a peculiar text, identified by a peculiar genealogy, signed by peculiar sacraments, peculiar people not excessively beholden to the empire, and not lusting after domestication into the empire (2).

Clearly, Brueggemann sees the situation of the modem Church on the analogy of post-exilic Judaism. He further sees three appropriate strategies and mechanisms for survival in such circumstances: 1) The recovery of memory and rootage and connectedness; 2) the intense practice of hope (e.g. apocalyptic); and 3) the intense and intentional recovery of the text of the community. Each of these identifies an alternative community and serves to preserve it. Each of these serves to bring theological dimension to an institution.

Unless the leaders of the Church understand their role, as Ezra did, as serving these ends, they will allow or encourage the institutions they lead to be so driven by management and systems that vision and calling will be lost, and the Church will be absorbed, chameleon-like, into society. It will continue to lose its voice and sign-bearing power. A Church leader who does understand her or his calling as serving the end of preserving the Church as a redemptive or alternative community, having a unique voice, will remember and remind others by word and action that the Church is a sign that humankind and creation are to be healed not broken, strengthened not burned out, inspired not organized, redeemed not managed. The authority of such Church leaders emerges from their vision, strength of purpose, and personal integrity; from their sensitivity to the gifts and capacities of those around them; from their identification with the gospel and with their constituents. It is persons of exceptional vision and integrity who remind the Church of its unique calling.

In this light, the Church leader is primarily a theologian and only secondarily and derivatively, a manager. In this light, Church leadership is radically refocused away from its current emphasis on maintenance and directed to memory, hope, and text. In this light, the Church itself will be helped to rediscover through its leaders its authentic voice for its own life and for the redemption of the cosmos. Only in this light can it hope to survive, let alone flourish as Church.

The Church has a unique vision (the Dominion of God), a peculiar sense of power (in weakness) and of truth in historical existence (incarnation). Theological education and all preparation for leadership must be carefully measured and defined for this particular time in light of that vision, power and truth. The images that are compelling in light both of the unique nature of Church leadership, and of the current perversion of that leadership, must per force affect theological education.

I propose that three images be used that are absolutely consistent with historic understandings of Church leadership, but are currently neglected in common practice. They are: 1) the Church leader as theologian; 2) the Church leader as teacher; and 3) the Church leader as representative. (1 Corinthians. 4:9 and 2 Corinthians. 5:20)

The Church Leader as Theologian

In the Autumn 1991 issue of *Theological Education*, Craig Dykstra said rightly that, "The larger whole of which we (theological educators) are and may be more critically a part is what we might call 'the practice of Christian theological education'." (3) This, he said, requires theological schools to conduct the academic study of theology, to educate the Church and the public in Christian faith and practice, as well as to prepare ministers for Church leadership. He based this on the conviction that the practice of Christian theological education is the practice of Christian faith itself, which in turn is a response to widespread and profound hunger for meaning and truth.

When I came to my present work in 1986, I met with fifteen groups across the country to survey the landscape. Each group was composed of parish ministers, lay educators and lay leaders who did not teach, but who cared about learning. One of the primary purposes of the gatherings was to learn the needs and hopes of the people in the churches. The findings were revealing and instructive. The greatest need that emerged again and again was expressed by lay leaders with stark clarity: "People have tremendous difficulty expressing their faith. We must find ways to let articulate faith arise out of the community." And another: "We're trying to give people answers before they have questions… they must be helped to ask the questions about truth, meaning, justice, and oppression."

Such a clear call for theological insight and focus must be addressed. We hear it all around whenever we listen. It reflects a deep hunger for meaning and purpose, for liberating truth and power in these rapidly changing times. It is a signal that the Church and its institutions must equip the saints for the work of ministry (Ephesians. 4:12). In order to do so, the ordained ministers, educated in theological schools, must be *theologians* — persons whose lives are devoted to the *practice* of the Christian faith, who can articulate and hear the searching questions of those around them, who can *wrestle* with and understand biblical text and story, who can see and express the relationship between the gospel and the realities of the world. That task is *theological.* The Church leader must be theological, rnust be a *theologian.*

The Church Leader as Teacher

The importance of the teaching of the ordained minister and of all Church leaders can hardly be exaggerated. It is as teacher that a Church leader presents the faith and tradition. It is as teacher that the Church leader equips the Church for the work of ministry. It is through teaching, together with preaching, that the gospel is brought to light and passed from generation to generation. In the Early Church a disciple was, by definition, a learner — one who learned how to live according to God's will. Teaching was directed both to the mind and to the will. It is in this sense that Jesus was a rabbi and teacher (John 1:38; 20:16). The Early Church tried at first to avoid the use of the word "rabbi" for anyone other than Jesus. But that couldn't last. The Church needed teachers and all of its leaders had to be teachers. "While there was a clear distinction between kerygma and didache, both belonged to both prophets and teachers. In the integration of teaching and preaching, the Church emerged." (4)

As the Church changed through the centuries, the teaching office became, if anything, more important for various reasons at different times — for purposes of apologetics, for the defense of orthodoxy, to illuminate scripture, creed, catechism and sacrament, and to nurture congregations. The teaching office is so central that the vow to teach is included in most, if not all, ordination vows. It is so important that it could be said that the Church is in peril if it neglects the teaching office. It could also be argued that it is now exposed to that peril, to the weakness and uncertainty that accompany the widespread absence of understanding of the symbols and texts of faith, to the abdication of the teaching office. There is now a growing, widespread awareness of the need for reclaiming the image of teacher for ministerial leadership. Robert Wood Lynn puts it clearly:

> If there was ever a timely moment to call for the recovery of the 'Teaching office of the church,' it is now in the 1990s. During this interim period when old line Protestants should be engaged in sustained and disciplined study of their fundamental problems, they will need teaching leaders whose commitment to teaching is so profound that it transforms not only the way they lead, but also the way church folk understand the concept of leadership. That is an assignment of awesome complexity. No other generation of church leaders in the twentieth century has been able to budge the crippling notion of leadership so deeply

embedded in our national culture. The new generation will require all the help it can muster from every quarter (5).

Dr. Lynn goes on to say that the way forward requires a "return to first principles and for Christians that takes the form of 'a critical inquiry into the Bible and the definitive theological foundations that have nurtured the Church in the past.'" (6) To that end, the nurture of teaching leaders who have the capacity to return to first principles requires that full, focused collaboration of educational institutions, especially the seminaries. Craig Dykstra adds to the litany calling for a thinking faith and therefore for teaching ministers. He has said:

> The times we live in require a thinking faith or no faith at all! If Christian faith in our times is not a thinking faith, it will not be Christian faith at all. It will be something else—something so flat and barren as to be the spiritual equivalent of despair; or something so external as to have no substantive effect on any dimension of our lives that does require thought.... The wisdom proper to the life of the believer has over the centuries, created a body of thought of immense richness, subtlety, and grace—a body of thought of enormous power to inspire and shape the human heart and will and of such beauty as to captivate and compel the mind. Thinking faith requires thinking on these things (7).

We need ministers who are teachers, and theological schools to prepare them for that role.

The Church Leader as a Representative

The Early Church had a rich array of images of the minister. Thanks to the Apostle Paul, we can never forget that the apostolic calling is first of all a matter of *being*. The apostle is a servant of Jesus Christ (Romans. 1:1, 1 Corinthians 4:1), an ambassador for Christ (2 Corinthians. 5:20), an earthen vessel bearing a treasure (2 Corinthians. 4:7), a planter for God (1 Corinthians. 3:6), a public spectacle where God's action takes place (1 Corinthians. 4:9). In all these, the one who serves is always transparent for God, pointing in her or his life and witness to another—to Jesus Christ.

Most current images of ministers emphasize what the minister does on her own or his own. To be a mentor or pastoral director is to act largely out of one's own center. That is also somewhat true to the image of pastor, teacher and preacher, though these latter roles/images derive their authority from Christ. None of the current images of the minister captures the transparency of the Pauline images or of the evangelists' picture of John the Baptist. It is the biblical images and a theological understanding of the ministry that must be desired by the Church, encouraged by theological education and cultivated in the Body of Christ. To put primary emphasis on the minister as a public spectacle where God's action takes place is to put the primary emphasis on *being* rather than on *doing*. The Church leader of the future must be a theologian, a questioning leader, and a transparency for the gospel.

Whatever else theological education must be, it must first of all exist and be designed to give definition and shape to the vocation itself, to the nature of witnessing and servant-hood, and treasure-bearing, to the cultivation and articulation of the life of faith, to the ways by which the minister is a sign to the world of the gospel. The purpose of theological education is to encourage theological inquiry, to invite intellectual honesty and modesty in the presence of mystery, to encourage the search for ultimate truth and meaning and hope. This is the purpose of all ministry: to be theologian and a questioning teacher, one who points to the truth of the gospel. It is the primary purpose *sine qua non.*

Conclusion

I have contended that in prevailing practice mechanistic images of Church leadership prevail, images that are oriented to organization, program, products and results. Charles Wood quotes Edward Farley's comment on such an orientation: "The more the external tasks themselves are focused on as the one and only *telos* of theological education, the less the church leader becomes qualified to carry them out." Wood goes on to say, "This is because the tasks of ministry require a judgment which transcends technical mastery." (8) To be a teaching minister (lay or clergy) and a representative of another reality (lay or clergy) is to transcend the technical, and address the ultimate purpose of the community of faith that is to be a redemptive community and an alternative community. The consequence of preparing teaching ministers and lay or clergy representatives of Christian reality is that theological education will be done in congregations and in denominational agencies as much as in seminaries. This is rarely a possibility given prevailing images of ministry.

This approach takes patience because it is not geared to results. Malcolm Warford has said: "The turning toward new options begins in our unwillingness to be rushed by the spirit of our age." His illustration is compelling. Thomas Merton, the Trappist monk, once explained the superb artistry of the Shakers: "The peculiar grace of a Shaker chair is due to the fact that it was made by someone capable of believing that an angel might come to sit on it." (9)

And so we seek and reflect and wait for a new day in the Church.

Notes

1. Lynn, Robert Wood, *Mid-Stream*, April 1992, 112.
2. Brueggemann, Walter, "Rethinking Church Models Through Scripture," *Theology Today*, July 1991, 137.
3. Dykstra, Craig, *Theological Education*, Autumn, 1991, 99.
4. Throckmorton, Ansley Coe, *Chicago Theological Seminary Register*, 21.
5. Lynn, *Mid-Stream*, 121.
6. Ibid, 122.
7. Dykstra, *Theological Education*, Autumn, 1991.
8. Wood, Charles M., *Vision and Discernment*, Atlanta: (Scholars Press, 1983.)
9. Warford, Malcolm L., *Living Between the Times: Notes on the Vocation of the Congregation*, United Church Board for Homeland Ministries, 35.

(*On The Way*, Vol. 11, No. 2, Winter 1994-95)

Susan Brooks Thistlethwaite

The Vision That Has Formed
the United Church of Christ (Part I)

Shifting Vision

It seems odd that I should be the one to begin this series of lectures when it was not I who was one of those whose vision did indeed result in the union that became the United Church of Christ. When Louis Gunnemann and others were dreaming of union, I had yet to finish grammar school. I belong to the next generation; those who have inherited what was wrought during the framing of the union. And to that formation we are responsible to add our own insights and energy to sustain this Church.

We are here to talk about the identity and uniqueness of the United Church of Christ. Yet, as I reflected on this theme, I became more and more convinced that one of the things we must take account of today in the UCC is that the relation of religion and American public life is undergoing a profound shift. Many of the problems that are currently labeled the "theological ferment in the UCC" (for lack of a better designation) are not unique to the UCC nor do they spring only from the identity of the United Church of Christ. As we look to the next twenty-five years of the union now called the United Church of Christ, we must be aware of the larger situation in which we find ourselves and we must interpret our own situation in light of this larger location.

Louis Gunnemann has written that "The formation of the United Church of Christ was a venture of faith, a response to a vision created out of the heritage of the past and in the context of new responsibilities." (1) This presentation is an attempt to expand on that insight from the perspectives now available in 1985. The two aspects to be expanded are the nature of our heritage from the past and the context of new responsibilities. The past we appropriate is the subject of intense debate among those who, as Barbara Brown Zikmund has titled her study, have "hidden histories." Furthermore, the history we appropriate is subject to the method we apply to its retrieval. In the mid-eighties, a method in use is to study the political and cultural impact of historical movements. Gunnemann also remarks on the crucible of the 1960s as an important point of departure for understanding the shaping of the institution of the United Church of Christ and its priorities. I agree that this crucible is crucial to our identity. It is also key to examine the crucible of today's situation in order to understand the pressures on the denomination and the possible responses available to us. I will postpone any extended discussion of the learnings from the 1960s until my second address when I hope we can discuss the alternatives available to some of our polity problems.

Robert Bellah and Ann Douglas (among others who study American Protestantism) note the profound change that took place in the nineteenth century when the major denominations were disestablished from public support. When Congregationalism ceased to be the state-supported religion of Massachusetts in 1833, churches became privately supported throughout the United States. While it was some time before the full impact of disestablishment made itself felt, the result by the late nineteenth century was that religion, like the family, was a place of private concern.

When John Winthrop and the other Puritans settled in New England, they came not to try to establish religious toleration but to found a "New Jerusalem," the "City on the Hill," in fact an ecclesiocracy. But after disestablishment, numerous factors conspired along with this legal step to separate religion from public affairs. Along with disestablishment came the rise of industrialization. The growth of a capitalist economy required public virtues (such as "dog eat dog" or "do unto others before they do unto you") to which the traditional values of Christianity were antithetical. Thus Christian virtues were relegated to the private sphere as well, and the values of the marketplace were differently dictated. The North American inheritors of a biblical tradition profoundly concerned with the public, political lives of nations and citizens now deemed Christian virtue to be a private, individual matter.

Yet, this is not the whole picture. While this history is certainly an important part of who we are in the Protestant churches, there is also a public role which Protestant churches have played in North American society. A clue to the fact that Protestant churches have had a public role in our society is the label "mainline Protestantism." This label indicates that several denominations (taken together) broadly define the main-lines of religious belief in North America.

The "mainline" churches have been close to the center of North American culture. The reverse is equally true. North American culture was close to "mainline" Protestantism. Catholics, in order to preserve a distinctive religious identity, chose not to enroll their children in American secular public schools because these schools socialized children into the distinctively Protestant character of American society.

Gunnemann quotes the Campbell-Fukuyama study of the late 1960s on the patterns of lay attitudes and church participation in the United Church of Christ. (2) Of particular significance is their third hypothesis that sought to determine whether the participants' religious orientation had any significance for involvement in the issues of society. This study found a high correlation between church participation in the United Church of Christ and attitudes that challenge cultural values. While the United Church of Christ is not the only Protestant denomination ever to challenge cultural values, it is distinguished in this respect from "mainline" Protestantism by this observation. It is well to recall this observation of the 1960s as we move to an analysis of the next twenty-five years, from 1985 to 2010.

Well into the twentieth century the Protestant character of North American public life was articulated by prominent spokespeople for these churches who often articulated issues in ways which were widely influential in the public realm as well. A Paul Tillich or a Reinhold Niebuhr spoke on public issues of concern to the entire nation It has been many years since such a public figure has emerged in Protestantism to speak on issues of concern to the nation at large. In fact, those who now articulate issues of national importance from a Christian perspective are the American Catholic Bishops. The Pastoral Letter on Nuclear War (and now the one on the economy) have come the closest to being a public forum on religious concerns.

Yet, there are important differences between the role a Protestant such as Reinhold Niebuhr played in articulating issues of national importance and these pastoral letters on the part of the American Catholic Bishops. A case in point is the Dunn Commission report. The Federal Council of Churches produced a study (largely written by Niebuhr) during the early 1950s on the churches' response to nuclear weaponry. The study ratified the position of the current administration that wholesale preparedness requiring enormous sacrifice was the only way to "safeguard freedom." As is well known, the American Catholic Bishops pastoral is a critique of the cherished doctrine of deterrence from the principles of "Just War" theory. While it is clear that Catholics have moved closer to the center of North American culture, they appear not to be nearly as captive to a wholesale identification between their religious values and those of American society as has been characteristic of Protestantism.

Part of the shifting vision of which we need to take account in the next twenty-five years in the United Church of Christ is to recognize the extent to which "mainline Protestants" are no longer the main line. Robert Bellah has made this case in his new study *Habits of the Heart: Individualism and Commitment in American Life*. We might be better off if we adopted terminology such as "sideline Protestantism" to accurately reflect the extent to which the Protestantism of which the United Church of Christ is illustrative, no longer represents the mainstream. (3)

In fact, what has happened in Protestantism is directly linked to what is happening in the larger culture. The "right" has captured the "center" and done so with more sophistication than that to which we have been accustomed. The older right has manipulated options so that what was the center now appears to be the "left" and a genuine left is out in "left field."

I

The alliance between white religious fundamentalism and the political right is evident in every major Protestant denomination. Each has its well-funded right wing which stresses "traditional family values" as a code name for attacks on feminism, racial justice, gay and lesbian concerns and a host of related rights issues. This is part of a larger national shift that is challenging the traditional center of American political life.

The seeds of this situation lie in the character of the liberalism that formed the foundation of the theological perspective of the so-called "mainline" Protestant churches. It is particularly crucial for us in the United Church of Christ to pay attention to the results of this liberal perspective, since the UCC came into being as a direct result of the outworking of these theological assumptions. Liberalism, as a theological perspective, is a reaction against the older orthodoxy that stressed discontinuity: discontinuity between God and the world, between the sacred and the secular, between Christ and humanity, between sin and grace. Life was a struggle between these opposing forces, with the Christian soul always in peril. By contrast, liberalism stresses continuity: God is in the world, the world as a whole is sacred, Christ was different from us only in the degree of his consciousness of God, and sin is lack of education. Getting "in tune" with this harmony is the goal of the Christian life.

The politics of each vision is not difficult to figure out. The older orthodoxy stressed a broad political vision in which good is struggling with evil with the fate of the nation in the balance. Liberalism, by contrast, dislikes conflict. The liberal political vision is a single issue politics: voting rights, environmental protection, etc. Since disestablishment, liberalism, the true heir of that disestablished compact between a public, political ethic and a private, personal ethic has not been able to gain a critical distance on

American society from which to provide a broad-based critique. Hence, the contrast between the Dunn Commission report and the American Catholic Bishops' pastoral. The first is primarily characterized by its assent to the public stance of the nation; the latter primarily by its dissent from one of the cornerstones of defense policy.

The pastoral on the economy is another interesting issue and provides additional contrast. Several streams in nineteenth-century thought gave rise to liberalism. Darwinian evolutionary theory gave liberalism its progressive slant, but it was romanticism that colored that progressivism rosy. In addition, romanticism is a viewpoint whose adherents regard both the family and economic relations as the realm of nature and not the realm of history. Simply speaking, this means that family relations and economic relations are fixed by natural laws (somewhat like the law of gravity and subject to about as much chance of change). They are outside the forces of historical change.

Therefore it is very difficult for liberalism to critique the economy as did the American Catholic Bishops. For liberals, the marketplace is governed by immutable laws which cannot be altered even should we try to do so. (An interesting variation on this theme, however, is that Catholics regard the family in the same natural law light as do Protestant liberals. This is evident in references to the issues associated with the family such as abortion or women's rights that receive oblique reference in the pastorals. The American Catholic Bishops cannot apply their own principles of economic justice to women.)

Thus, liberal Protestant denominations have not been able to provide the kind of far-reaching ethical guidance that the American Catholic Bishops have attempted in their two pastorals. Members of so-called "mainline Protestant denominations" are left with the impression that their faith does not speak to a great many aspects of American public life, in striking contrast to the work of some of the most influential of Protestant spokes-people throughout its history.

The United Church of Christ is no exception to this scenario I have painted of our shifting situation. Brought into being by the main impulses of liberalism, we share both its strengths and its weaknesses. In the past two decades the shifting public situation of religion in North American public life, so glaringly evident in the last election campaign, necessitates that we begin to analyze this situation, our position in it, and the extent to which we can move effectively to define a new role for the "sideline Protestant" church that faces an uncertain future.

Notes

1. Gunnemann, Louis H., *The Shaping of the United Church of Christ: An Essay in the History of American Christianity*, New York: (United Church Press, 1977), 197.
2. Campbell, Thomas C., and Fukuyama, Yoshio, *The Fragmented Layman*, Philadelphia: (United Church Press, 1970).
3. For a discussion of the "eclipse" of the Protestant "mainline," see Dorothy C. Bass, "Faith and Pluralism in the United States," in *On The Way*, Vol. 3, No. 1, Summer 1985, 12f.

(Presented at a theological colloquy of the Wisconsin Conference, UCC, in the Summer of 1985 at the Pilgrim Retreat Center of the Conference, Green Lake, Wisconsin.

Published in *On The Way*, Vol. 3, No. 2, Winter 1985-86.)

Susan Brooks Thistlethwaite

The Vision That Has Formed
the United Church of Christ (Part II)

Authority and Accountability

In the foregoing address, I briefly alluded to the crucible of the 1960s which Louis Gunnemann has observed (in *The Shaping of the United Church of Christ*) was such a significant factor in the institutional formation of the United Church. I want now to reflect jointly on the history of that decade and to examine some of the learnings that need to be challenged. In the sixties, as most of us remember, there emerged the discovery of political confrontation as a means of social change. From Rosa Parks to draft card burning, minorities came to a consciousness of their identity through group work. They confronted institutions that had systematically excluded and exploited them.

The sixties for me are both memory and history. I therefore found the section in Gunnemann's book on the appearance of James Forman (and his presentation of the "Black Manifesto" on behalf of the Black Economic Development Conference) at the Seventh General Synod of the United Church of Christ in 1969 to be illuminating reading. I will repeat a short section of that description and then move to analysis.

> Delegates gathering in Boston... for the Seventh General Synod had been forewarned to expect a different kind of synod. James Forman's supporters had received prime space in the news media by use of a sit-in in various national offices of major American denominations to underline the "reparations demands" of the Black Economic Development Conference. Both the Board for World Ministries and the Board for Homeland Ministries offices of the United Church had been occupied. Nevertheless, Forman's appearance on the speaker's platform at the synod with a group of supporters heightened the tension that had been

nourished by reports and rumors throughout the opening hours of the session (1).

Gunnemann comments on "an entirely new style of operating." I would like to argue that this is where we learned to do theology by caucus in the United Church of Christ and that this learning of the tactics of caucus and confrontation have debilitated theological creativity in the UCC (as well as in other Protestant denominations).

In order to argue this point, I should like to refer to what is popularly called "theological ferment" in the United Church of Christ. As one of the signers of the so-called "Letter of the 39," (the letter written to the Executive Council by thirty-nine theological educators urging them to institute sustained mechanisms for theological reflection in the UCC), I have been involved in lengthy correspondence with several of the signers including Frederick Herzog, Barbara Brown Zikmund and Sharon Ringe. In one exchange between Brown Zikmund and Herzog, she made a point with which I have been so taken that I want to repeat it to you here and then to expand on it.

On November 22, 1983, Barbara Brown Zikmund wrote to Frederick Herzog:

> ... I agree that we do have a theological vacuum in the United Church of Christ and that we need to do something about it. The ad hoc efforts are no substitute for some clear, agreed-upon consensus. . .as we deal with public issues, ecumenical relations and ecclesiological decisions. However, I cannot sign the statement because of the means it proposes to develop a consensus. One of my own learnings in the past decade relates to the inductive methodology used in the WCC Study on "The Community of Women and Men in the Church." For centuries the Church has shaped its theological stance in councils and commissions. Given the limitations of literacy and communication in past eras, this was understandable. As a church historian I cherish the legacy it created. But I also know as a woman (and with new sensitivity to the pluralism of the Christian community in the UCC and world-wide) that I cannot support "top down" theological formulations in these times. I believe that there is theological energy that needs to be released in our church. I would be happy to sign the statement if paragraph 3 on page three would ask the Executive Council:... "to develop a comprehensive program for assisting the UCC in its local congregations, Associations, Conferences and Instrumentalities to develop theological consensus

which would explore the central faith affirmations of our church
. . .and consider how these affirmations nurture and discipline.

The earlier drafts of the "Letter of the 39" proposed one way to approach "theological ferment" in the United Church of Christ. That way (a Theological Commission), would have been elitist, traditional and would not have taken pluralism seriously. Yet, the idea of a Theological Commission not only represents traditionalist thinking, but would have been a means to exacerbate the kind of paralyzing "theology by caucus" that now exists in the United Church of Christ and which, in my view, is a product of the 1960s. Let me explain what I mean. A Theological Commission would have had to be appointed and the appointees would be drawn, fairly enough, from the various constituencies of the Church. Having been the "women's concerns" representative on far too many committees, commissions and the like, I can tell you that this type of balancing act rarely leads to genuine creativity. It more frequently results in a trade-off posture on the part of the participants and the result holds no consistent line of development.

A consensus-building process would be a response more faithful to the actual polity of the United Church of Christ and would have a real chance to develop meaningful faith expressions. "Theology from below" is not merely the newest catchword of theologians of liberation. It is a description of what many are striving for in their religious lives today and was part, in my view, of the original vision of the United Church of Christ.

A related learning of the 1960s was to question authority. I can remember wearing a button with just such a motto. The type of authority brought into question during that period was one whose exercise was synonymous with exclusion and hierarchialization. This questioning was necessary for new structures to emerge. Yet, a distrust of all forms of authority has resulted in a radical atomism in which there is no mutual accountability across the Church for the decisions taken by the Church as a whole.

It is interesting to me to read in Gunnemann's work that a significant part of the discussions of the nature of the polity of the UCC that would follow on the union, concerned the cherished autonomy of the congregation. This concern for autonomy is consistent with the strong stress on individual autonomy in North American culture. And like the culture that it so strongly resembles, the Protestant church is suffering the same lack of commitment that an over-balanced stress on individual autonomy brings.

It is necessary to reclaim some sense of the corporate authority of the Church, but to do so without falling into the error of identifying authority with hierarchy. It is entirely symptomatic of the contemporary situation that authority needs to be defined carefully. Modernity is characterized by both an erosion of authority and by a lack of clarity about the meaning of authority. Another characteristic of modernity is the ability to turn everything into something else by redefining it. This I will attempt to avoid doing while reclaiming some aspects of the nature of authority that are ignored in contemporary usage.

The conservative view is that authority is always exercised through coercion and therefore that an authoritarian order must be hierarchical. The liberal view has been that authority is vested in an order of persuasion by reason and therefore must be egalitarian. But, on the one hand, the use of coercion to enforce obedience means that the ruling order has lost authority and cannot expect free obedience, needing to demand it by force. This is most obviously the case in totalitarian regimes in which the rulers must substitute terror for authority.

On the other hand, argumentation or persuasion equally evidences an erosion of authority. Authority does not explain itself—it must be immediately recognized as authoritative to exist at all.

One of the most enduring sources of authority is neither force nor argumentation, but tradition; a connection to the past, to what has gone before us. The Church, in its distant past, defined authoritative teaching as "what everywhere, always and by all" has been believed. While this was a necessary fiction (as all historical reconstruction is to some degree), what has gone before clearly has the unquestioned force that is authority. The Church has exercised authority in this manner. So did the Romans, on whom the Church modeled itself. The authority of the traditional has been most often administered through hierarchical orders.

Yet, there is no absolutely necessary connection between hierarchy and authority. The thrust of the last four centuries has been to question authority and consequently undermine the authority of tradition. But the loss of one dominant tradition need not necessitate the loss of the past. In some instances, the loss of tradition has been the welcome destruction of bonds holding each succeeding generation to a predetermined pattern. The danger comes not necessarily from the loss of any particular tradition, but from a loss of memory. Augustine was correct when he claimed that the seat of the mind is in the memory. To be conscious of the past is not necessarily to be determined by a particular tradition. We can mine the past selectively. We must search our past for traditions that can excite our imaginations and lend our institution the force of authority.

Part of the vision of the next twenty-five years of the United Church of Christ must be a reclamation of memory. The authority of the Church lies in the connectedness in the memory of the people of the Church to the significant events of Christian history as these are revised and reworked in contemporary context.

One of the key issues in the relationship of Church structures to the question of authority is the nature of accountability. Accountability, in my description, is an acknowledgment of the claim posed on the contemporary Church both by its past and by the whole communion of the Church. Historical consciousness and collective consciousness need to be fostered in the community of the Church to counter the type of radically present-oriented individualism that dominates our encounters with one another and which results in theology by caucus.

Mutual accountability both in history and through history does not result in stratification into hierarchies. On the contrary, it is my opinion that radically atomistic individualism is the best seedbed for hierarchy because each is jockeying for position over against the other.

An example of learnings on organic structures has come out of the women's movement in recent years. Several years ago a significant article appeared by Jo Freeman entitled "The Tyranny of Structurelessness." She pointed out that women had discovered that while unstructured interaction might work for consciousness-raising groups, it did not provide a means for the accomplishment of tasks, such as starting a crisis center. Immobilization, hidden and non-accountable leadership or elitism, were often the result. Groups would bog down in the "pit of process" or leaders would emerge whose personal charisma singled them out, but who were not representative of the group as a whole.

The more recent years of the women's movement have been characterized by a search for structures that facilitate action, but that are open and accountable. It has become evident that the choice for organizations is not exclusively between authoritarian or non-authoritarian structures, but between authority exercised autocratically (whether overtly or covertly) and authority exercised responsibly and in clear and open structures of accountability.

The authority of a church which understands itself to be rooted in Christian history but always undergoing the challenge of the Spirit can be authority exercised in accountable and participatory structures that are clear and identifiable. Authority need not go hand in hand with hierarchy, but it does require ordering for its exercise.

For the United Church of Christ, we have to be clear that the Church is a community that is mutually accountable both to its history and to its members. Each one's church is not solely under his or her "hat." Consensus building in the Church is, as in many ways it always has been, a matter of doing theology from below. Participation precedes confrontation, though confrontation is not ruled out. Caucusing, however, does not define our ways of acting together. Broadened participation in clear, accountable and accessible structures, coupled with a strong effort to reclaim an historical consciousness of the pilgrimage of the Church in all its diversity, is a diagram for the vision of the United Church of Christ in the next twenty-five years.

Note

1. See Louis H. Gunnemann, *The Shaping of the United Church of Christ: An Essay in the History of American Christianity*, New York: (United Church Press, 1977,) 85.

(Presented at a theological colloquy of the Wisconsin Conference, UCC, in the Summer of 1985 at the Pilgrim Retreat Center of the Conference, Green Lake, Wisconsin.

Published in *On The Way*, Vol. 3, No. 2, Winter 1985-86.)

M. Douglas Meeks

Sound Teaching in the Church

The celebration of the 450th anniversary of the Augsburg Confession is a time for deep appreciation and deep criticism of Augsburg. (1) More particularly, it is an occasion not only for celebrating one of the most important doctrinal origins of the United Church of Christ but also for asking whether the United Church of Christ has a doctrinal future. (2) This is tantamount, I believe, to asking whether the United Church of Christ has a future at all.

My thesis is that the UCC is and *should be* a confessional and doctrinal church. By "is" I mean to state a historical fact. The traditions and denominations out of which the UCC has been generated are doctrinal. By "*should be*" I mean to acknowledge that the current self-understanding and common-sensical perception of the UCC often seems to be that it is not a confessional, doctrinal church. It is sometimes claimed that confessions such as Augsburg have long ago proved their irrelevance to the modern world and that, furthermore, the UCC is an "open and free church" in which the consciences of its members are not constrained by written statements of belief. The slogan from the Ritschlian School and the Social Gospel, "Deeds, not creeds!" still has wide currency. I appreciate and want to maintain the critical attitude toward creeds, confessions and doctrine which has been attained with considerable theological integrity and suffering in the UCC. Nevertheless I want to argue that the future of the UCC depends on its reaffirmation of its character as a confessional, doctrinal church. Augsburg can teach us that the church cannot live without confession and doctrine (which I am going to call "sound teaching"), even if Augsburg, taken by itself, cannot be our confession and doctrine today.

The issue, it seems to me, is whether doctrinal statements are to be understood as the *foundation* of the Church or whether confession and doctrine *function* as necessary elements of the Church's mission in the world. I argue for the latter understanding of doctrine as *function* of the Church's faithfulness to its mission. Confession has to do preeminently with how the triune God binds the Church in freedom for its common tasks in the world. Doctrine always has to do with that felicitous definition of a people or community given by Augustine in *The City of God*: A "people is an assemblage of reasonable beings bound together by a common agreement as to the objects of their love… In order to discover the character of any people, we have only to observe what they love." (3) Doctrine and confession are dynamic processes by which the Church discovers its character and its possibility for being a real historical community living to change the world by stating for itself and others the objects of its love.

The tendency of many Protestant traditions has been to perceive doctrinal statements as the *foundation* of the Church. Already within a few years after it was written, the Augsburg Confession was considered, in the words of the "Formula of Concord," as "pure doctrine," a "pure Christian symbol," written by "pure teachers." (4) The chief writer of the Augsburg Confession, Phillip Melanchthon, said in his "Apology": "(I)n our confession we covered almost the sum total of all Christian doctrine." It is true that the "Formula of Concord" aptly speaks of Augsburg as "the symbols for our time." (5) But the clear tendency of the tradition has been to hold Augsburg as the very foundation of the Church on a par with the scriptures themselves and the present experience of the Holy Spirit.

For two reasons I believe this conception of confession and doctrine as the *foundation* of the Church should be rejected. The first reason is that the evangelical tradition itself demands that we be totally critical of all doctrinal and confessional statements by means of and for the sake of the gospel. The evangelical tradition knows that the gospel must be *traditioned,* that is, faithfully handed down from generation to generation and that it must be professed, preached and taught in the language of our own time. All that is necessary. The evangelical faith loves the tradition because it knows that gospel and faith are mediated through the tradition. But it knows that tradition can be dangerous and potentially destructive to the gospel and to faith. Of course, Augsburg wanted to make that point. But have not the last 450 years shown that Augsburg may have itself become the very thing it criticized, namely, a hardened tradition which may at times foreclose and enervate the gospel for a new time and a new place? (6)

The evangelical tradition knows that the tradition, the preacher, the teacher, and the theologian may be the absolutely most dangerous distorters and enemies of the gospel. What is closest to and most necessary for the vitality and future of the gospel is at the same time potentially the most threatening to the integrity and the truth of the gospel. The closer doctrine is placed in value to the gospel, the greater chance doctrine has to eclipse or replace the gospel in the present. The gospel must be free in every time and place to make its point, namely, that the only foundation of the Church is indeed its head, the Living Lord, Jesus Christ. In existing to make clear that the foundation of the Church is the gospel of the crucified risen one, Jesus Christ, doctrine functions as does John the Baptist in the Isenheim altar by pointing with outstretched finger to the crucified one: "You must increase, but I must decrease."

The second reason that the conception of doctrine as the foundation of the Church should be rejected is that the symbols of the past creeds are broken symbols. That does not mean they have no power to serve as crucial guides to the truth in our time. But the symbols of past doctrinal statements cannot be spoken immediately by the discourse of our culture for another reason, namely, because the language of our culture is broken. Thus if we try simply to restate traditional doctrine in our time as the way of expressing the objects of our love, we shall preclude the doctrinal and confessional work which we must do. The task of confession and doctrine is to restore the broken symbols of the Word of God, but that cannot be done uncritically as if we could ignore the brokenness of our own culture and of ourselves.

Augsburg was indeed "the symbol" of the Church for "that time" and it will behoove us to study carefully the meaning of this fact. Like any great confession, Augsburg expresses the shared truth and shared meaning of its time and furthermore is still open to the future referring action of the Holy Spirit. Augsburg is not a "pure symbol" in the sense that it is a perfect, final and closed symbol but is rather an open symbol, which has the creative power to contribute to our confessional and doctrinal task today.

Confession

How, then, should we understand the nature and function of confession? Confession functions to make the Church historical, that is, to bring the Church into being in a time and a place and to make the Church aware of its time and place. Confession is the way we express our willingness to bind ourselves in order to be free for God's mission in the world. Without giving an account of our hope in every new historical situation, we will be "tossed to and fro, carried about with every wind of doctrine." (Ephesians 4:14) To use the language of Acts 15 (the earliest confessional language), confession is our way of saying, after the assembly has… spoken, listened and kept silence, "it has seemed good to the Holy Spirit and to us…" (Acts 15:28) "Having come to one accord" (v. 25) through confession is the condition of the Church's mission actually making an impact on the world. A confessional church ties some things down, that is, it agrees on what is necessary for it to fulfill its mission in the world, its overall *strategy*, and thus it becomes free for expression of and debate about important differences of mind within the church about its *tactics*. A non-confessional church ties nothing down. Because everything remains suspended, it constantly replaces its overall strategy with first one tactic and then another.

Creeds and confessions are not finished repositories of truth. Rather they are agreed-upon guides. They are the instruments of the gospel's creation of the Church through the presence and power of the Holy Spirit. The first function of every Christian confession is to make clear for our time and place who is the Author of the Church. The second function is to say what it means for the Church to be faithful to its calling in the world at this time and place. Thus confessions function *hermeneutically*, heuristically and poetically.

1) Through confession the Church makes a decision about the most truthful way for reading and understanding the Bible here and now. Confession gives direction to and is itself part of the Church's hermeneutical task, that is, the task by which the Church brings into relationship what the scriptures and the Church's mission meant *then* and what the scripture and the Church's mission mean *now*. In our time this task is doubly crucial and considerably more difficult than in the time of Augsburg.

The first problem is that we experience a great distance between the world of the gospel's original text and our own world and its culture. The second and more difficult hermeneutical problem is that we experience, living as we do after the iconoclastic critique of our culture, a deep alienation from the content of the gospel itself. Marx, Nietzsche and Freud have submitted our culture to a devastating critique. We are left with the realization that there is no world that immediately and un-problematically corresponds to the gospel and that there is no present culture which can immediately and un-problematically express the gospel. We have not only to understand the text across twenty centuries but also to restore meaning to the text in relation to a world in which the gospel can be read and heard truthfully and meaningfully. Confession in our time would have to include the Church's decision on directions for going about this task.

The gospel itself claims that God the Holy Spirit creates the world, the context, in which the gospel's text can be understood. The gospel does not make sense without its reality reference to God's creation of a new world. Otherwise, belief in the gospel is merely an intellectualist or idealist activity. The hermeneutical task is to point to and engage in the Holy Spirit's creation of the gospel's world. This means that, more than ever, confession today would have to claim that understanding the gospel and participating in God's transformation of the world are one and the same activity. There is no understanding without conversion of ourselves and of the conditions around us. Confession is a performative understanding of the gospel's text by which the Church discerns and participates in the Holy Spirit's creation of a new world and in a new language situation in which the gospel "interprets itself" by converting human beings and their life conditions.

2) Through confession the Church makes a decision about where to follow up the truth it knows in its mission to the world. It engages in the heuristic, exploratory task. The truth that the Church knows has to do with its giving itself to the world. It does not grasp, possess, and fully know the truth and then engage in action; but rather it comes to know the truth only as it follows up God's promise and command that have sent it into the world. So it was with Abraham who set out into the wilderness without a map, leaving everything behind, in order to find himself and God by following nothing but a promise and a command given by God. So it was with Moses who inquired about the source and being of the strange command coming from a burning bush to liberate slaves in Egypt, but who received no complete ontological definition of God. Moses received only the assurance that he would find out who God is by following up God's promise and command of liberation in the actual historical struggle for freedom. So it was with the first disciples who encountered the risen Lord. No one believed in the risen Lord except those who were sent into mission. The obverse is also true: No one was sent into mission except those who believed in the risen Lord. Knowing the risen Lord and his truth takes place through keeping his commands: "Go into the world." "Feed my sheep," etc. Through confession the Church explores and searches out the peculiar context for its mission in the world of its time.

How do the mainline Protestant denominations in North America decide on their mission in the world? Often it is by a process of voting on priorities that have been derived from sociological surveys. The resulting "priorities" for mission often leave out the most troublesome economic issues and show no contact with the actual situation of the poor and oppressed. But does the Holy Spirit intend to leave these issues and these situations out of the picture? Is not the Holy Spirit calling the Church in North America to learn the truth of the gospel precisely in the context of economic justice and the poor? But the Church must be free and able to risk exploring the truth in these dimensions of reality and it cannot do that without engaging in the heuristic confessional task.

3) Through confession the Church makes a decision about how to participate in God's shaping of the world for a future of freedom for God's

creatures.   It engages in the poetic task for a new awareness of God's politics. It speaks confidently the gospel to the world in assurance that the gospel is a word with a surplus of meaning; a word that has the power through the Holy Spirit to create a new world. The Church's confession itself is a symbol which should be full of possibility; a symbol which means more than it says; a symbol which stimulates the imagination of every believer to find the real objective possibilities of God's transforming love of the world precisely in his or her own life-situation. Confession is the way in which we accept the full gifts of the Spirit promised and given to the Church and use them as the means of proclaiming the gospel to the world.

The gospel is a creative word. It is not proclaimed merely to create faith but also to create hope for and love of the world. That is, it is proclaimed in order to create new persons and new worldly conditions. Evangelization can be satisfied with nothing less than bringing new historical life into being. Confession is about the imagination of the Holy Spirit and the empowerment of prayer. In confession the Church is open to an imagination that shows us how actually to live into the gospel's promise of life in a society that is in love with death-serving systems. In confession the Church brings together the possibility of the gospel and the impossibilities and negations of the world and reminds itself that it has more than enough resources to do what it has been called to do. "He who did not spare his own Son, but gave him up for us all, will he not also give us all things with him?" (Romans 8:32) Confession is the way in which the Church lives in the furthest reaches of imagination to find out how the Holy Spirit really is making available what is necessary for justice so that people and the creation may live.

Confession is the way the Church in every time and place should rediscover the nature of God's cruciform power and learn to discern the various claims to power in its environs. If the Church will have fewer monetary resources in the near future, as now seems likely, we shall have to learn more about the power and resources which do not come from our own production. That happened to Peter and John when, upon hearing the plaint of a lame beggar at the Temple gate, Peter replied: "I have no silver and gold, but I give you what I have; in the name of Jesus Christ, walk." (Acts 3:6) Confession discerns and publicly expresses the power which is available for the Church's giving Itself to the world.

Doctrine

We have discussed three aspects of confession: the *hermeneutic aspect* or the way the Church agrees on how to understand the gospel's truth for our time and place and its authorization for the Church's mission in the world; the *heuristic aspect* or the way the Church agrees on why and where and to whom to engage in mission to the world; and the *poetic aspect* or the way the Church agrees on how to engage in mission to the world and with what actually existing power and possibilities to do this. I believe these aspects of confession lead immediately to the necessity of doctrine or "sound teaching." It would help us to remember that "doctrine" means "teaching" and that "doctor" means "teacher." A physician who teaches patients about their health may be called a "doctor." But in a period when this seems to be the last thing on the mind of many physicians, perhaps this functional title "doctor" should be recalled from physicians. Has the Church, too, given up its "teaching" office? When ordained clergy give up teaching, does that also signal a new relationship in which clergy merely "operate" on laity with various professional skills without teaching them so that they can take full responsibility for their life in faith and their own calling?

Confession and doctrine implicate each other. Confession makes public what we believe. Doctrine makes clear the public implications of what we believe. In confessing, we acknowledge Jesus publicly before all human beings (Matthew 10:32) and say why we belong to him as a matter of life and death (Romans 10:9). This immediately creates a forum in which the conversation of teaching explores what the confessed reality means for the believing community and for the world to which it is called. Confession always prompts questions, by confessors and non-confessors in any historical situation and thus demands the open, free space of doctrine in which responsible answers can be given. Confession without doctrine is a mere idealistic, wordy claim that shows no interest in historic embodiment. Doctrine without confession is an intellectual scheme or plan of action that has no committed agents to put it into practice. Confession should lead to new doctrine just as new doctrine will require new confession. When I say that the most urgent question of the future of the United Church of Christ is whether it will reclaim its confessional and doctrinal character, I mean that the most urgent task of this church is restoring "sound teaching."

But if I say that the Church's confession leads to the necessity of doctrine and that doctrine is about Christian education, I run the risk of gross misunderstanding because we have so trivialized the meaning of the teaching office and of Christian education. Teaching refers to the process in which the Church is brought into being and sent into the world (*educatio* = leading out). Should we not let down our defenses and habitual thought patterns and let our imaginations work toward restoring the biblical certainty of teaching —not as arid scholarship, not as information-giving, not as control of the learner, not as how-to for the manipulation of persons and nature, but as the comprehensive process by which the preached gospel creates the Church through the power of the Holy Spirit for solidarity with the poor and the transformation of the world?

But does the United Church of Christ really need "sound teaching?" Is the matter really as urgent as I am claiming? I will try to make one point toward the case for the urgency I am indicating. The UCC has been an action-oriented church. It was as if this young church assumed from its inception that there could be real uniting only by leaving behind the creedal definitions of the past and resolutely focusing on the common agendas seemingly dictated by the signs of the times. But the more relevant it has become to the world, the more it has fallen into an identity crisis. Merely because the Church is "meaningful" or "relevant" to society does not necessarily mean that it knows and practices the truth. It may simply mean that it is accommodated to the world.

History could play a dirty trick on this most "avant-garde" denomination in North America. The United Church of Christ's self-perception, which is shared widely by other Christmas, is that it has always been on the front lines in the crucial political and social crises of the last two decades, leading the way on civil rights, legal rights, human rights (when defined politically), and the questions of the health and integrity of democratic processes. It has led the way also on the issues of cultural oppression in racism, sexism, ageism and the repression of the handicapped. The traditions of the UCC, once they flourished on American soil, appropriated and richly enhanced the great struggles for democracy and the philosophical traditions behind these struggles (such as the tradition of John Locke). The UCC, even when it did not engage in theory or public discourse about these traditions, could depend upon them in its life and action because they were deeply rooted in its heart and mind.

But I think history could change this self-perception overnight, as it were, because the questions of *economic justice* are already clearly the questions that will determine the quality of the future of our nation and the world, indeed they will determine whether the world has a future at all. With few notable exceptions (such as perhaps the Social Gospel movement) the United Church of Christ does not have a rich tradition of economic justice, that is, of applying the gospel to the questions of work, production and property. Do not most public statements of the UCC still tend to speak as if the Church has only something to say about how we spend or manage the wealth we have, not about how wealth is made in our society? In this way we continue the assumptions and language of Andrew Carnegie. (7)

We tend to treat work as defined by the present job market rather than as a mode of life that has everything to do with whether persons, families and communities are genuinely human. We still tend to look upon property as a sacred right to protect the individual rather than a sign of responsibility for the vitality and future of the community and its coming generations. Part of the reason that we are unprepared for the epoch of economic justice, which is breaking out all over the world and which all our wishing to the contrary will not be able to hold back, is that we have not thought through work, production and property in our own time in relation to what God in Christ through the Holy Spirit is doing in our world. That is a doctrinal question. That is a question of "sound teaching," on which the future of this church depends.

To put it more pointedly, I would say that *the* main question of sound teaching is always, "How can the Church be obedient to the gospel in our time and our place?" And, I believe, that this question has to be asked in face of the present and coming massive increase of poor people in our country and throughout the world. Our processes of secularism, stoked by a blind technocracy and governed only by an ideology of progress, make people poor, physically and spiritually. We live in abstract notions of secular progress and of democratic freedom—that is, we cannot even see that this progress and this freedom are regarded as nothing or even as demonic by those who do not have enough bread for their children or work that gives them dignity.

Are we not even now being convicted by a deep failure of imagination to understand what is going on in Iran and in our own country? Fanatic, ugly, self-destructive religion is again rising throughout the world. The more one crisis inherent in the world economic order follows upon another crisis and the more our blind belief in progress thrives on these crises, the more religious passions will erupt in our societies. Religion as the *sigh* of the oppressed, as the *protest* of the oppressed and as the *opium* of and for the oppressed is beginning to appear in a magnitude not even imagined by Karl Marx. It seems at the moment to be the decisive world phenomenon. False, idolatrous, and dehumanizing religion is not dead but only coming into its own. The "Moral Majority" and other conservative movements, which in the final analysis are opposed purely and simply to economic justice even though they mask their protest with such issues as abortion, sexuality, and prayer and "evolution" in the schools, threaten to tear the last threads of a communal fabric which is the precondition of our nation moving toward economic justice. What we must learn quickly is that we can no longer counter either the manic protest or the oppressive masking of religion with Enlightenment rationality and certainly not with the idolatries of American "civil religion." The great majority of the world's people does not think in the categories of the Enlightenment or of technical rationality or of scientific method and they simply do not believe the doctrines of American civil religion.

It may not be too long before this is also the situation in our country as well. Iran, Ireland and Guyana are signs of the latent reality of our society. Our so-called secular age may be over. We are learning that in what we called our "secular" society actually only a very few were "secular," that is, mature, responsible and capable of determining their own future. The many have been assigned to a life of immaturity, of dependence, and of no control over their future. Their existence patently contradicts the notion of a secular society. Like Augsburg, our main doctrinal question is the *conflict of religions*. For some time now teaching in the Church has been absorbed with the question of the *relevance* of the Church to a secular society. But now "sound teaching" in the Church will have to be more and more concerned with the question of *truth*. No other way promises us liberation from the religiosity that the human heart seems so adept at producing.

As our welfare state continues to disintegrate and as our society is faced by the question of what to do with surplus people (that is the people who are not needed for and cannot be supported by the secular processes of a highly technological, profit-and growth-oriented corporate society), (8) the Church will simply not be able to live and act on the "stored up" teachings of the tradition. In this new situation the Church will either accommodate even more to the destiny of the dogmatically closed secular society or will, through its own counsels of despair, simply follow already detectable signs of atrophy in spirit and institution. Is there an alternative to these tendencies? Yes. We still have eyes to see and ears to hear that hope is the energy which God, the Holy Spirit, is giving us to invest ourselves in sound teaching throughout the Church, to find out what the obedience of the Church to the gospel means for its life in this new situation in the world.

Sound Teaching in the United Church of Christ

A remarkable document appeared in the life of the United Church of Christ at the beginning of its third decade. Entitled "Toward the Task of Sound Teaching In the United Church of Christ," it is probably the closest thing to a confession that has emerged in the UCC in the last few years. (9) It demonstrates our point that confession and doctrine are inseparable. Furthermore, it shows that confession, polity and the Church's claims about justice in the structures of human society can not be separated. They are of "one piece." (10) This document makes a giant step forward in pointing out what should be the focus of confession in the UCC and is aware that the crucial issue is the character of doctrine or teaching in the Church.

There are two kinds of teaching already implicit in the Augsburg Confession and still extant in the UCC. As is widely known but not deeply considered, it was Emperor Constantine who called the Nicene Council in 325. Why did this emperor call these theologians together? What did he want from them? What Constantine wanted from the bishops was a definition of "unity" in the godhead that could be translated into the political unity of his empire. As is widely known but not deeply considered, Emperor Charles V called the council at the Diet of Augsburg in 1530. What did he want from these Reformation theologians and church leaders? What Charles V wanted was "a united front in his military operations against the Turks, and this seemed to demand that an end be made to the religious disunity which had been introduced at home as a result of the Reformation." (11) What he got from the pen of Melanchthon with the approval of Luther and the other subscribers was an ambiguous answer.

On the one hand, those elements of the Augsburg Confession deriving from the so-called "Torgau Articles" lead to the definition of the nature of the Church as a minority covenant community: "The Church is the assembly of saints in which the Gospel is taught purely and the sacraments are administered rightly. For the unity of the Church it is enough to agree concerning the teaching of the gospel and the administration of the sacraments." This conception of the Church remains true to the Reformation starting point in the cross and does not facilely serve the functions of a civil religion of Charles' empire. On the other hand, those elements deriving from the so-called "Schwabach Articles" are attentive to how a national-cultural church could serve a public duty to the prince and civil society. For a church that understands itself to be in fact defined by civil and residential territories, by the secular calendar, and by the cultural givens, that is by the "parish," evangelization and mission are contradictions in terms, since everyone in this "Christian" society is already by definition a latent Christian. The nature of the Church gets caught in a squeeze here and becomes conflicted on levels of its life: Invisible and visible church, spiritual and organizational church, community and institution, congregation and bureaucracy, theology and polity, grace and law.

This tension inherent in the Augsburg Confession is still very much alive in the United Church of Christ and is reflected in recurring questions in its life: Is the UCC an organization for everyone in the United States, a church for the masses, or at least for everyone in the middle class? What is the function of baptism? Does baptism still function to initiate a new Christian and a new citizen simultaneously into church and civil society? Is the Lord's Supper basically closed to those who cannot fit into the ethnic and class definitions of the local church? How urgent and necessary are evangelization and mission to the North American society? If the Church should be understood chiefly as a pluralistic, national-cultural church, one kind of doctrine will be necessary. If the Church should be understood as a minority covenant community, another kind of doctrine will be necessary. This is a period in history in which the United Church of Christ will have publicly to confess its faith and in so doing decide what its character is. The reason I suggest that the "Sound Teaching" document is much like a confession is that it makes such a public statement and definitely decides that the Church is not a mass church which gets its definition from the state, from society, or from prevailing notions of culturally defined ministry. Rather the Church is the (minority) congregation shaped in covenant with God's righteousness for justice in the world. And thus it makes clear that the emergency issue is the question of doctrine or sound teaching which can serve the realization of what is confessed. Of course, it remains to be seen whether this proposal for confession will spread widely in the church so that it would prompt a broad confessing in the UCC. If this were to happen it would depend in large part (just as the Augsburg Confession depended in large part) on regaining nerve for and concentration on the teaching office in all dimensions of the church.

Reformation in the United Church of Christ should proceed, I believe, by a new concentration on the promises that are publicly given in baptism and the Lord's Supper. Reformation will depend, at least in part, on understanding that ordination is *primarily* a commission to sound preaching and sound teaching in the congregation of those who are striving daily to keep their baptismal promises. We are at the beginning of a struggle in the Church to overcome the detrimental results of the "professional ministry movement" which in many ways has eclipsed the chief responsibilities of ordinal commissioning in the life of the congregation. To be ordained does not mean to enter into a professional-client relationship in which services are rendered to a passive people with religious needs or in which psychological or sociological skills are employed to manage and control a pre-defined organization. Rather, to be ordained means to accept responsibility to teach in the midst of a congregation called through baptism to take part in Jesus' messianic mission in the world and to cooperate through the power of the Holy Spirit in the struggle of God's rule of righteousness in the world. "Teaching" and "teacher" cannot in this context derive their meaning from what has happened during the last four hundred years in Paris, Berlin, Oxford and Harvard. Rather, "teaching" will refer to the whole task of bringing the congregation into being and leading it into its mission, and "teacher" will refer, in the words of Erik Erikson, to the "mature," "generative" person who is given the task of being the "chief learner" in the congregation and of conveying whatever is necessary in the dialectic of biblical text, tradition and context for the ministry of all persons in the congregation (12). "The Lord God has given me the tongue of those who are taught, that I may know how to sustain with a word him that is weary." (Isaiah. 50:4)

The "Sound Teaching" document, I believe, has correctly pin-pointed "justice" as the primary focus in the process of regaining nerve for the teaching office. We can conclude with some notes on this process:

Justice Hermeneutic: The teaching office in the congregation should move from an exclusive emphasis on the questions of the *meaning* or *relevance* of the biblical text/church tradition to the question of the truth of God in history. When the biblical text is read only with the question of how it is relevant to the growth, development and domination of our capitalist systems, then the question of God's justice as truth does not appear. Nor does the question, "Who is God?" appear. Who God is we know from the narrative of God's history of liberating the oppressed for justice. God's name is a history; a story of justice being done: "I am the Lord your God, who brought you out of the land of Egypt, out of the house of bondage." (Exodus. 20:2) God's righteousness, that is, God's power for life, is the content of the name of God. When we want to say truthfully who God is we tell the story of God's justice. The righteousness of God as displayed in the history of Israel and in the story of Jesus as it today effects justice is the truth (though we do not possess this truth exclusively or finally). The question of "meaning" and "relevance" is the question of how this world is to be transformed into conformity with the truth as God's justice rather than the question of how God's Word can conform to the actually existing world of injustice.

Sound teaching in the United Church of Christ should center around God's claim of justice and human rights. In order to bring about abundant life for every human being, God takes sides with those whose rights are most denied in the present. The UCC Pronouncement on Human Rights (General Synod XII) says:

> All human beings have equal human rights by virtue of their
> being created in the image of God. Because of God's claim upon

all creatures, human rights have to do with the basic answerability or responsibility of being a human creature. To be created in the image of God means to be called to be God's representative to the creation. It means to be called to care for God's whole creation according to God's intention. Therefore the fundamental human right that gives the human being his or her dignity is also an obligation: to serve and to help in the creation of the conditions of life in the whole creation. The fundamental human right is the right to be held responsible by God... In view of God's claims on God's human creatures, rights are given by God as the means for all human beings to fulfill their duties before God's righteousness.

Thus human rights are what human beings must have in order to do justice. That means, in order to be human. The fundamental hermeneutical issues of sound teaching have to do with understanding God's righteousness in terms of God's justice struggle to make God's image human.

Justice Heuristic: The teaching office in the congregation should focus on the congregation as a "school for learning justice." Sound teaching is concerned not only with justification; how God makes us just, but also with sanctification; how God makes us ready to do justice. Sound teaching leads to learning how to do justice in the congregation for the practice of justice in the world. We are often mesmerized in local churches by frenetic communication overloaded with every conceivable whim and spirit from our culture. Sound teaching must be concerned with detecting and naming those things that keep us from learning justice in a genuinely free community. Most of these obstacles center around the definition of the *homo Americanus* in terms of the dominant conceptions of work, production and property in our society. No one is likely even to be sensitive to what in our society is enslaving us middleclass North Americans unless he or she is living in a community in which the issues of justice in its own life are being uncovered. This means that the teaching office will have to become much more tied to a transformed *diakonia* in the congregation. *Diakonia* is actually giving persons the justice they need to be human. This excludes all forms of making persons passive and manipulating them through "serving" or "caring for" them.

A congregation that is not producing a deadening ennui by turning in upon itself will be constantly searching for systems, organizations and movements open to justice. Such exploration is always necessary since the church cannot create conditions of justice in society by itself. But in order to do this the congregation must itself be an open system for justice. The congregation discovers the direction and conflictual location of its mission in the world by already practicing justice for the poor in its own life.

Justice Poetic: Sound teaching in the congregation has to do with pointing to the real objective possibilities of cooperating in God's justice in the world. The question of *authority* in the congregation finally comes down to the question of whether there is an Author, a Poet, a Creator whose Word creates a new world actually containing possibilities for obedience to the lordship of Jesus Christ, God's incarnate justice. Without imagination, the Church always succumbs to the world around it that it describes as the *real* thing to which it must conform. Sound teaching points to the poetic power of the gospel as that which is most real. And therefore it imagines a different world, a just world, that is, a true and real world. Sound teaching is not thereby utopian, but rather points to the gospel's power to disillusion us about untrue claims of an unreal world of injustice. Perhaps the hardest thing to learn *in* our congregations today will be that sound teaching is basically *praxis*. It does not suffice to know the meaning of justice in the abstract. Nor does it suffice to practice justice only in the congregation. Everything is aimed at finding the power and the means to do justice in the world. Those who are liberated by the justifying power of God's grace and sanctified by the Holy Spirit in the community of saints for mission will also look for God's creation of the possibilities of justice in the world. This is also part of sound teaching. Those who accept the responsibilities of the ordained pastoral and episcopal offices and thus become chief teachers in the mode of chief learners will have as the greatest of their responsibilities the task to find the poor and oppressed in their region of leadership and to lead the people in their struggle for justice in the midst of the poor.

It is only important here to stress that the "justice poetic" is not the last in a series of educational steps. It has the priority, since everything begins with God's passion for the world, with God's poetic to create a new world of justice. Doctrine, sound teaching, therefore begins and ends with the realization: "To know God is to do justice."

Sound teaching means the *reformation of the Church*. In that we can completely agree with Augsburg. Only now the churches that must be reformed are the very churches that were in part engendered by Augsburg: our churches. Would there be any other conceivable way of expressing gratitude and allegiance to Augsburg except by continuing the Reformation in our time by new confessing and sound teaching?

Notes

1. Useful studies of the Augsburg Confession are: George W. Forell, *The Augsburg Confession: A Contemporary Compassion*, Minneapolis: (Augsburg, 1968); Joseph A. Burgess (ed.), *The Role of the Augsburg Confession: Catholic, and Lutheran Views*, Philadelphia: (Fortress, 1980); Wolfgang *Bartholomae, Einfuhrung in das Ausburger Bekenntnis*, Gottingen: (Vandenhoeck & Ruprecht, 1980); Leif Grane, *Die Confessio Augustana. Einfuhrung in die Hauptgedanken der lutherischen Reformation*, Gottingen: (Vandenhoeck & Ruprecht, 1980); Harding Meyer (ed.), "The Augsburg Confession in Ecumenical Perspective," in *Lutheran World Federation Report*, 6/7, December 1979, Geneva: (Lutheran World Federation); Fredrich Wilhelm Katzenbach, *Augsburg 1530-1980*, Munich: (Chr. Kaiser Verlag, 1979).

2. The Preamble of the United Church of Christ Constitution says that the UCC "claims as its own the faith of the historic Church expressed in the ancient creeds and reclaimed in the basic insights of the Protestant Reformers." For the UCC, these "basic insights" of the Reformers are mediated especially through the Augsburg Confession, Luther's Small Catechism and the Heidelberg Catechism. See Douglas Horton, *The United Church of Christ: Its Origins, Organization, and Role in the World Today*, Philadelphia: (United Church Press, 1962), 59ff; Hanns-Peter Keiling, *Die Enstehung der "United Church of Christ" (USA)* Berlin: (Lettner-Verlag, 1969), 167-176; 190-194.

3. Augustine, *The City of God*, Bk. 19, par. 24.

4. Tappert, Theodore G., (ed.), *The Book of Concord: The Confessions of the Evangelical Lutheran Church*, Philadelphia: (Fortress, 1959), 520.

5. Ibid. 465.

6. And thus at its inception the UCC, in order to be a united and uniting church, refused to understand received creeds and confessions as a "test of faith." This does not mean, however, that faith in the UCC does not need confession and confessing. Christian faith must be publicly expressed. That is, in the first place, the simple meaning of confession.

7. In an essay entitled "Wealth" published in 1889 in *The North American Revival*, Carnegie argues that the way human beings acquire wealth is determined by the laws of competition, individualism and the survival of the fittest. These laws are inexorably embedded in nature and it would not behoove the Church to try to change human nature. Once one has earned one's money, however, it is then possible to assert the rules of charity for the dispensing surplus wealth to the poor. The "man of wealth" with a good will knows best how to effect the most beneficial results for the poor and the community as a whole.

8. See Richard Rubenstein. *The Cunning of History: Mass Death and the American Future*, New York: (Harper and Row, 1975).

9. "Seminar Report: Toward the Task of Sound Teaching in the United Church of Christ," The United Church Office for Church Life and Leadership. The complete document can also be found in the Appendix of Frederick Herzog, J*ustice Church: The New Function of the Church in North American Christianity*, (Maryknoll, N.Y.: Orbis Books, 1980), 139-154.

10. "We understand that confessions of faith are not free- floating formulations detached from the structures of' human society. They are of one piece with a polity that reflects

this faith in the context of human organizations." See Herzog, *Justice Church*, "Appendix, Seminar Report," 143.

11. *Book of Concor*d, editorial Introduction to "The Augsburg Confession," 23.

12. John T. McNeill shows that pastoral care from the New Testament perspective is chiefly a matter of teaching understood as healing and preparation for life in the world through the total formation, of the congregation. *A History of the Cure of Souls*, New York: (Harper and Row, 1951), 67-87. For his view of the relationship of teaching and generativity see Erik H. Erikson, *Childhood and Society*, 2nd ed. New York: (Norton, 1963), 266ff. ad passim. See Juan Luis Segundo, *The Liberation of Theology*, (Maryknoll, N.Y.: Orbis Books, 1976), 110-122 for a conception of "*deutero*—learning" as "learning to learn" justice in the congregation as opposed to modern concept of learning ruled by the Baconian dictum, "Knowledge is power."

(This undated monograph was a contribution to the theological "ferment" that took place in the United Church of Christ in the 1980s and 1990s, following several significant theological developments, including the publication by the UCC Office for Church Life and Leadership of a document called "The Task of Sound Teaching in the United Church of Christ.")

Frederick Herzog

New Spirituality as Grass Roots of New Doctrine

The misunderstanding of theology might already have been the real issue when Emil Brunner in the early 1950s published "The Misunderstanding of the Church." A vast Himalaya of words has accumulated since. If anything, understanding theology has not improved. The misunderstanding is that theology is the be all and catch all of Christian thought. In many denominations it has become a surrogate of spirituality and doctrine. The early medieval church developed the creeds. The Reformation produced confessions. Modern liberal scholarship often intimated that creed making and confession writing had spent themselves. Has anything arisen in their place? It cannot possibly be theology, since increasingly it is an individual and very private enterprise.

Circumstances have recently developed that put Christian doctrine in the foreground again. There is a new process of teaching formation, a new step in Christian thought. Its final shape is not yet fully clear. Now creeds and confessions apparently are not immediately looming on the horizon. But there is emphasis on sound teaching. In certain quarters it is seen as arising ultimately only as accountable teaching—Christians joining minds and hands in helping each other understand the core of their witness in a new teaching mode, directly making each other accountable for the witness. Theology is no longer in the driver's seat. It turns out that it can only be a second step trying to make old and new doctrine more transparent.

It needs underscoring that the new shape of teaching is an outgrowth of the new spirituality growing at the grass roots. It suggests that new doctrine in the church arises from new discipleship, from what I like to call "God-walk"—distinct from "God-talk." Perhaps in the early 1960s it could still remain hidden that the Civil Rights struggle born in the God-walk of the black church had much to do also with doctrine. Yet as soon as an articulate response to Black Power occurred (Cone's and Wilmore's work among others), it was clear that doctrinal issues were at stake. Today, South Africa is adding to the same doctrinal churning. On the foil of the Reformed apartheid teaching, a new truth/untruth struggle is arising. Similar things could be said about the women's struggle, and other examples abound.

The core of the process is a new spirituality, not a new dogma, not new concepts for the sake of concepts. There is a new sensibility among Christians moving closer in on each other and joining hands with all humankind. The ecumenical movement is one of its expressions. But more important yet, Jesus is encountered anew in situations of dire need throughout the world. The base communities in the Third World are one dimension of the new encounter. The new teaching mode tries to offer a new center of spirituality. Under its aegis, a phrase like "Light of light, very God of very God" (Nicene Creed) now appears not as a mere dogmatic formula, but more like a mantra of Christian spirituality. The World Council of Churches has a parallel formula, though for somewhat different purposes: "Jesus Christ, God and Savior." In our situation of global poverty and dire need we might instead be moving toward an affirmation like "Jesus, refuge and refugee."

From the Grass Roots Up

New Conversations (a journal of the United Church Board for Homeland Ministries), offers its Spring 1985 issue under the theme, "Toward Theological Self-Understanding in the United Church of Christ," an intense dialogue between conservative, liberational, and confessional groups at the grass roots. In several respects it is a prism of what is happening in other North American churches by way of teaching formation. The "United Church of Christ may be a good case study of the unique ways in which theology is changing in the modern world." (Barbara Brown Zikmund). Our point cannot be that one denomination presents an ideal model of what ought to be happening in other North American denominations. What is crucial is that a number of denominations reflect a new step in doctrine formation. People are teaching each other and learning from each other. "There is a vast reservoir of insight in the rank and file UCC pastoral and laity leadership." (Gabriel Fackre). The process of teaching is no longer moving hierarchically from the top down, but corporately from the bottom up. Spiritual formation at the grass roots is evoking a new teaching formation.

We presuppose new spiritual formation when we give an account to each other on our diverse thoughts that emerge from our varied praxis. There is a distinct difference from the way such a process developed in the past. Early medieval teaching formation climaxed in synods or ecumenical councils—the Emperor at times imposing a heavy hand. In the Reformation, individual theologians usually determined the formation of confessions. Melanchthon is a good example. Today we work with a keener sense of corporateness. Christians on all levels of church structures are struggling with each other for a new root metaphor of faith in keeping with the Tradition. "Jesus, refuge and refugee," could be one such metaphor.

As soon as one turns one's attention away from the struggle of church people to understand the "real presence" of Jesus today, one is caught up in the nightmare of what Ronald Goetz (*The Christian Century*, April 6, 1986) has called "The Rise of a New Orthodoxy." Whatever shade of new orthodoxy may be emerging one can only say: "God forbid." In these trying times there is the temptation for the theological guild to pull together, shore up its defenses, and start working on a new system which turns out to be a new straight-jacket. The opposite temptation is to let everything ride and to leave it to pluralism.

Some liberation theologians have suggested that instead of orthodoxy, we had better first consider *orthopraxy*, a new grasp of God arising not from sheer abstract argument, but from the argument of our lives. God-walk might, for example, turn the old theodicy logic around. The old theodicy asked, "*si deus, unde malum?*" "If there be God, where does evil come from?" By way of deduction from an abstract notion of God, one tried to tackle evil as a theoretical issue. Today, the whole thing might be turned upside down: "*si malum, unde deus?*" "If this be evil, where does God enter the picture?" The most basic contemporary doctrine formation begins with the denigration of humanity, the debasement of persons, the non-person. It is in this relationship that at the grass roots people begin to think anew. The new God-question is evoked by the struggle with injustice.

In the struggle itself we might not find any answer, but as Christians we are enveloped by the "real presence" of the Christ struggle in history. Thus, instead of our *orthopraxy* we need to begin with the *Christopraxis*. The burden of the justice struggle does not lie on our shoulders. The Eucharist makes this clear to us time and again. We sense that Jesus offers us help as God's right hand in the struggle. While we do not see that Jesus always mitigates evil, we realize that he always litigates evil. There is controversy of God with evil throughout the world. Jesus spearheads it.

God's Deprivation

So there is a little "theodicy reservation" before we scurry off to answer the question of evil on the old theodicy model. It is so small we almost do not notice it. And yet it makes all the difference in the world. We cannot come to grips with the theodicy question, for example, unless our spirituality has been revamped. Spirituality is the soul turf on which we exercise our conscience in new relationships to God, others, and the world as a whole. Spirituality is indwelling our true relationships. Yet, it is never without the Tradition.

We had better not seek the security of the Tradition. Yet, unless we "secure" our new insights in the cues our Tradition offers us, we lose our bearings. If it were not for "mantras" like "truly God and truly man" or "*homoousios*"—as they emerge from the Nicene and Chalcedonian faith accounts—we would perhaps not even be aware of the need for new root metaphors in accountable teaching.

The awesome difficulty of First World theology to come to grips with new doctrine formation arises from its inability to indwell the spirituality of God's justice struggle in Jesus—the divine litigation of evil. God's justice struggle is never without God's solidarity with the non-person. Yet, the non-person thus far never appeared as a crucial factor in teaching formation. So today the non-person is almost a brutal interference on the playground of the theologians. There has been the almsgiving type of generosity to the poor, also the Social Gospel passion for the underdog. But ultimately the non-person stayed relegated to the field of ethics; the application of dogmatic theory, if related to anything theological at all. Non-persons had no place in dogmatics (just as Albert Schweitzer's famous dog had no place in ethics) and therefore played no doctrinal role whatsoever. It has been forgotten completely that Jesus is a refugee; a homeless one.

Being compelled to hear the word of God in the non-person evokes a new phase in Christian thought. Not only is the root metaphor different, but the elementary relationship to God in Christ is changing. That is why theology is changing in the modern world and is being relegated to a second step. First comes a new grasp of spirituality. So Christology and Christian anthropology will also need to be revamped by the new spirituality. Incarnation is still a buzz word. We think we know what it means. But pontification on incarnation without specification of God's solidarity with the non-person is utterly inappropriate today. First the *Christopraxis*, Jesus' struggle, engages us. There is no leisure to reflect abstractly on the suffering of God. Jesus leads the caravan of the despised trying to do battle with evil. Nicea and Chalcedon did not let Jesus as refugee, as the homeless, the non-person, through the lofty Christological grid. So Jesus in the dogmatic tradition hardly appears as a particular human being, but at best rather abstractly as impersonal person (as in the old doctrinal notion of *enhypostasia*.) Nicea and Chalcedon dealt with the divinity of Jesus, but not with the "humanity of God" in the streets—God in solidarity with the poor, wretched, human being.

In some respects, we are still very much where we were at the beginning of the twentieth century when Schweitzer wrote, *The Quest of the Historical Jesus* (1906). We remember how he stated the problem: The dogma "had first to be shattered" before we "could once more go out in quest of the historical Jesus." Meanwhile, there have been several, even gigantic, attempts to reconstruct the dogma. But all around there is the nagging feeling that we have not as yet achieved a workable meshing of history and dogma. What is more (in Schweitzer's words): "We have not yet arrived at any reconciliation between history and modern thought-only between half-way history and half-way thought. What the ultimate goal towards which we are moving will be, what this something is which shall bring new life and new regulative principles to coming centuries, we do not know."

Meanwhile, we have at least a glimpse of what brings new life and new regulative principles to coming centuries because of God's solidarity with the awesome poverty that stares us in the face everywhere on our globe, largely brought about by modern thought. The new quest of the historical Jesus has not helped us very much in coming to grips with this new "environment." It is rather from *Christopraxis* (God-walk, discipleship) that we learn new Christological thought. It is from here that the question of God's suffering becomes acute; not in retrospect. In the struggle of the poor we encounter Jesus first of all as God's right hand of justice. Here God litigates evil. In the *Christopraxis* of the poor Jesus, we learn that the dynamics between Jesus as non-person and Jesus as person is as crucially thought-provoking as the Nicene-Chalcedon dynamics between true God and true man. God's justice struggle is not the primary issue. This is not a theoretical point. Evil is being litigated, coped with.

God's own deprivation in Jesus, God's impoverishment, is a correlate of God's solidarity with the poor and oppressed in the justice struggle. Many of us orient ourselves and act out our lives in keeping with some root metaphor that compacts what we deem reality to be like. For medieval times or the Reformation grasping reality hinged on Chalcedon's "true God and true man." Here was the ruler of the universe, the heavenly Emperor, the *Pantokrator*, and the final Judge. How the young Luther cringed before Jesus as Judge! Jesus as refugee; homeless and non-person, was not part of it. Jesus' humanity not only paled, his human person no longer existed. Says Schweitzer: The supra-mundane Christ and the historical Jesus of Nazareth had to be brought together into a single personality at once historical and raised above time. That was accomplished by Gnosticism and the Logos Christology... When at Chalcedon the West overcame the East, its doctrine of the two natures dissolved the unity of the Person.

Now, when the Third World "overcomes" the West as well as the East, the doctrine of Jesus as refugee, as homeless non-person, might reinstate the unity of the person. As the divine person enters human deprivation in the non-person, the deprived non-person Jesus also constitutes God as person—instead of disappearing as person in his "privation." So God as person is constituted also by the homeless, the faceless, the throwaway; the non-person. Only on these grounds does it make sense to puzzle about the suffering of God.

God's promise is crucial: There is nothing worthless. The most despicable creature in human eyes is of equal worth with the humanly most honorable. The person is not meant to be merely an object of charity. The Hebrew people before Jesus' day already sensed why the "impoverished" Servant of God shows no form or comeliness (Isaiah 53). Jesus underscores it. God resists evil.

This is also the point of the unity of Jesus' person. The unity lies in the oneness of the personal divine deprivation and the non-person's deprivation. It is not an end in itself. It seals the worth of the worthless. We are not allowed to reject even the most ragged "shred" of the human. God gives infinite worth to the worthless. Whatever countermands it is evil and needs to be resisted. We do not first of all hear the word of God through non-persons. We meet the "very God" in the non-person, struggling for justice. That is what the struggle for mutually accountable teaching and learning is all about. The dignity of each human being is at stake, especially that of the most despised. God did not become merely "man", but a despised refugee. Along with him into exile went the parents. A woman was part of the "flight into Egypt." So God is present also in the despised women: battered, illiterate, and tilling the land without owning the land, bearing children often forced to die in men's wars.

We do not as yet have a common grasp of a new root metaphor. The professorial guild will not produce it for us. It will emerge from the toils and trials of the people. It will have a lot to do with God in deprivation litigating evil. It will make us choose between our comfortable cult Christ and the street Jesus. If God in person is a refugee, how can we deny sanctuary to the refugee? If God in person is homeless, how can we ignore the street people?

The Confessional Situation

This is a time of waiting. The main task now is to grasp the revamping of our spirituality. The mutual accountability in teaching we sense today opens our eyes to the new spirituality developing. We need to listen to what is going on in our own denominations in this regard. No longer can conservative, confessional, and liberational groups treat each other as non-persons. In a more elementary way yet, we need to hear the pain of the Third World mediated, for example, through Gustavo Gutierrez (*We Drink from Our Own Wells*, 1984). Here we inescapably encounter new spirituality in new relationships. God appears in solidarity with the non-person. We can think of the new situation only in fear and trembling. There are still the old expectations with which others approach us. There are countless people we will fail on the old and even the new terms. The dynamics of failure, grace, and forgiveness will forever be with us as the Eucharist will time and again make clear to us. Yet, we cannot avoid the new situation.

The full understanding of the new spirituality is still in the future, yet we are already struggling over its validity. The relationships constituting the new spirituality shape a new selfhood that contradicts the way we usually see ourselves. We are quickly moving into a situation where those who are caught up in the new selfhood clash with those who still see themselves differently. Robert McAfee Brown suggests that we have reached the *"status confessionis,"* a confession situation "in which the church, in order to be true to itself and its message, must distinguish as clearly as possible between truth and error. There are times, particularly if public policy is concerned, when Christians may disagree. …Christians (in the United States,) for example, frequently disagree about tariff policies or interest rates. But some issues are so fateful that no disagreement or compromise is possible." (see *Saying Yes and Saying No: On Rendering to God and Caesar*, 1986). As examples, Brown points to nuclear weapons and the demands of the national security state expressed in the United States invasion of Grenada. Behind all the concern over the present *status confessionis* lies the struggle over a new spirituality. Some theologies still take for granted the conventional wisdom about our elementary relationships. Yet that also implies agreeing to a God who legitimates the present power arrangements in our world, essentially unconcerned about the fate of the non-person.

The lines of the struggle are clearly drawn. Christians have many concerns today. There is the sanctuary movement aiding refugees in our national backyard. There are the farmers forced off their homesteads in our national front yard. We become increasingly aware of South African blacks exiled from their "homesteads" to so-called "homelands." Yet, in our medical sanctuaries in the West, millions of fetuses go down the drain—unborn non-persons. Part of the breakup of the family in the United States is unwed teenage mothers—often also non-persons. We are not getting a handle on our permissive society coming apart at the seams. We may ponder the need for an alternate spirituality. And yet subliminally we may still be satisfied with our "junk culture" (*Time Magazine*).

God is present to the fetus as non-person is to the battered woman who should not be forced to become a mother. Only an impoverished God who is not an idol can turn us around and wrest awe from us, so that we want to become new human beings. Only the homeless Jesus can heal our broken homes.

"Doctrines function as rules." (George A. Lindbeck). They thus function only in a church of mutually accountable teaching. The mutual accountability is possible only where a new spirituality prevails. Here, ethics is no longer an appendix of dogmatics. In God's justice struggle, at the grass roots, dogmatics and ethics are fused. In minimal ways, we are already learning that these two strands of Christian thought can be tackled from the bottom up. It is not too late for any church to let its accountable teaching trumpet give no "uncertain sound" (1 Corinthians 14:8).

(Unpublished monograph that appears in this volume through the kindness of Dr. Kristin Herzog, Durham, North Carolina.)

Susanne Hein

The Public Witness of Women
in the Confessing Church: 1934-1945

With women you don't make a church struggle (*Kirchenkampf*).
We leave that to the men!

This was said by Kurt Scharf, the President of the Confessing Church of Berlin-Brandenburg. (1) It was said to the Gestapo, the secret service of the Nazis. Of course, Pastor Scharf used this as a way to get his secretary out of jail. But if you look at the meetings and the committees of the Confessing Church, you could think this truly was the reality. At the famous Confessing Synod of Barmen in May 1934, there was only one woman, Frau Stephanie von Mackensen from Stettin in Pomerania. The leading committees within the Confessing Church were called *Bruderräte* (Councils of Brethren). The representatives on the committees were men: Dietrich Bonhoeffer, Martin Niemöller, Kurt Scharf and so on. And if you look at the books and research projects about the Confessing Church, this impression will be confirmed.

Given this background, it is remarkable that you have included the public witness of women in the Confessing Church as part of the agenda of this theological gathering today. Yes, there have been of course sisters among the brothers during the struggle of the churches against Nazism! They did the *practical* work within the congregations and the practical *illegal* work. For understanding this you must know that female theologians were not allowed to be ordained or to serve congregations as pastors; neither in the "official church" of the "German Christians" ("Deutsche Christen") nor in the Confessing Church.

Because of the contemporary women's movement, interest in the role of women in the Confessing Church has increased. Nowadays you can find some writing about the "Women of the Confessing Church." (2) Most accounts are based on interviews with those women witnesses who had been active in the church at the time (1934-1945). The results of two research projects related to these witnesses will be published this year. Rather late. So I can't give you an extensive view, but I will try to offer some ideas on the witness of women in the Confessing Church. Who were "the sisters with the red card," the membership card of the Confessing Church? They were female theologians, spouses of ministers, secretaries in local churches, female parish workers, volunteers and so on. I would like to tell you a little bit about some of these "sisters" who can stand for the countless confessing women.

Vikarin Katharina Staritz

Katharina Staritz was a theologian with a doctorate (Ph.D.). She was one of the first female theologians within the Evangelical Church of the Old Prussian Union (3). She worked in Breslau (today this city is in Poland) as a so-called *Vikarin* (Assistant Minister). In this time in Germany women could study theology, but were not allowed to serve as pastors in congregations of the Protestant Church in general. Even the Confessing Church didn't break with this tradition. A female theologian could work in a congregation as a *Vikarin*. This is the name given to a pastor who is still in training. But as such, a *Vikarin* was not allowed to preach on Sunday, or to baptize or to confirm. Her responsibility was especially the work with women and children within the congregation (4). I will come back to this point later.

In her local church, Katharina Staritz was responsible for looking after so called "non-Aryan" church members. Since 1939 within Germany there were twenty-one church offices that were in charge of the baptized Jews. From September 1941, all Jews older than six years had to wear in public the Star of David. In a circular, the Deacon of Breslau asked the pastors, in cooperation with Katharina Staritz, to act in solidarity with those members of the church who were affected by this police regulation. Katharina Staritz asked them not to expel those marked people from church life. Practically, the pastors were asked to help those who had now to come to worship or Sunday school with the Star of David. The official instructions of the German Evangelical Church, however, said that the congregations were responsible to see that the baptized non-Aryans stayed away from the church. Katharina Staritz was fired. Six months after this circular, she was arrested and put into the concentration camp at Ravensbrück for one year.

Vikarin Klara Hünsche

Klara Hünsche was one of the Confessing Church's most significant theologians. She had been a teacher. As a second career, she studied theology and was examined by the Confessing Church in 1935 and again in

1937. Then she was "consecrated" in Berlin. She couldn't be ordained because she was a woman. As a *Vikarin* she was responsible within the Confessing Church of Berlin for the concerns of schools, for example, the further vocational training of teachers of religion. Especially within the "school struggle," she fought for teaching both the Old and New Testaments and against the preaching the "Aryan" Christ in the schools. This was very difficult but important work.

When, in November 1938, the Nazis forbade Jewish and baptized "non-Aryans" to attend public schools, parents organized (together with the Confessing Church) school lessons for those children. The idea that baptized children had to go to a school for Jews led the Confessing Church to become active. Klara Hünsche led such a school and there she offered religion classes. Because of her illegal examination in the Confessing Church, she had to work at a military office at the beginning of 1941. At the school she continued to teach secretly. This was very dangerous. Finally she experienced the powerlessness of the Confessing Church. Nearly all of the children were deported and killed.

To be a witness to the Word of God was the basis of her work. Klara Hünsche didn't fear danger. But for Jewish and other non-baptized, non-Aryan children, she did not intercede. Klara Hünsche had wanted with all her heart to be a pastor within a congregation. She was deeply engaged in the discussions within the Confessing Church about ordaining women. She liked to preach. At the end of World War II she was allowed to preach for her brother. But she had to give this up again in 1946 because by then there was no longer the emergency situation of the war. Once again, female theologians could not be full pastors.

Senta Maria Klatt

Senta Maria Klatt worked ten years as a secretary in the illegal office of the Confessing Church in Brandenburg. She worked especially for Kurt Scharf and Otto Dibelius. Before this, she had led a church day care center. In 1934, she had to prove that she had an Aryan descent. She could not because her mother was Jewish. So she immediately lost her position. Senta Maria Klatt typed the correspondence and statements of the Confessing Church. She ran many errands and was responsible for the bookkeeping. This office work was extremely dangerous because it was illegal. She was summoned more than forty times to the Gestapo. She herself knew that the role of the Confessing Church began on the level of practical work. Once when she was arrested, Kurt Scharf went to the chief of the Gestapo in Berlin (Alexanderplatz) in order to protect his secretary. Scharf explained to him: "With women you don't make a *Kirchenkampf*; we leave that to the men." On the same day Senta Maria Klatt was released.

Every Sunday the Gestapo tried to confiscate the offering of the congregations of the Confessing Church because this was the financial basis of its work. Once Senta Maria Klatt had to revise in the accounting book all receipts for one year. Together with a *Vikarin*, she worked on this through the night. The next day, Kurt Scharf had to go with this forged offering list to the Gestapo. To their surprise it worked. Several times the office in which she worked was searched by the Gestapo. Often she was able to hide documents for which the Gestapo was looking. Once she had to carry a letter from Otto Dibelius to Admiral Canaris, chief of the counter intelligence service and active within the resistance movement. (Canaris was engaged in the assassination attempt on Hitler in July 1944.) Just as she was preparing to leave, she was arrested. The letter was hidden in her muff. During the questioning she had a moment alone. It was then that she ate the letter.

Another time, in 1944, at the offices of the Gestapo, she was presented with a committal to the concentration camp at Ravensbrück. With a trick she was able to rescue herself. But then she had to work in a military company until the end of the war. Nevertheless, she remained an active member of the Confessing Church.

Margarete Magdalena Grüber

A fundamental element in the Confessing Church was the confessing parsonage. Spouses, in addition to their traditional work within the congregations of their husbands, secreted documents of the Confessing Church, delivered information or letters, hid Jews and so on. Sometimes, the pastoral families had six or seven children. Usually the spouse was responsible for financing the daily life of the family. This became very difficult when the pastor worked illegally for the Confessing Church and did not receive a periodic salary. Such a family was often supported by the congregation. People gave them money or food.

Margarete Magdalena Grüber was the spouse of Heinrich Grüber, a pastor in Kaulsdorf, near Berlin, who founded the *"Buro Grüber,"* an office for people who were persecuted because of their race. Katharina Staritz worked for this office in Breslau. At first this was a private activity. Grüber asked his wife whether she agreed that they put all their private money into this work. She did. In 1937, Pastor Grüber was arrested for the first time. She was allowed to visit him in the Gestapo jail. They were permitted to say goodbye with a kiss. In this moment she would pass money to her husband. This was usually just before the first of the month, and being without this money for the remainder of the month was not easy for her.

Pastor Grüber was able to rescue some Jews and bring them to safety outside Germany. Often, the Grübers had such persecuted persons for a night or longer in their house before they could be hidden by members of the local Confessing Church somewhere else. Margarete Magdalena Grüber worked with her husband on this although they had three children. When her husband was arrested again at the end of 1940, he was sent to Sachsenhausen. He was then brought to the concentration camp at Dachau. During the three years he was imprisoned, Margarete Magdalena Grüber organized the work within his congregation. In an interview in 1984, she expressed the feeling that the Confessing Church didn't support her enough in this very difficult time.

Else Niemöller

Martin Niemöller was one of the guiding lights of the anti-Nazi Confessing Church. He often discussed his sermons and presentations with his wife, Else Niemöller, needing the dialog with her. They had seven children. As their daughter Hertha said in an interview in 1984, Else Niemöller bore alone the responsibility for the upbringing of their seven children. She was supported by a maid. She had to work alone on the financial problems the family got into when the church did not pay a salary once Pastor Niemöller was not allowed to speak in public and after he was sent to the concentration camp. It was especially difficult to have no money for the children when they were to go to school.

In 1937, Martin Niemöller was arrested in Berlin-Dahlem. He spent the next eight years in concentration camps. The oldest of his seven children at the time was seventeen. The youngest was two years old. At first, according to their daughter, Hertha, Martin Niemöller tried to relate to his family from prison. But Else Niemöller soon had to make decisions alone because only she knew the reality outside. The family moved in 1943 to the south of Germany, to Starnberg. From there Else Niemöller regularly went to Dachau to visit her husband. The journey took four days. Hertha says that her mother never spoke to her children about her fear. "She took it!"

Hildegard Hannemann

Hildegard Hannemann came from a Social-Democratic family. She had a business training. In her free time, she was responsible for a group of ten children within her local church. In 1938, at the age of twenty years, she became a member of the Confessing Church. She attended courses for young Confessing Church members who were preparing to take responsibility in a *Bruderrat*. Later she was a member of the *Bruderrat* of her congregation. Because of the war, the number of women in the *Bruderräte* (in the local churches) grew. This was different on the level of the supra-regional boards where fewer women were represented.

In 1938, with the death of her pastor, the Confessing Church was thrown out of the parish house. They were able to find rooms in the Gössner-Mission. In 1941, when Jews had to wear the Star of David, Hildegard Hannemann tells that they had a discussion in her Confessing Christ congregation on how to react. They decided that the parish members with the Star of David should sit during the service among the congregation. She belonged to the group who insisted that the so-marked church members be able to serve the Lord's Supper as before. But they couldn't push this through. She tells how they brought those people home after the Bible study group.

Another point of disagreement in her congregation was whether they should read the intercessions for arrested Confessing Church members during the Sunday service with all names or without names and whether they should read all recommended announcements. As a result of this discussion the congregation split in two. Some members went back to the former congregation, especially those (like officials and businessmen) who feared the conflict with the government. Hildegard Hannemann remained.

In 1938, during the Czech crisis, the Confessing Church wrote a special prayer liturgy. The Gestapo tried to hinder the delivery of this prayer for peace and it persecuted congregations where this prayer was read as part of the liturgy. Hildegard Hannemann tells that she helped to copy the text. And once, while she was sitting together with her children's group, the Gestapo came. "We all sat on this prayer liturgy. It was hidden under the cushion we sat on. We were singing as the Gestapo looked for the sheets but they didn't find them."

These few examples show how different was the role of women within the Confessing Church. They were very courageous but had their limits too. They were carried by their strong faith but must have experienced fear also. They tell about the good and deep community within the congregations of the Confessing Church and speak about being disappointed.

The Association of Female Theologians

The Association of the Female Pastoral Theologians in Germany discussed the church struggle but didn't decide to become part of the

Confessing Church. They supported the Barmen Declaration but wanted to be neutral. So every theologian had to decide on her own.

It is important to see that the Confessing Church involved not only the confession and public witness of famous public figures. The Confessing Church was composed of confessing congregations. And in the congregations, especially during the war, the women were active! That is to say, a congregation of the Confessing Church without women is not imaginable nor did it exist.

As I have indicated, women did the *practical* work in the congregation and the practical *illegal* work. They were in danger like the men: They copied the pastoral prayers for persecuted members of the Confessing Church, copied information for the reports at the beginning of Bible study, and the recommended prayers which had been forbidden. They organized as lay people the work of the congregations especially during World War II. They kept the members together when they were thrown out of the church buildings. They kept people in contact with each other. They passed information in letters. They kept the offerings in safe places. (5) They hid persecuted people. They hid Jews, often without the support of the Confessing Church. They organized the food permits for hidden Jews. A spouse who had hidden many Jews in her house said in an interview: "What was a burden for me in living together with those hunted was not the fear of discovery but to feel their fear. And the shame of being a part of this terrible guilt knowing that your people watch silently the million-fold crucifixion of the Jew, Jesus."

As theologians, women were not fully accepted. They were called by a church law *Vikarinnen*, although they had taken two examinations required of pastors. This title gave them an inferior status. The Confessing Church, as well as the "Deutsche Christen" ("German Christians"), had a conservative idea of women. Important was the role women held as mothers of many children, the preservers of the home, marriage and family, and supporters of their husbands.

The Confessing Church was brave yet weak. They dissociated themselves from the women's liberation movement like the Nazis did. In 1936, when female judges and lawyers were not allowed to work any more, they did not respond. This you must know for understanding the discussion within the Confessing Church about the ordination of women.

To study theology had been permitted since the first years of the twentieth century. (In the United States, women have studied theology since early in the nineteenth century.) After long discussions, the Evangelical

Church in Germany (1927) passed a law that a female theologian could become a *Vikarin*. This meant females were consecrated for service as pastors for women and children but with preaching, teaching and pastoral care only for them. They were not ordained, so they were not allowed to preach in the Sunday service, to baptize or confirm or to lead a congregation. Instead of a pastor's robe, they wore a black dress. They were allowed to teach the confirmands in their first year but not in the second. Usually they led the Sunday school but they were not allowed to do this in all congregations. They were not members of the church boards. They received about seventy-five percent of the salary of male pastors. When they married, they had to retire from their calling (celibacy). To this, most female pastoral theologians agreed. There were only some who argued for the general ministry of women.

The Confessing Church worked on the basis of this church law (which, as noted above, had been passed in 1927). In correspondence with the National Socialist idea of women, some Protestant churches withdrew this law so that female theologians could not work in the church anymore at all. For example, in Bavaria the Church chose not to examine female theological students anymore. In the first years of the Confessing Church, for the *Vikarinnen* the question of their possibilities of working as pastors was secondary. They first were thinking about the destiny of their church in general. They did not think about themselves. So they worked in the con-gregations with women, girls and children.

This changed with the beginning of the war in 1939. Congregations were wondering about how they would be served when the pastors were drafted as soldiers. So people didn't think first about equal rights of women but discussed whether female theologians would be allowed to stand in for a pastor. This was the main question of the *Vikarinnen* too. They had to face the daily problems. Who should do the confirmation? Who should do a funeral? Who was allowed to sign documents? And so on. So it became necessary to find general regulations about substitution for a pastor. The *Bruderrat* of the Confessing Church said in October 1939 that the district *Bruderrat* was allowed to give a certain *Vikarin* the right to stand in for a pastor for a certain time and a certain responsibility. This didn't solve the practical problems of the *Vikarinnen*. A synod in Leipzig in 1940 said they could not decide this question without a fundamental theological purification. So they ordered a theological certificate and got some other statements on this. But the synod in 1941 in Hamburg still could not decide. They formed a committee that discussed fundamentally whether women could be ordained in the time of a war. The main arguments against the ordination of female theologians in such an emergency situation had been the understanding of the role of women within the Bible (1 Corinthians. 14:33-37; 1 Timothy. 2:11-15), understanding of activities and services, reaction of the congregations (men could not imagine that a woman would preach in a Sunday service.)

The Synod of the Confessing Church of the Old Prussian Union decided in 1942 nearly like the *Bruderrat* had already done in 1939. New was that a *Vikarin* now was allowed to give the sacraments to women, youngsters and children. But the *Vikarinnen* were only allowed to preach on Sunday when there were no men available. They had to apply for this. They were not allowed to lead the entire worship. Some *Vikarinnen* who had argued for the general ministry were very disappointed. They said: "Now we are theological skilled deaconesses!" In protest against this, Kurt Scharf ordained *Vikarinnen* in 1943. Berlin-Brandenburg let *Vikarinnen* stand in for pastors. They often worked for several congregations. But there was no basis for this by law and only seventy-five percent of the male's salary was paid to the *Vikarinnen*. Women had to be very strong to work in such a situation. To be "recognized" in this way was a difficult and heavy thing.

Imagine, Germany was living within a terrible war. Yet, people within the Confessing Church discussed for three years the possibility of ordination of women only as "stand-ins" in for pastors! And then they came up with this conservative result! The main reason for this behavior must have been the fear that if more liberal regulations were proved in the daily congregational life, perhaps they couldn't be canceled after war. People noticed that the congregations accepted the *Vikarin*. In interviews some of them said that people in the congregations liked having female pastors because they were more open. They were not such authoritarian representatives of the church. For example: "Traditionally when the pastor came for a visit people invited him to come into the dining room. We talk to our church members in the kitchen where they really live!"

Why is the public witness of women in the Confessing Church fifty years later important for us? Some reflections on what is important with the public witness of women in the Confessing Church may explain: There is the example of the limits of men and women in supporting Christian Jews. The struggle of women like Katharina Staritz, Klara Hünsche and many others for the Christian Jews was a part of the limits of the work of the Confessing Church. One of the *Vikarinnen* said in an interview: "We read the Bible together and have the Lord's Supper together with our church members with the Star of David. We gave them the gift of friendship and community. But when they had to gather to be transported to Theresienstadt, (6) nobody said anything. It seems to me so absurd: These people have been in extreme danger! And our help was only that we read together the Bible and had together the Lord's Supper."

The same thing might be said of Klara Hünsche. Her aim was to give the good message of Jesus to all baptized children, independent of their race. She struggled against the Nazis on this point valiantly. But she didn't protect the Jews from their ultimate fate. She was not able to offer political resistance.

Neither the men nor the women of the Confessing Church wanted to offer political resistance. There were a few exceptions. But, primarily the Confessing Church fought only against the attempts of the Nazis to influence or rule the church and the persecution of members of the Confessing Church, who were baptized Jews. Not even for them, the Confessing Church did enough or could do enough. For the Jews in general the Confessing Church did not do anything! As Klara Hünsche has said: "My experience is that under a total government you can't avoid being a part of the guilt of your nation. A clean slate is an impossible dream, even within the resistance!" This part of the history of the Confessing Church teaches us, men and women, to be awake and alert to the scorn of all people, not only of the members of our church.

Let me return for a moment to some of the women issues: Because of World War II, some female theologians received the opportunity to stand in for a pastor - after a long discussion. This gave them self-esteem, especially to manage their calling under the difficult circumstances of a war. This experience now became part of the history of women in the church. In 1945, they lost the possibility of working as *Vikarinnen* in congregations again. But women kept on it! It took until the 1950s, 1960s and 1970s for female theologians to be given their equal rights. In Germany we say women are like the "folding chairs" of society. You use them when there is a shortage of people, but you fold them up when there are too many men looking for work. The same is happening at this hour in the East of Germany. After the unification (1990), women were the first who were fired. Now there is a rate of unemployment of women of twenty-two percent. It is the same as the Church did in its history! We have to be awake and alert that this doesn't happen nowadays again.

And it's certain that if the women had argued together for the full ministry already in the Confessing Church they would have achieved better results. Research into discussions within the Confessing Church show that the majority of the theologians were simply too undemanding in regard to their own interests. We can learn from them.

Women were very, very important for the work of the Confessing Church. But the Confessing Church did not act in solidarity with the women. Since 1988 we have the ecumenical decade "Churches in Solidarity with Women." In Germany, many women are working on this but they miss the interest, activity and commitment to change among men and in the Church. Yet women continue to hope that the Church will confess solidarity with them.

Notes

1. The Confessing Church in Germany was composed of Lutheran, Reformed and United Church pastors and laity. It was a minority in the German Evangelical Church and looked to the Barmen Declaration of 1934 (written largely by Karl Barth) as its confession of faith. The church was strongest numerically in the Rhineland, Westphalia and in certain regions in Prussia. Even where it did not hold the majority in certain regional churches, there were small circles of support for the Confessing Church. Victoria Barnett points out that by the end of 1934, "90 percent of the active Protestants in Westphalia - some 500,000 people - held red membership cards" (in the Confessing Church).

2. See, for example, Victoria Barnett's wonderful book, *For the Soul of the People*, New York-Oxford: (Oxford University Press, 1992) especially 74-77, 93-94, 161-176, 203-204.and Michael Phayer's *Protestant and Catholic Women in Nazi Germany*, Detroit: (Wayne State University Press, 1990) especially 138-156, 162-168, 184-189, 197-202, 239-242).

3. The Evangelical Church of the Old Prussian Union became known as the Evangelical Church of the Union (Evangelische Kirche der Union [EKU]) following World War II. In 2003 it became part of the Union of Evangelical Churches (UEK) within the Evangelical Church in Germany. At synods in Berlin in May and June, 1980, the EKU affirmed *Kirchengemeinschaft* (Full Communion) with the United Church of Christ (USA). The following year, the United Church of Christ, at its General Synod in Rochester, New York, took similar action. This ecumenical expression of the Church remains vital to this day. (Editor)

4. Victoria Barnett has pointed out that "At the beginning of the war, there were about 100 active *Vikarinnen*... in the Berlin-Brandenburg Church; and there were several hundred women throughout Germany who had completed their theological education in the 1920s and 1930s. They remained barred from many vocational opportunities, including parish ministry. The rapidity with which the status of theologically trained women changed after 1939 illustrates how badly the church needed these women during the war years. As the number of wartime vacancies grew, the regional churches began 'ordaining' or 'consecrating' lay elders, deaconesses, and women. These 'ordinations,' however, were seen as exceptions,... and those 'ordained' were still barred, in most cases, from preaching and giving the sacraments."

5. The collection of offerings for the Confessing Church was illegal. The offerings were received nonetheless and were used to support the "illegal" Confessing Church pastors, vicars, and their families.

6. Theresienstadt was a transport camp near Prague from which Jews were shipped directly to Auschwitz.

(*On The Way*, Vol. 12, No. 2, Winter 1995-96)

Hans Berthold

Confessing Christ in a Multi-religious and Multi-cultural Society

I would like to begin this essay with two stories that, I believe, are significant for the difficult situation in which Christians find themselves today in Germany.

I

Two days after Christmas last year, Herr D. met his old friend who is a very successful businessman, a prominent member of the Christian Democratic Union and the Rotary Club. When he had seen and admired his friend's magnificent villa, the English-styled garden with its old trees, the exquisite taste his friend and his wife had been able to demonstrate by combining antique and modern furniture, it so happened that Herr D discovered a book near the Christmas tree that at once found his interest and attention. The title of the book was: "Reincarnation: Evidence from India for Life after Death."

Perplexed for a minute or two, and not without hesitation, Herr D. asked his friend; "Haven't you been active with me years ago in our Christian youth group where we had Bible studies and then, since 1980, marched for peace because of our Christian convictions?"

"Oh yes, that's true. I shall never forget it," his friend answered, "but the world is different now and so is Germany since the end of the Cold War. The company I am working for operates in Europe, America, and Australia. I now wear a Swiss watch, Italian shoes, an English suit. My computer was made in the United States, my camera in Japan, my car in Germany. Why should I continue to obtain my religious belief exclusively from German Protestantism?"

"Perhaps not from German Protestantism", Herr D. conceded, "but from the Bible and Martin Luther's Reformation, I would suggest, which in fact means directly from the Jewish and Christian revelation. Remember our former Bible studies, and how we decided to continue—in the context of justice, peace and the integrity of creation—the struggle of the Confessing Church against the Nazis.

"True enough," his friend admitted, "but this is all history, and it now tends to be narrow-minded. Tradition no longer fits my present way of life, nor is it in accordance with Europe's unification and the worldwide activities of my company—in short, with modern globalism. I can assure you that I will always think admirably of Jesus. And the Bible is, and always will be, number one on my book list. However, at the same time, being in a responsible position in my company, I really need for my physical and psychological survival the art of meditation as taught in Zen Buddhism, and I am also very interested in the teachings of Hinduism. The pastors I know are rather vague about Christ's resurrection and its implications for daily life, the future of humankind, and God's creation."

II

Pastor M. was invited to a group meeting of very able men and women who had tried once again to put into practice the concept of what had been named "Open Church in Our City." Frau N. was the chairwoman of the group. Summarizing the impressions of the group members, she informed Pastor M: "Friday evening last week, we enjoyed every minute of a new form of divine service. First of all, the unique atmosphere in our fourteenth century church made a deep and lasting impact on each one of us. Second, the organ, playing Mozart—not Bach—was a treat. Third, there was this fascinating arrangement of candles and flowers, together with your non-clerical and comforting voice, Pastor M. Finally, and most important, thank you for not preaching a sermon, filled with all that theological stuff we are just all fed up with. The new form of service enabled our group to really listen to our inner voices. That truly is God's voice, isn't it? There was no obstacle, no hindrance, no barrier to deeply perceive texts from the Bible and German poetry, treasures old and new we thought. Preaching or interpretation would have spoiled the whole evening. It would have destroyed our feeling and intuition, blocked our sensitivity and imagination, wiped out our being near to God and his Holy Spirit. On my way home I was reminded of Goethe: 'Feeling is all there is: words are but sound and smog.' There can be no doubt that we need more of these new evening services."

Up until now, Pastor M. had been convinced that confessing Christ as the "One Word of God" (Barmen Declaration) was the center of all activities in his congregation, including the endeavors for peace, justice and the integrity of creation. But now and for a couple of weeks, he feels a growing uncertainty as to the objectives of his pastoral work because a growing number of church members tend to be fascinated by those evening services.

Some of them often quote the dictum of Karl Rahner, S.J., "The Christian of the future will be a mystic or he/she will disappear altogether."

III

These two stories, I must admit, are not "true" stories in the sense that everything happened exactly in the way I have told you. But they are not merely fictional stories either. As a matter of fact, they are true in so far as they indicate new tendencies in present German church life and theology. I composed these stories by carefully selecting and re-assembling significant results of discussions and experiences which I had with German pastors in recent years during which I have had the privilege of serving as the director of the Institute for Continuing Education and Pastoral Studies (*Pastoralkolleg*) at Iserlohn, Germany. I have listened and I have learned that Christians in Germany, and pastors in particular, are having to grapple, at the end of the twentieth century with two fundamental questions: 1) How can we live as Christians in an increasingly pluralistic, multi-cultural and multi-religious society? And 2) How can we confess Christ in this new context, remaining faithful to our biblical and Reformation oriented origins?

The society in which we find ourselves is often referred to as "secularized" society. But this term can be misleading. Compared with the two decades after the Second World War, there is indeed a growing tendency towards secularism. But it is worth noting that more than eighty per cent of the inhabitants of the western part of Germany are still members of either the Evangelical or the Roman Catholic Church. They are not likely to give up their membership in the forseeable future. Yet there are, of course, different degrees of interest, allegiance and loyalty. About one third of church members are said to be connected with the life of the church, whereas the other two thirds participate only occasionally or don't feel any need to do so at all. However, there are indications that the number of regular church attendants is on the increase. Is this due to the greater variety of church activities, new services with more emphasis on liturgy and spirituality? Or is it the result of combined ecumenical efforts, Feminism, "Justice, Peace and the Integrity of Creation," caring for the sick, the disabled, the unemployed? May these improvements be the fruits of evangelization and church growth? There is currently a hot debate about these questions in Germany. This debate is usually followed by discussions about general strategies for the future.

The picture, however, is different and rather saddening in East Germany, the former German Democratic Republic. In April this year, *Time*, the U.S. newsmagazine, published a well-informed and exciting article on this problem, the title of which was: "Shattered hopes—Germany remains a divided country." This assessment of the present situation is not only true of the economic and social tensions in East Germany, but it also mirrors the reluctance and even resistance of many East Germans to the Christian message. By and large, this is the legacy of twelve years of Nazi terror and Nazi ideology, plus an additional forty years of Communist atheism. Whether we like it or not, this is the context in which Christians in Germany have to witness today to what the Church is, whereby it is recognized, and which specific contributions to the life of the individual and society can be expected.

At any rate, church membership can no longer be taken for granted in Germany. Despite atheism, agnosticism and an increased indifference towards the Christian message, the churches of the Reformation are still faced with a host of expectations. Some people expect the churches to be institutions of safeguarding traditional beliefs and identities. Others see the churches as engines of social change or as advocates and helpers of people in need, under pressure, or in critical situations. A third group expects the churches to provide ethical orientation on the fundamental issues of life. So the beginning of the twenty-first century presents risks and opportunities for Christians and the Christian churches in Germany.

IV

On September 27, 1998, general elections will be held in Germany. One powerful weapon that is now often used in the election campaign is to attribute the development of a multi-cultural and multi-religious society to the four million Muslims who presently live in Germany as well as to the influx of hundreds of thousands of non-Christians asylum seekers from eastern European countries since the end of the Cold War. This sort of generalization is highly dangerous because of its hidden prejudice against non-Germans. Moreover, it is only a part of the truth; the part that is "above the sea level," as we say. Yet ninety per cent of the iceberg is always beneath the surface of the sea and this is, in our case, the all-pervasive change of thinking and feeling, values and attitudes that is often referred to as "postmodernism". Postmodernism is exerting an unrivalled, deep and long-lasting impact on all social institutions, the Church included.

In July 1995, the influential German monthly *Psychologie Heute*, published a long article entitled "What God is, I decide." The title was not, it is important to note, "Who God is, I Decide." This is significant in the sense that modern religiosity insists on not being limited in its range of experience by the boundaries of traditional concepts of God, Christian or others. At the end of the twentieth century we find ourselves in the "global village" where traditional religion is moving towards a new religiosity. This religiosity can be lived in a multitude of different forms and according to one's individual needs. As I tried to explain in the two introductory stories, it is the individual person who assembles his/her belief from different sources. By and large, a syncretistic religion is the result. It is the individual person who wants to decide whether religious traditions are still acceptable or not. Traditions of the past are likely to be rejected as soon as they are seen to be at odds with what seems to be the modern person's holy grail, one's personal right to choose and to revise one's choices. So postmodernism has the tendency to say "Yes" to religion, but "No" to the God of the Bible. (Johann Baptist Metz, *Gotteskrise—Versuch zur geistigen Situation der Zeit*, 1994).

V

It was from Ulrich Beck and other sociologists that I learned to understand the irreversibility of our way into the "new modernity". Beck introduced a specific usage of the term "individualization" to describe the current changes in society and in the lives of individual persons. (*Die Risikogesellschaft—Auf dem Weg in eine andere Moderne*, 1986).

Generally speaking, "individualization" denotes the transition from traditional patterns and courses of life that, in the past, were predetermined by the class and the gender into which a person is born in "individualized biographies." Today a person can and must choose his or her course of education, his or her living arrangements, his or her degree of participation in society. In every-day life as a consumer, he or she can choose from a wide range of goods and services. Under this aspect, individualization is a gain in freedom and very attractive. On the other hand, individual choices are subjected to the all-pervasive economic law of supply and demand, which is the governing principle of neo-liberalism and modern capitalism. Personal ties such as being attached to one's partner or family, to neighborhood and workplace, to regional culture or church membership are subordinated - and often have to be sacrificed - to the requirements of the market in order to secure one's market-mediated existence. This is why there are both attractive opportunities and an increase of risks in modern individualization. The experience of personal achievement and happiness can easily turn into an unexpected personal crisis, even chaos, as well as into a collective disaster like mass unemployment (Ulrich Beck/Elisabeth Beck-Gemsheim, *Das ganz normale Chaos der Liebe*, 1990).

In short, it is the ambivalence of individualization that we should be aware of (G. Schulze, *Die Erlebnisgesellschaft—Kultursoziologie der Gegenwart*, 1992)." Individualization is a double-sided gift of our time. The increased freedom to choose goods and to enjoy life is matched by a growing unwillingness to remember the sufferings of the poor, the unemployed, and the needy. Individualization is also responsible for the way in which we continue to destroy God's creation and the future of coming generations.

VI

Politicians fighting a general election campaign cannot tell people "the truth, the whole truth, and nothing but the truth." That's how it is, and it would be sheer hypocrisy to blame this fact exclusively on the politicians. It is for this reason that I am grateful for the "Joint Statement by the Council of the Evangelical Church in Germany and the Roman Catholic Bishops' Conference" of February 1997. It offers a vision that is apt to counterbalance the negative aspects of individualization and neo-liberalism. "For a Future Founded on Solidarity and Justice" is the challenging title of this statement. Right at its beginning the Joint Statement declares that it does not pretend to be "an alternative expert opinion or another annual report on the economy. The churches are not a political party. They do not aspire to political power in order to implement a specific program. Their mandate and their competence in the field of economic and social policy is to work for a value orientation serving the good for all." In other words, it is the common good over against individualism and egoism that the Joint Statement advocates. This is very important in face of the high rate of unemployment (twelve to twenty per cent and even more) in Germany. This is why the Joint Statement says: "The persistent unemployment is dangerously explosive in the lives of individuals and their families - especially in much of eastern Germany - and for social peace." The Joint Statement, therefore, summons Christians and the Christian churches to remember the dual command to love God and one's neighbor (Luke 10:25-37), the preferential option for the poor, the weak and the helpless (Matthew 25:31-46), as well as the social principles of justice, solidarity and sustainability.

VII

Against this backdrop of the political and social problems in Germany, it becomes evident that what is needed among the postmodern diffusion of worldviews and introverted religiosity is an identifiable witness to the Christian faith. In spite of postmodernism and neo-liberalism, the institution of the Church will remain important provided it gives a clear, discernible, consistent, and "prophetic picture" of what Christian belief is about.

Harking back to the problem of how to live as an individual person in a multi-cultural and multi-religious society, it is important to understand that individualization does not necessarily imply the replacement of traditional forms of belief by non-Christian convictions. Rather, it claims that traditional

Christian belief which in past centuries was firmly institutionalized in ancient creeds, liturgical texts and otherwise, is now losing its significance, where it is not based on individual choice and needs. In principle, the call for personal choice and decision is well in accordance with the New Testament and the Reformation. The danger, then, with which individualization confronts the Christian faith, is the diffusion of the content of its message. There is the danger that the Christian message will be more and more at the disposition and mercy of the individual's pragmatic needs. So, whether we like it or not, the dividing line between truth and error must sometimes be drawn, even though the churches, afraid of possible tensions in their ranks, often tend to withdraw from what has to be said. They tend to preserve peace and unity by avoiding critical issues rather than by taking positions on matters of faith. But the Christian message is based on a determinate and an identifiable truth that is not compatible with all sorts of opinions, ideas, and positions. To give but two examples of exclusive concepts which also make a difference in practice: One cannot believe in the Jewish and Christian God, considered as the Lord over all of history, and at the same time have an individualistic view of the world and human life. Another example from the scene of our multi-cultural and multi-religious society is the Christian belief in Christ's resurrection and the modern esoteric as well as the Hinduistic belief in reincarnation that are mutually exclusive.

VIII

"Perceptions without concepts are blind," said Kant. The perception of postmodern forms of belief remains in our case "blind" as long as it does not press forward to a theological concept of the Church of Jesus Christ. But Kant also said: "Concepts without perceptions are empty." The concept of the Church remains in our case "empty" as long as it is not related to the real problems within the Church of Jesus Christ. In other words: A theological concept of the Church can be determined by different interests. It can be drawn up to support the Church's self-understanding. It can be intended to defend the church against heresy. It can be developed to compare Protestantism with Roman Catholicism, or to compare one denomination with another. Last but not least: a concept of the Church can be the vision of pastors, priests or laypeople. "Every concept of the Church must therefore raise the question, and allow it to be raised: whom is it intended to benefit, and for whom and whose interest is it designed?" (Jurgen Moltmann, *Kirche in der Kraft des Geistes—Ein Beitrag zur messianischen Christologie*, 1975).

These are important questions, but they can only be answered when they have been linked, as M. Josuttis has shown, with distinctions between a) the church as organization, b) the church as "milieu" of the local congregation, and c) the church as the body of Christ in the sense of Romans 12:3-21, 1 Corinthians 12:12-31, Philippians 3:20-21; Colossians 1:13-14. (Manfred Josuttis, *Unsere Vokskirche und die Gemeinde der Heiligen*, 1997). The result of these distinctions must then be discussed within the framework of christological affirmations, which means on the basis of confessing Christ as the "one Word of God which we have to hear and which we have to trust and obey in life and death" (Barmen Declaration). Confessing Christ is indeed the most indispensable and most needed Christian response to the development of a multicultural and multi-religious society, characterized by diverse and mutually competing orientations of faith outside and inside the Church. Confessing Christ, "as he is attested to us in Holy Scripture" (Barmen Declaration), is the very center of Christian faith (cf. Matthew 10:32-33; Romans 10:9; Philippians 2:11). It is both the basis for the critical stance of the Church towards all tendencies denying the Gospel of Jesus Christ as the foundation of faith and life, and for its constructive cooperation with all men and women of good will.

The Barmen Declaration also says: "The Church's commission, upon which its freedom is founded, consists in delivering the message of free grace to all people in Christ's stead, and therefore in the ministry of his own word and work through sermon and sacrament." This is why confessing Christ involves freedom from the constraints of making self-realization and self-determination the sole criterion of successful individualization and achievement. There is no reason why Christians should be ashamed of the biblical message and hesitate to say openly that Christ is our Lord and Savior, and always will be.

Finally, confessing Christ in a multi-cultural and multi-religious society will lead to prophetic criticism as the Joint Statement of 1997 shows. Christians are commissioned to not remain silent but rather to intervene where human dignity, human life, and the integrity of creation are being infringed upon and violated. This commission motivates Christians also to take a stance in issues of politics and in questions of the economic and social order. Their prophetic criticism will, however, only be credible if it is not proclaimed in an authoritarian and clerical manner. This is why Christians and churches ought to expose themselves to the criticism of the Bible and seek direction and renewal for themselves by listening to Christ's voice in the gospel.

IX

In his letter from Tegel prison, dated April 30, 1944, Dietrich Bonhoeffer wrote to his friend Eberhard Bethge: "What is bothering me incessantly is the question what Christianity really is, or indeed who Christ really is, for us today." This is the most important and the most pressing problem of christology for us, too, and it has to be pursued in the changing conditions of society at the end of the twentieth century. At this point it is not sufficient for the theological assessment of the present situation to merely mention the deficiencies of the political, economic and social order in both the United States and Germany. As Christians, we have to look first of all at the "other side" of Western civilization. For every civilization has its reverse side, which is barbarism; every victorious history has its costs, which is the misery of the defeated; and all progress has its price. The "other side" is generally neither seen nor heard. Who bothers about the victims at whose expense one is living? This, for example, is the all-pervasive question of T.C. Boyle's great novel *The Tortilla Curtain*, 1995.

In our age of economic globalism, the tendency to forget Lazarus, "longing to satisfy his hunger from what fell from the rich man's table" (Luke 16:21) is almost everywhere on the increase. And this problem can by no means be confined to the United States. What do you feel by reading Frank McCourts Irish memories that were published under the title *Angela's Ashes* in 1996?

Christian theology would not be Christian and would not be christological if it did not become the advocate of people who are living "on the other side." Christian theology has to concern itself with the crises and contradictions of our civilization, and the people who suffer from them. This is a necessary implication and actualization of confessing Christ today.

At the moment we are living with the contradictions between the nations of the "Third World," which are getting poorer and poorer, and deeper and deeper into debt, and the rapidly developing rich industrial nations of the "First World." This is not a temporary crisis but rather a congenital defect of the civilization itself. The inequalities and injustices of the world-wide economic system are not diminishing. They are growing. But the community of the Christian church is made up of people in the "Third World" and in the "First World."

Therefore Christian theology cannot merely ask: "Who is Christ for us today?" It has also to find out: "Who really is Christ for the poor of the 'Third World?'" And: "Who is Christ for us, when we make use of their poverty, for our own purposes?" The main problem for us here is not our own world — what Bonhoeffer termed "the world has come of age." Our main problem is the world that we have made incapable of coming of age. If liberty is the central theme of modern European theology and philosophy, then for people in the "Third World" this means "liberation from oppression and apathy. (see Jürgen Moltmann, *Der Weg Jesu Christi—Christologie in messianischen Dimensionen*, 1989).

I close my presentation referring not to Bonhoeffer, but rather by reminding us of Oscar Romero, the people's bishop in El Salvador. He was consecrated priest in 1942 and bishop in 1970. In 1977 he was appointed Archbishop of San Salvador. At that time presidential elections were being held in El Salvador. The ruling military junta rigged the results, and the other parties protested in a demonstration. They were shot down by the National Guard. Two weeks later, on March 12, 1977, a priest was murdered for the first time in El Salvador. Father Rutillo Grande SJ, was the parish priest of Aguilares. Romero hurried to the place of this murder and spent the night with the murdered priest's parishioners. He said later that this was the night when he "was converted."

Romero was 59 years old. Up to then he had been a conservative churchman. Now he recognized the connection between the persecution of the Church and the repression of the people by the ruling minority in his country and their "death squads". He began to go to the poor people and became "their" bishop. "What is really persecuted is the people, not the Church," he wrote, "but the Church is on the people's side and the people are on the side of the Church." He believed in "the God of the poor", writes his biographer, Jon Sobrino. Romero learned to hear the gospel of the kingdom of the coming God in the signs and the protesting cry of the poor. The poor "evangelized" him. The cathedral of San Salvador became the place where the people gathered; a place of liturgy and hunger strike, a hospital for the wounded. Romero understood why and how the people were moving towards becoming an "organized people." He supported the "popular organizations" of the farm workers, the smallholders and the workers. For him "the people's project" was a solution to the problems of his country. And this meant he was drawn into the political conflict. Archbishop Romero was shot during mass by a paid assassin in front of the altar in a chapel in March 1980.

X

All I might wish to say to you in this essay has been said more concisely and more consistently in Hebrews 13:7-9. There we read: "Remember your leaders, those who spoke the word of God to you; consider the outcome of their way of life, and imitate their faith. Jesus Christ is the same yesterday and today and forever. Do not be carried away by all kinds of strange teachings; for it is well for the heart to be strengthened by grace."

(A monograph projected for *On The Way* in the Pentecost-Trinity Season of 1998. This issue of the journal remained unpublished.)

Reinhard Ulrich

Reflections on the Role of the Confessional Tradition in the United Church of Christ

Earlier this year, the church school staff of one of our prominent "old Reformed" congregations in the Wisconsin Conference asked me to join it in a study of the "beliefs and practices about confirmation and the sacraments commonly held in our own congregation and in the United Church of Christ." There was much reminiscing about what they, themselves, had been taught. Some expressed regret at losing the direction and identity which "being Reformed" had once given to their congregation and its teaching mission. Others expressed frustration with the dissonance created by the new orthodoxies of constantly changing programs and emphases. The question, "What should we teach?" soon turned into each person's story of what she or he had been taught.

So, I told my story: As a young pastor, I served Eden Evangelical Lutheran Church (UCC), a Volga-German congregation in Chicago that took its ethnic and confessional heritage quite seriously. One-third of the congregation still attended German-language services regularly. At German communion service, tradition reigned supreme. There were "Lutherans" who knelt at the altar rail and without touching the host or the cup, received the elements from the pastor. There were the "Reformed" who stood at the rail and took bread and cup into their hands from the pastor. And in between, there were a number of "Lutherans with arthritis" who were unable to kneel, yet refused to take the elements in hand: they expected to be served by the pastor. For their young minister, the German communion service was a definite learning experience. Yet, I always thought of Eden Church as a wonderful model of the household of God, where there was neither "Jew nor Greek," but Christ in all.

The old liturgical traditions were important and respected, yet they were not essential marks of the community of faith. The meaning of the Eucharist transcended usage. It was clearly understood as being contained in the word and promise of Christ. Almost everyone knew the words of the service "by heart," in both senses of the term. I learned from them the power of those words when, at their sick beds, the older sisters and brothers would join me in confession and absolution, in the "great prayer," the words of institution, the thanksgiving, and the *Nunc Dimittis*.

Among our church school teachers, the question of the Eucharist quickly reduced itself to the practical problem of what to do: What should be done about requests for children's communion? The group discussed the matter at length and settled on a pluralistic solution: We agreed to disagree! This, of course, did not answer the original question of what church school teachers should be teaching the youth of the congregation. Finally, a clearly frustrated member of the group turned to the pastor and asked: "Why doesn't the Conference tell us what we believe?"

Far from being facetious, that question is touching the central problem of faith and order in the United Church of Christ today. The classical doctrines (generally accepted teachings) of the Christian Church are not just a tale that is told. They preserve what our ancestors called the *casus confessionis*, the case for taking a confessional stand, that is, those teachings of the faith "which are (or should be) most certainly held among us" if we are to bear the name of Christ.

A "Christian community" without normative statements of its faith is a contradiction in terms. In the form of catechetical instruction, doctrines transmit the "tradition of the faith" (the "*regula fidei*") to future generations. In the form of confession and celebration, they gather and inform the community at worship. As imperatives of action, they give direction to the church's life and work. "To do the good," said Socrates, "you must know what it is." By the same token, to proclaim the gospel, Christians must know and understand what the good news is.

The practical issue of children's communion translates into a theological question that cannot be settled by an appeal to child psychology, that is, by discussing how individual parents or children in the congregation "feel." The answer hinges on the community's understanding of the sacrament. If that understanding is "catholic," the holy communion is efficacious in and of itself (*ex opere operato*). It seems reasonable then to allow baptized children to fully participate. If, on the other hand, that understanding is "Protestant," believer's baptism (or "confirmation" of baptismal vows) is an essential requisite of participation. Either position is defensible. Yet both require that the community develop its doctrinal position, state its theological understanding(s) clearly, and transmit them as doctrine and confession to the community and beyond. Here, as elsewhere, the devil may be in the details, in the "*adiaphora*" or "non-essentials."

In spite of our present aversions against prepositional language, the classical and modern statements of the Christian faith are not the enemy of Christian action. Theological language is inherently no more divisive than celebration of "praxis." Conflicts over the agenda, over "what should be done," in the church are fierce and frequent. On occasion, they may even yield to the "doctrine" of God's love or to Christ's presence at the table of the Lord. A classical axiom holds that the effect cannot be greater than the cause. Our fading memories of an identifiable "tradition of prophets and apostles" may well be the most serious threat to the ongoing life and mission of the United Church of Christ.

I. The Present Condition

The Sunday school teacher's frustration with our much-celebrated diversity reflects the dilemma of "mainline" Christian churches. We are faced with a situation where pluralism and inclusiveness are rapidly becoming litmus tests of a new post-Christian culture religion. Specific theological claims are viewed as divisive; substantive confessions of the Christian faith are often dismissed as embarrassing or irrelevant. Human action has replaced religious faith as the only good work. Pelagius would be pleased (Maybe not; he was a very serious monk). Even within traditionally "confessional" or "biblical" churches, commitment to classical understandings of the Christian faith is increasingly considered a private matter which Christians are reluctant to share for fear of offending others or of exposing themselves to ridicule.

During a recent interim assignment, I asked my confirmation class to memorize the Apostles' Creed. We discussed the history and structure of the most popular creed of the Western Church and its influence on other creeds or statements of faith, including that of the United Church of Christ. One of the deacons, who had been listening at the door, pulled me aside after class and said: "I can't believe you still teach that stuff about the Trinity."

The new culture religion rejects all formal statements of faith and all theological commitments in favor of a vaguely perceived religious feeling. "Feeling is all there is; words are but sound and smog, darkening the brightness of heaven," the German poet Goethe wrote two hundred years ago. In the marketplace of religious ideas, the current favorites are eclectic and inclusive manifestations of the human experience. There is little room for particular revelations, for the scandal of the cross, the inconvenience of tragedy, not to speak of pervasive social evil and human sin. Christians are invited to shed the narrow confines of their creeds and embrace the broader ecumenism of all other religions. It is almost as if we were being transported back to the first century.

The most serious threat to the Early Church may very well have been, not its enemies but, its Hellenistic friends. Where all things are Christian, nothing is Christian! Yet, the central affirmation of the Christian gospel, that God is in Christ reconciling the world to God-self, violates the canons of the religion-in-general. Religion-in-general has no place for the incarnate Christ of faith. It is troubled by the ethical idealism of the Jesus of history. Jesus becomes just another portrait to be placed in the religious "hall of fame." Friedrich Nietzsche contemplated the consequence of this loss of transcendence, of the triumph of the *homo naturalis*: "If God is dead, everything is permitted."

In the 1930s, the Confessing Church struggled with an earlier manifestation of the *homo naturalis* in Germany, where the neo-pagan "Faith Movement of German Christians" proclaimed a fascist social order based on the promises of "positive Christianity" in the Nazi party platform. In retrospect, this seems absurd of course. It did not seem so at the time. Very few people outside or within the Christian community perceived the dangers of this new idolatry as clearly as Dietrich Bonhoeffer did. The new religion of feeling has no room for the "otherness" of God. God is in our words, our will, our actions. Yet, where humans speak for God, God is silent.

A pastor friend of mine regularly asked in his pastoral prayers that "God meet our every need." I hope and trust that God will think this over carefully! We may regret tomorrow receiving what we thought we needed today. The same may be true of re-imagining the story of the faith in the light of our present experience. (The "German Christians" re-imagined an Aryanized Christian scripture purged of Jewish influences. Really!) In the brave new world of the new age religion, theological understandings of scripture are giving way to the hermeneutics of our moment in history.

There is nothing all that new about the apparent conflict between biblical and cultural theology. The Early Church's encounter with classicism is the prime case in point. In our time, H. Richard Niebuhr's study (*The Social Sources of Denominationalism*) has shown that the theology and practice of North American churches are strongly influenced by cultural and ethnic factors. None of this is surprising. We have this treasure in earthen vessels! It is surprising however that, on all sides of the theological spectrum, we are now turning our cultural and political preferences into contemporary doctrines of the Christian faith. Thus, in the former "mainline" churches, euro-centricity is out, inclusiveness is in; classical confessions are out, openness to all points of view is in; academic theology is out (unless, of course, it is your own), the fresh winds of the Holy Spirit are in (unless, of course, they speak in tongues). Irenaeus is out, Origin is in; Augustine is out, Plotinus is in. The list goes on.

Apart from the obvious difficulty of reconciling diversity and inclusiveness within a single community of faith, it seems to me that unqualified religious pluralism cannot become a unitive principle for those who claim that God is active in human history, Christian or otherwise. The faith affirmations of the historical religions become "inclusive" only if their unique theo-logies are "explained" away as historical or cultural irrelevancies, that is, by questioning the theological substance of what a given community seeks to affirm. Again, if everything is Christian (Muslim, or Jewish), nothing is Christian (Muslim, or Jewish). The attempt to explain a particular faith in terms of religion-in-general does not bring people together. It destroys religious identity and generates its own set of enemy images. *"Und willst du nicht mein Bruder sein, so schlag ich dir den Schaedel ein."* ("And if you will not be my brother, then I shall have to crack your skull.") This old German saying unfortunately seems to describe the divisive temper of the times more adequately than undifferentiated visions of global harmony. Not all myths are created equal!

There is a vast disparity between the visions of the new culture religion and our actual experience of an emerging new tribalism in a crumbling social order. The world and nations are becoming not less but more divided. Our problems are aggravated by the analytical tools we use to make sense of our contemporary dilemmas, that is, our solutions seem to be part of the problem. Principles no longer guide action; action becomes the tool of political will and personal feeling. Borrowing heavily from the social and behavioral sciences, we have been limiting ourselves to a method that reduces religion to experience. We find it increasingly difficult to even access theological propositions such as "God is in Christ reconciling the world to God-self" and often dismiss the language of faith as poetic license that ultimately is meaningless unless it serves our ends.

A recent study document of the United Church of Christ envisions the Church of the twenty-first century as a global Christian society, where unity and diversity are reconciled in a universally acclaimed "righteous empire" (to borrow Martin Marty's phrase). To bring it about, the document lays out an ambitious social action plan "of justice, mercy, and peace so that lives may be renewed, spirits revived, and worlds transformed." (See below)

To read this document in the fiftieth anniversary year of the end of World War II is a sobering experience. No one seems to notice that we have not yet mastered the previous lesson, as if there had been no Holocaust, no Hiroshima, Khmer Rouge, Rwanda, Yugoslavia. There seems to be no humility, no sense of the tragic limits of the human condition, no sense of the cross, no heartfelt sorrow for sin. One thinks of Bonhoeffer's words about grace that comes too cheap. The document ignores a truism well known to our mothers and fathers that the finite is not capable of the infinite (Calvin) apart from the gift of grace. Where the human limits are ignored, there is no need for the cross, and the world remains un-reconciled. To be fair, each of the four main points of the UCC study document begins with the words, "by God's grace." Yet, this is followed by what is essentially a contemporary "statement of strategic goals and objectives for the 21st century." God seems to serve as a preamble of the Church's agenda; of our global action plan.

There used to be a popular hymn: "God has no hands but our hands to do God's work today." As a pastor and teacher of the Church, that hymn has always bothered me. Luther, who had less to be humble about than most of us when it comes to faith and action, asked God, "only do thou not forsake me, for if I am left to myself, I will certainly bring it all to destruction." The history of this "century of progress" eloquently makes the point that even well-intentioned "*homo naturalis*" more often than not ends up creating the whirlwind.

We are gathered to reflect on the fiftieth anniversary of Dietrich Bonhoeffer's death. This has given me an incentive to look at his *Ethics* again. Reading Bonhoeffer again confirms my suspicion that we may be asking the wrong questions: In his *Ethics*, Bonhoeffer warned against separating the truth of Christ from the love of Christ; the person from the work. Or, against his teacher at Union Seminary, Reinhold Niebuhr, the Christian tendency to draw too sharp a distinction between "moral man and immoral society." Push this a little further and the same warning applies to the distinction between faith and action. The truth of Christ cannot be separated from the love of Christ. This means that the teachings (doctrines) of the faith must inform Christian actions, and what Christians do must reflect the teaching of the crucified and risen Christ.

II. Faith and Action

Where action has primacy over theological reflection, doctrine becomes the enemy. Theological intransigence, of course, may also be an enemy of the Church. Philip Melanchthon prayed: "Lord, preserve us from the ravings of the theologians!" But the imperatives of action, even Christ's mandate of selfless love, can easily be turned into a means of human domination or control (Emil Brunner). The scriptures do not teach a primacy of action over faith. Rather, the New Testament teaches the essential unity of faith and action, in that order! "Good works do not make a Christian, but a good Christian (cannot help but) do good works" (Luther). The Christian gospel cannot be separated from its roots in the ancient "teaching tradition of prophets and apostles." Nor can the Christian Church, as a human institution and community of faith, be understood as if there were no historical context. We have this "treasure in earthen vessels," says St. Paul. It is a curious perversion of Paul's meaning to argue that therefore the enduring affirmations of the Christian faith about the person and work of Jesus Christ are relative, that they have no power to bind the Christian consciousness or conscience. Nor does it mean that each and every phrase and story in the canon is created equal. Nonetheless, the abolition of dogma is not the cure for doctrinal rigidity.

In his introduction to the 1960 edition of Williston Walker's venerable *The Creeds and Platforms of Congregationalism*, Douglas Horton warns against abusing the principles of individualism and of local autonomy. Local churches and their agencies, he says, are "secondary causes, which would not take place if Christ had not entered history." Horton continues: "It is Christ who gives the Church power, feeding strength to the local church through the whole company of churches and to the whole company through the local church. He is immediately present alike to each church and to the whole."

Elmer J. F. Arndt wrote "of the things that are most surely believed" among members of the former Evangelical and Reformed Church which (in 1957) united with the Congregational Christian churches to form the United Church of Christ: "The (Evangelical and Reformed) Church seeks to be loyal to the biblical message…It wishes to keep ever before itself the faith that Christ is the way, the truth, and the life; and to understand the Bible in such a manner that this central proclamation will be brought into the foreground… Its doctrines are those expressed in the ancient creeds and confessional books… which are revered as conformable to the teaching and as historic expressions of the Christian faith. They are understood as the response of a faithful and devout church to God's revelation."

Twenty years earlier, Bonhoeffer had recorded his impressions of church-state relationships in the Anglo-Saxon world. North America (and to a lesser extent, British political institutions), he said, are not burdened with the "two swords theory" (secular and sacred) which plagued church-state relations on the European continent since Christianity became an established religion in the fourth century and gave rise to the political concept of the *corpus christianum* or Christian state. The concept of Christendom was challenged first by the Protestant Reformation which destroyed the claim of the absolute spiritual authority of the Church, that is, of the spiritual sword; the Church as an institution of salvation, and second, by the French revolution which swept away the concept of a divinely ordained sovereignty of the feudal state. Together, the Re-formation and the Enlightenment laid the foundations of the modern national and secular state.

According to Bonhoeffer, North American political institutions were shaped by people who understood the doctrine of original sin. In sharp contrast with the early optimism that propelled the French Revolution, the framers of the United States Constitution provided safeguards against "the evil which lurks in human hearts," that is, checks and balances against the natural thirst for power of both the rulers and the ruled. The constitutional concept of a "division of powers" has its roots in the Calvinist doctrines of a divinely ordained sovereignty and of a pervasive inclination of humans to sin that must be curbed by divine and human law. In North America, these principles are linked to basically opposing ideas borrowed from the British dissenters. God's realm of righteousness cannot be founded on human wisdom or on the power of government. The vision of God's realm of righteousness is found only in the congregation of believers, that is, in the gathered Christian community. The Church's mission therefore is to proclaim the principles of a divinely sanctioned social and political order. The mission of government is to find the means to carry them out.

This scenario, says Bonhoeffer, blends the distinctly different callings of the spiritual and the secular powers which inevitably entails an ongoing process of secularization. Writing in 1940, Bonhoeffer concludes that "the claim that the Christian community knows how to rebuild the world on Christian principles is bound to result in a total surrender of the church to the world, as even a cursory look at church life in New York will show." The only reason why this claim has not triggered radical hostility against churches in the United States, says Bonhoeffer, is the fact that in North America no clear distinction exists between the church's spiritual and the secular "office" or calling (see his *Ethics*, I, 43). In other words, the political role of the churches in North American society has not been given a definable institutional form or expression. Bonhoeffer concludes that this is why in North America "godlessness tends to be more hidden" than in Europe.

III. Christianity and Culture

Almost sixty years have passed since Dietrich Bonhoeffer visited the United States and wrote these lines (above). The threatening "surrender of the American churches to the world" has been a hotly debated, yet hardly understood, issue ever since. This struck me in a special way a few years ago as I was attending Sunday worship with a group of East German visitors in one of our stately churches in New York City, not far from where Bonhoeffer had been living in the early thirties. During the service, the pastor asked for volunteers to help him fill two buses for a trip to Washington, DC. The purpose was to join a demonstration in support of increasing government funding for AIDS research. So far so good. Yet both my friends were embarrassed and offended when the pastor supported his bus trip citing Martin Niemoller's famous words at the height of the German church struggle: "... first they came for the Communists and I did not speak up because I was not a Communist. Then they came for the Jews and I did not speak up because I was not a Jew. Then they came for the trade unionists and I did not speak up because I was not a trade unionist... Then they came for me and by that time no one was left to speak up." When it comes to the depth and the cost of discipleship, there is a vast difference between a lobbying trip to Washington, DC, and Niemöller's seven-year journey to a Nazi concentration camp.

So, what are we teaching the coming generation about the nature of Christian faith and practice?

In ecumenical conversations, particularly in the ongoing "Lutheran-Reformed Dialogue," our ecumenical partners have expressed reservations about baptismal practices in the United Church of Christ. Changes in the baptismal formula, which seem to be prompted by the demands of the new culture religion, are fast becoming a major roadblock to Christian unity, even within the UCC. How can we be sure that our children are properly baptized in the triune name? Is it important to do so? What does the sacrament of baptism mean? Is the liturgical form another local option or a matter of personal preference of local pastors? The answers to these and similar questions may well contain the future of the Church. The ancient axiom may still be true: *lex orandi, est lex credendi* (The way we worship determines what we shall believe).

Five years ago, work began on a seven-volume series entitled, *The Living Theological Heritage of the United Church of Christ*. The first volume, "Ancient and Medieval Legacies," is being published this year by Pilgrim Press. The initial task was to decide whether a "living" theological heritage needs a volume on the ancient and medieval church. Some felt that ancient theological disputes have little relevance to a contemporary religious community that defines itself in terms of actions rather than words; that theological inquiry is inherently divisive, and that classical Christian doctrines are relics of our cultural past. It is interesting that we feel compelled to measure our theological heritage, even those elements of the faith that have sustained the community for nearly two thousand years and beyond, by the perishable orthodoxies of this fleeting moment in history. For the Christian Church, the central and perennial question remains theological: It is the question Jesus asked his disciples: "Who do you say that I am?"

As mentioned earlier, a recent study document of the United Church Board for Homeland Ministries, "A Church Attentive to the Word," presents four points for theological reflection by pastors and congregations. Expository articles follow on these points:

1) A Church attentive to God's Word: By God's grace, we will be an attentive church. We commit ourselves anew to listen for God's word in Holy Scripture, in our rich heritage, in faithful witness and in the fresh winds of the Holy Spirit so that we might discover God's way for us.

2) A Church inclusive of All People: By God's grace, we will be an inclusive church. We commit ourselves to be a church for all people and, in Christ, we celebrate, affirm, and embrace the rich diversity of God's good creation.

3) A Church responsive to God's Call: By God's grace, we will be a responsive church. We commit ourselves to be a church of justice and mercy and peace so that lives may be renewed, spirits revived, and worlds transformed.

4) A Church supportive of One Another: By God's grace, we will be a supportive church. We commit ourselves to strengthen Christ's body through renewed resolve and mutual support in our common ministries.

The document focuses on the scriptural mandate to love the neighbor. It sets before us the prophet's vision of peace and justice (Micah 6:8) "for all people everywhere." All this, of course, is part of the church's agenda. Yet, the document speaks of the church's mission in the coming century almost in the language of social ethics. Christians are to be "peacemakers in the global community." The emphasis is on what we shall do, not on what God has done. The tone is decidedly utopian, not eschatological. We are told that God calls us to right action, not to right belief, as if one excluded the other. According to the document, the church shall become a model community, committed to deeds of "justice and mercy and peace so that lives may be renewed, spirits revived, and worlds transformed." Certainly, the vision of a peaceable kingdom is an essential part of the promise of God's realm to come. Yet is this vision adequate to the task? To one who has lived through much of this "monstrous" century, the statement expects too much of us and too little of the crucified and risen Christ.

Again, we may get some direction from Dietrich Bonhoeffer's *Ethics*:

> The basis of Christian ethics is not the reality of my own self, nor is it the reality of the world; it is not even the reality of ethical norms or values. Rather, it is the reality of God revealed in Jesus Christ. This is the decisive challenge facing all those who wish to make the problem of a Christian ethics their own. It leads to the ultimate decisive choice, the question of what kind of reality shall really matter in our lives; the reality of God's revealed Word or the reality of the resurrection or the reality of death? (Bonhoeffer I, 56)

The answer to the problem of Christian ethics, writes Bonhoeffer, is making Christ real in the world: "The problem of Christian ethics is how the reality of God's revelation in Christ can become real among God's creatures. Just so, the problem of dogmatics is how the reality of God's revelation in Christ can be regarded as the truth." (Bonhoeffer I, 57)

Note the radical shift in how the question is framed. Bonhoeffer's primary emphasis is on the theological problem of God's action in Christ, not on the ethical problem of our action, even human action sanctioned by God's grace. For Christians, all theological and ethical discussion begins and ends with the reality of God's revelation in Christ. Are faith and action contradictories? Of course not! Christ is still calling the disciples to make Christ's presence real and Christ's word true in this world. Bonhoeffer understands theological ethics and Christian dogmatics in functional terms. The task of Christian ethics is to make God's revelation "real." The task of dogmatics is to witness to its truth of Christ. Either way, the reality of God's self-disclosure in Christ is the given and the starting point of faith and action. We are called to be Christ for our neighbor.

Yet it is Christ, not we, who makes God's peaceable kingdom possible in spite of our very real experience that "in the world (we) have tribulation." (German: *Angst*) Luther still makes eminently good sense: "Faith is the only (and the most difficult) good work!" Apart from the Christ of faith, the vision of global peace and justice remains a utopian dream or an ineffectual wish to be better off than we are. Or worse, in the hands of the right demagogue, it becomes the blueprint of a brave new world.

IV. The Role of the Confessions

A christological approach to Christian faith and ethics is impossible without serious theological engagement with biblical and historical understandings of the Christ of faith. Christianity is a historical religion. It cannot be understood, proclaimed, or practiced without being part of the "ecumenical" experience of the communion of saints in their pilgrimage through time. In short, there is no way of doing Christian ethics teleologically (i.e. looking to the future) without the ancient and implausible story that God was and is in Christ reconciling the world to God-self. For it is that reality; Christ's reconciling presence in the world, that Christ has called his disciples to make manifest in faith and action. We are still quite clear about this in the "Preamble" to the Constitution of the United Church of Christ:

> The United Church of Christ acknowledges as its sole Head, Jesus Christ, Son of God and Savior. It acknowledges as kindred in Christ all who share in this confession. It looks to the Word of God in the Scriptures, and to the presence and power of the Holy Spirit, to prosper its creative and redemptive work in the world. It claims as its own the faith of the historic church expressed in the ancient creeds and reclaimed in the basic insights of the Protestant Reformers. It affirms the responsibility of the church in each generation to make this faith its own in reality of worship, in honesty of thought and expression, and in purity of heart before God. In accordance with the teaching of our Lord and the practice prevailing among evangelical Christians, it recognizes two sacraments: Baptism and the Lord's Supper or Holy Communion.

Here, the church is seen as belonging to Jesus Christ. Christ, not we, calls us to membership in the communion of saints by word and sacrament. Whether we like it or not, confessing Christ and no other defines the boundaries. The question before us is not who should be included in the United Church of Christ, but whether the UCC continues to confess Jesus Christ its sole head, the Son of God, and its Savior. If the latter is questionable, the former becomes meaningless.

There is a story in Matthew 16: Walking with his disciples outside Caesarea Philippi, Jesus asks, "Who do people say that I am?" The answers are diverse. They sound like an opinion poll: John the Baptist, Elijah, Jeremiah, etc. Jesus asks again, "Who do you say that I am?" "You are the Christ, the Son of the living God," answers Peter, and he hits the jackpot. "Blessed are you Simon Bar Jona! Flesh and blood has not revealed this to you, but my Father who is in heaven." I believe this passage cuts through a lot of nonsense about the role of confessional statements in the life of the Church. Clearly, when Jesus turned to his disciples, he was not conducting an opinion poll. He was asking for confession and commitment. The story of Peter's discipleship confirms both the glory and the dilemma of Christian faith and action.

For Christians, the good news of God cannot be reduced to an agenda of human progress, no matter how noble the purpose or intent. The gospel is contained in the scriptural affirmation of God's reconciling presence in Jesus Christ. Throughout history, Christians have always given account of what their faith is all about. The record of their understandings is the story of dogmatics. Karl Barth defines dogmatics as "the discipline (science) in which the Church, in accordance with the state of its knowledge at different times, takes account of the content of its proclamation critically, that is, by the standards of the Holy Scriptures and under the guidance of its confessions." Dogmatics is our way of asking who we are, what we are to teach and preach, and how we are to act in our personal and social lives in order to live and do the gospel.

Christian doctrine, says Barth, did not drop from heaven. It is something we do. Yet, even the founders of modern liberal theology have consistently argued that, though understandings of faith are constantly changing, the constant of the gospel must be identifiable. Friedrich Schleiermacher (d. 1834), for instance, challenged the traditional idea that creeds and confessions are objective statements of "the truth about God." Instead, he said, they are expressions of "religious consciousness" subject to historical circumstance and change. Doctrines develop as the Christian community seeks to account for what it believes to be true. The official pronouncements of churches and synods, says Schleiermacher, are "declarations of what is considered valid by a given church association (*Kirchengesellschaft*) at a given time." Yet, Schleiermacher also insists that change implies a constant. The constant is Christ as redeemer: "Christianity is a teleological, monotheistic religion which is distinguished from all other religions of its kind in that it is related to redemption accomplished by the person of Jesus of Nazareth" (Introduction to *The Christian Faith*). In our own history, Philip Schaff (d. 1893) spoke of the classical creeds of Christendom "not (as) a word of God to men, but (as) a word of men to God, in response to God's revelation" (*Creeds of Christendom*, Vol. 1, 16).

What then is the constant? What are the essential affirmations of the Christian faith? The United Church of Christ and many other Protestant churches reject "tests of faith" as divisive and inconsistent with Jesus' mandate to love the neighbor. Many Christians insist that the Christian life is more important than verbal confessions and forms of worship. Perhaps that is so. Yet, liberal Christians in the late twentieth century, often act as if the "present consciousness" is all there is. We treat the cultural context, "what is considered valid at a given time," as if it were the definition of the faith. The call for total inclusiveness may be the cultural mandate that threatens our very identity as a community of faith.

The subject of dogmatics, says Barth, is the Church. To do theology, one must be part of the believing community. Christian doctrine cannot be understood without sharing the faith. "All Christians have the Church as their mother," said Cyprian, the third century bishop of North African Carthage. Across the centuries, Christians have continued to proclaim "redemption accomplished by Jesus of Nazareth" in the theological language of the scriptures and of the early Christian community. Today, we may appreciate that language, demythologize it, or try to explain it away. Yet, the centrality of Christ as expressed by the ancient Trinitarian affirmations continues to define the global Christian community. Nothing in the Church can therefore be more relevant.

It has been said that revisiting ancient creeds and controversies is not helpful; that all normative expressions of the Christian faith are inherently divisive. Since the language of dogma presumably threatens the bond of peace, some people believe it should be avoided at all cost. To be sure, theological controversy can be as acrimonious as any other form of human conflict. At the Seventh Ecumenical Council (787 A.D.), Greek and Latin monks are said to have engaged in a major fist-fight on the steps of the Church of St. Sophia in Constantinople. The cause of the brouhaha was the Holy Spirit, or more precisely, the Trinity. The question was whether the Holy Spirit proceeds from the Father alone (Greeks), or whether the Holy Spirit proceeds equally from the Father and the Son (Latins). Theologically, it was a draw. At the council, where they kept score, Eastern and Western representatives agreed to disagree. Yet, if they had to fight, at least they were fighting over an issue of substance. By their fights you shall know them. *Book of Worship* (published by the United Church of Christ in 1986), still preserves this ancient argument. It contains a translation of the Nicene Creed that affirms that the Holy Spirit "proceeds from the Father (and the Son)."

It is important to note that in the history of the Church, theological debate has not been the major enemy of Christian unity. Human arrogance and intolerance have been. The love of Christ may be made manifest where there are differences. An absence of theological discussion has almost always been a sign of apathy. Christian theology is an ongoing reasoned conversation about what matters to people of faith at any given moment in history. Where people are trying to understand eternal things, the things that really matter, there will be moments of harmony and discord. Yet, there will also be room for the Holy Spirit to fulfill Christ's promise: "I am with you to the end of the age."

I find it utterly amazing that Christians living today share a common faith with their sisters and brothers across the centuries. There is a "living" content, a perennial theology that "distinguishes the Christian religion from all others." Karl Barth called these essential understandings of the faith… *"das Dogma"* (the dogma) and distinguished it from *"die Dogmen"* (human doctrines) that are subject to cultural and historical change. There is a healthy tension between dogma and its expression in the historical doctrines of the Church. There are no fixed boundaries between them. The wind blows where it will (John 3:8). At first, Christians made no attempt to chisel their teachings into tablets of stone. Later, as sectarian disputes and heretical attacks threatened Christian unity, testimony hardened into test. The lesson of history seems two-fold: A "religious association" which uses its own understanding of the gospel as an exclusive test of truth, is in danger of separating itself from the world Christ has come to save. On the other hand, a "religious association" which lives by the human wisdom of its moment in history, loses its ground in Christ and separates itself from his body.

Each generation of Christians must make "the reality of God revealed in Jesus Christ" its own. It can do so only "in the language of the church, in the language of the scriptures and of the Christian tradition in which in the course of centuries the Christian church has gained and upheld and declared its knowledge… One thing is certain, that where the Christian church does not confess in its own language, it usually does not confess at all" (Karl Barth).

(*On The Way*, Vol. 12, No. 2, Winter 1995-96)

Hans-Jurgen Abromeit

Three Life Choices of Dietrich Bonhoeffer

Confessing Christ Today" raises the question: Who, then, is the Christ who shall be confessed? I am going to try to contribute to the answer to this question by looking into the background of the life and theology of the pastor and teacher of the Church, Dietrich Bonhoeffer. The decisive question in Dietrich Bonhoeffer's life, according to his famous letters from Tegel prison to his friend Eberhard Bethge, is this: "Who is Jesus Christ for us today?" (1) This focus can be followed through the whole life-work of Dietrich Bonhoeffer.

Already in 1933, in his lectures in Berlin on "Christology," he centered on the question concerning the person of Christ: "Who is Jesus Christ?" This problem, he tells the students - rather than all those deliberations about the coincidence of human and divine nature - is the central issue.

The book that made Dietrich Bonhoeffer well known during his lifetime, *Nachfolge* (*The Cost of Discipleship*) makes clear that the question cannot be put in an abstract way, but only in its relevance for us. Speaking of Christ always means also speaking of the life of Jesus Christ within us. Christ has taken residence in the hearts of those trusting in him: "His life on earth is not finished yet," Bonhoeffer insists, "for he continues to live it in the lives of his followers." (2) This is the leitmotiv which kept Bonhoeffer "in motion" in his life and thinking. The goal of his ethics shapes, as he puts it, "the way in which Christ takes form among us here and now." (3) Bonhoeffer's ethics is the ethics of reconciliation. He wants to show how to live out the "New Reality" which has become real in the reconciliation of Christ in this world: "To live and to increase in love is to live in reconciliation and unity with God and with men; it is to live the life of Jesus Christ." (4)

In the biography of no other theologian of the twentieth century have life and theology been linked so closely to one another. Bonhoeffer, in different situations in his thinking and living, actually responded to the question: "Who is Jesus Christ for us today?" Let us explore an answer to this question by examining three life choices of Dietrich Bonhoeffer:

In 1932, he experienced Christ as the One who claims the whole life: speaking and doing, believing and acting. Christ is the Lord who calls into discipleship. Dietrich Bonhoeffer, consequentially, chose discipleship to Jesus Christ.

In 1939, in the face of the emerging horror scenario, the war of extermination arising from Germany, Bonhoeffer decided not to trust the present reality, but Christ, the Real. He chose the way of resistance.

In 1944, in Tegel prison, Bonhoeffer experienced Christ as the One who shares in the suffering of the oppressed and of the weeping; the victims of the Third Reich. The compassion of Christ is there at the cross. But after the cross follows the resurrection. After the ruin of the national socialist terror regime, a new beginning. This, Bonhoeffer firmly believed, will be possible. Bonhoeffer chose the future.

It would be a misinterpretation, and not Bonhoeffer's way of thinking, if one considered only the first decision as a decision for Christ. In his view, all three decisions are decisions for Christ, even those, which—in our view—are political or secular. (5) In all three decisions, he attempted to learn what it means to confess Christ.

I. Christ, the Lord

In an attempt to understand what his decisions were, we have to know where Bonhoeffer was coming from. He clearly identified with his German "Fatherland." His older brother, Walther, had voluntarily signed up for the front in World War I and, within weeks, lost his life there. In the same spirit, seventeen-year-old Dietrich also participated in military exercises: "... today I am already a soldier. Yesterday, just after arriving (here), we were fit out and got our stuff. Today, we got grenades and guns... We don't receive wages. My address is: Rifleman (not Stud. theol.) D.B. Ulm 13. Infantry, 10. Company 1, Corporalsquad." (6) Indeed, Bonhoeffer's military career only lasted fourteen days. Nevertheless, the perspective that appears in the fore-going quote can be found five years later in a lecture held by the twenty-two year old vicar in Barcelona: "Basic issues of Christian ethics." Ethics seems to the young Bonhoeffer to be "a matter of blood and history…There are no actions which are bad in themselves, even murder can be justified…" With regard to Jesus' Sermon on the Mount, he wrote: "It is the greatest of misunderstandings to make the commandments of the Sermon on the Mount into laws once again by referring them literally to the present…. If a people needs more territory, is a war absolutely justified, even a war of aggression… the power is from God and the might and triumph…, for God himself is eternally young and powerful and victorious." (7)

With this theology—glorifying nationalist aspirations and justifying imperialist conceptions, Bonhoeffer did not stand alone. He simply expressed a way of thinking broadly held in theology and the church of his time, e.g. present in the so-called *"Neu-luthertum"* ("New Lutheranism"). The religious validation of the idea of "das Volk" (the people), which sounds so strange to us today, was a concept shared by the majority in German Protestantism during the first half of the twentieth century. (8)

In Professor Reinhold Seeberg, Bonhoeffer's teacher in Berlin, who called himself "modern positive," a theology can be found that glorifies the German state and the German *Volk*. (9) The young Dietrich Bonhoeffer had picked up these views also among some of his other teachers. However, from 1924-25 onward, another influence is to be found. By then, Bonhoeffer had come into contact with "neo orthodox" theology, especially as expressed in Karl Barth. Barth stated that God, by no means, should be absorbed in human ideas and wishes, but that God confronts human life as a "totally different" being. Above all, God is crisis and is judgment on all human ideas and concepts of God.

Visible differences first appear during a year of study at Union Theological Seminary in New York during the 1930/31 academic year. Bonhoeffer not only appeared to be a protagonist of the theology of Barth. It also becomes clear, through many lectures given in local congregations at this time, that his Christian responsibility for peace now gained prevalence over his national bonds. Certainly he confessed to being "a German who loves his home the best of all... who confesses gratefully that he received from his people all that he has and is. But before the cross of Christ and his inconceivable suffering, disappear all our external differences; we are no more rich or poor, wise or simple, good or bad; we are no more Americans or Germans, we are one large congregation of brethren." Because of this, he opposes war and speaks out against nationalism, class or race hatred: "It must never more happen, that a Christian people fights against a Christian people, brother against brother, since both have one Father." (10)

A fundamentally new approach, however, would not be taken by Bonhoeffer until the year 1932. This was the year before Hitler's ascension to power; a year during which Germany was stuck in a serious economical and political crisis. Bonhoeffer, at that time, was teaching confirmation classes in a district of Berlin where the parents were too poor to buy confirmation clothing for their children. At the Technical University, Bonhoeffer, himself only 26 years old at the time, was pastoring students of the Natural Sciences, to whom the word "God" was unknown. In May 1932, he preached on 2 Chronicles 20:12: "We do not know what we shall do, but our eyes look upon You." In these Biblical words, he discovered his situation and the situation of the Church adequately described.

Day by day, the economic and political problems were increasing. The criteria for distinguishing the right from the wrong solutions were more confusing than ever. Also in the private sphere, everything was being shaken: How should one live one's life? Is marriage an adequate way of life or is it an antiquated fashion? How do we need to educate our children? How can young people live their sexuality in a responsible way? At that time, Bonhoeffer did not know any of the answers. "We do not know what we shall do." But he knew the only thing that could help in this situation was to look to the crucified and risen Christ: "But our eyes are looking upon to you." Bonhoeffer wrote to a friend: "The problem for me becomes more and more critical and unbearable. Recently I preached about 2 Chronicles 20:12. I dumped all my despair there. But even with this I have not gotten a step further."

Four years later, he wrote to a woman friend how he had advanced: "I plunged into work in a very un-Christian way, lacking any kind of humility... (I was) deprived... of my fellows' love and confidence. In that time, I was terribly alone... (it) was very bad. Then, something happened; something that has changed and transformed my life to the present day. For the first time, I discovered the Bible. And again, it is very hard to say that. I had often preached, I had seen a great deal of the church, and talked and written about it – but I had not yet become a Christian, but (rather) wild and untamed, my own lord. I know that at that time I turned the doctrine of Jesus Christ into something of personal advantage for myself and for my crazy vanity. I pray to God, that that will never happen again. Moreover, I had never prayed, or prayed only very little. For all my abandonment, I was quite pleased with myself. Then, the Bible, and in particular, the Sermon on the Mount, freed me from that. Since then, everything has changed. I have felt this plainly and so have other people about me. It was a great liberation. It became clear to me that the life of a servant of Jesus Christ must belong to the church and, step by step, it became plainer to me how far that must go... I suddenly saw as self-evident the Christian pacifism I had recently passionately opposed." (11)

Prepared by the theology of Karl Barth and the experience of ecumenical Christianity, the twenty-six year old Bonhoeffer encountered a revision of life and thinking by reading the Bible. In the light of the Bible, he realized that up to now, he had exploited his being Christian for his own purposes and that, actually, he had "not become a Christian". This decision of Bonhoeffer's can be called "the decision for consequential discipleship."

In his book *The Cost of Discipleship*, published in 1937, he interpreted discipleship from his own experience: "Jesus summons men to follow him,... there is no road to faith... only obedience to the call of Jesus... It is nothing else than bondage to Jesus Christ alone, completely breaking through every programme, every ideal, every set of laws. No other significance is possible, since Jesus is the only significance. Beside Jesus nothing has any significance. He alone matters. When we are called to follow Christ, we are summoned to an exclusive attachment to his person." (12)

Thus, Dietrich Bonhoeffer experienced Christ as the Lord of all spheres of life. The bond with him embraces everything, including politics. Thus, in an important ecumenical conference in 1934 in Fanö (Denmark), he could uncompromisingly demand disarmament: "How does peace come about? Through a system of political treaties? Through the investment of international capital in different countries? Through the big banks, through money? Or through none of these, for the single reason that in all of them peace is confused with safety. There is no way to peace along the way of safety. For peace must be dared. It is the great venture. It can never be made safe. Peace is the opposite of security. To demand guarantees is to mistrust, and this mistrust in turn brings forth war. To look for guarantees is to want to protect oneself. Peace means to give oneself altogether to the law of God, wanting no security, but in faith and obedience laying the destiny of the nations in the hand of Almighty God, not trying to direct it for selfish purposes. Battles are won, not with weapons, but with God. They are won where the way leads to the cross." (13)

Having committed himself to Christ in this way, it became clear to Bonhoeffer how impossible it is to give any theological justification to war. He now took the Bible with profound seriousness, including the Sermon on the Mount. What he had refused vehemently in 1928 in Barcelona, now appeared to him to be a compelling necessity. He wrote: "Suddenly, Christian pacifism dawned upon me as a matter of course."

Bonhoeffer believed himself to have finally found a basis for his life. In 1935 he writes to his oldest brother Karl-Friedrich: "I now believe I know at last that I am at least on the right track for the first time in my life. And that often makes me very glad... At present, there are still some things for which an uncompromising stand is worthwhile. And it seems to me that peace and social justice or Christ himself, are such." (14) These last words are worth noting. In the dialogue with his agnostic brother, who was closed to the faith but very open towards the social question, Bonhoeffer identified peace and social justice with Christ. In other words, considering even the present challenges, Christ is peace and social justice.

II. Christ, the Real

The second crucially important decision was made by Dietrich Bonhoeffer in 1939. It was the decision for resistance. Bonhoeffer saw that Hitler wanted to push the world into war. As a Christian objector to military service, Bonhoeffer would be executed. At that time he received an invitation to give a set of lectures in the United States. He grasped the opportunity to leave Germany. But after only six weeks, he returned. What provoked this sudden return? His friend, Eberhard Bethge, had at the beginning of the year gifted him with a book of daily scripture readings. It is very revealing to follow along in his diary of the USA trip, noting how Bonhoeffer, by listening to the readings and praying, struggled for the right way. He questioned himself, whether he had not just run away out of cowardliness and disobedience (16.6.) Finally, on the twentieth of June, he refused a position as a professor in the United States, which would have guaranteed him a continuous stay in the United States. In his diary he wrote: "So the decision has been made. I have refused. They were visibly disappointed and somehow angry. I suppose that for me this signifies more than I can preview at the moment. God only knows." (15)

Bonhoeffer surely had anticipated his return to Germany would signify more than just a continuation of his former educational activities. After the beginning of the war; in spring of 1940 when the young vicars of the Confessing Church were being recruited to the military; he had to sever completely his work at the seminary of the Confessing Church. He also knew that a return to Germany could only mean a struggle against the inhumanity of the state under Hitler. What only God knew was that Dietrich Bonhoeffer would give his life in this fight.

After his arrival back in Germany, Bonhoeffer, through the mediation of his brother-in-law, Hans von Dohnanyi, for years a personal consultant to the minister for justice of the "Reich," was involved in the preparation of upheaval. Hans von Dohnanyi found Bonhoeffer a position in the counter-intelligence department of the military (*Wehrmacht*) as camouflage for his subversive activity.

Bonhoeffer himself was frightened when he realized where his way had led him. Could he, a pastor and a Christian, become involved in a conspiracy? Bonhoeffer responded, that "as a pastor I do not only have the duty to console the victims of a driver who has turned mad, driving his car on a populated road, but I am obliged to try to stop him." (16)

During the time of his conspiratory travel and activity for the intelligence service, he worked on "Ethics." From the fragments handed down to us, we know that Bonhoeffer, as a Christian, intentionally opted for the resistance (even the armed resistance). Again, it is the person of Jesus Christ from where his thoughts began. Jesus Christ, the Son of God, who has become a human being for us, who for us was crucified and resurrected, is in the center of his deliberations,

By the incarnation, God shows us that He loves all humans in the same way. By the incarnation, God has taken up all humankind in Himself. If God loves all human beings, the worst enemy is the despiser of humanity, as he appears in the shape of Adolf Hitler. Christians who believe in the God who made Himself human, will fight with all their power to stop crimes against humanity. If the Church or if an individual keeps silence in the face of the violation of human rights, he/she sins against Christ (*wird schuldig an Christus*".) As the Church has kept silence in the face of Nazi politics against the Jews (*Judenpolitik*), Bonhoeffer wrote in October 1940, "she is guilty of the deaths of the weakest and most defenseless brothers of Jesus Christ." (17) Bonhoeffer, however, not only points to the others. He sees himself included in this confession of guilt. The persecution of the Jews is one of the essential reasons for him to take part in the resistance.

By the crucifixion of the Son of God, God shows us that success is not the measure or justification of all things, but the judgment of God. Only what passes God's judgment is of consistency. But this judgment can only be passed by those who submit to the event of Golgatha. Bonhoeffer said: "Jesus is not concerned with success or failure, but with the willing acceptance of God's judgment. Only in this judgment is there reconciliation with God and among men." (18)

Undoubtedly in the war until now - in the eyes of most Germans - Hitler had been very successful. (19) Bonhoeffer, however, wanted to look beyond this superficial reality. His question was how to put God's being Lord of history and the success of the antichrist Hitler together. A little later (in September/October 1940), he notes: "The successful man (Bonhoeffer thinks of Hitler in this instance) presents us with accomplished facts that can never be reversed..." Assessing the situation theologically, one has to state: "The figure of the crucified invalidates all thought which takes success for its standard." Precisely, the cross is the judgment on that success. Therefore, peace is not to be achieved by success but through the judgment, which has been executed at Golgotha: "Only by God's executing judgment... can there be peace between Him and the world and between man and man." (20) God's judgment on success helps the disciple of Jesus Christ put him/herself into a critical position towards such success. So God's judgment leads from the deification of success into the resistance.

In the resurrection of Jesus Christ, God shows us that life is more than what happens on this side of death: "God's love for man has proved stranger than death." On the other hand, however, it appeared already in Bonhoeffer's time—and how much more today!—that absolute power is ascribed to death. All that is important is supposed to happen on this side of death (*Todesgrenze*). Death is the last (being) and puts itself into the place of God. Bonhoeffer speaks of the "idolization of death:"

> "But wherever it is recognized that the power of death has been broken, wherever the world of death is illumined by the miracle of the resurrection and of the new life, there, no eternities are demanded of life, but one takes of life what it offers, not all or nothing but good and evil, the important and the unimportant, joy and sorrow; one either clings convulsively to life or casts it frivolously away. One is content with the allotted span and one does not invest earthly things with the title of eternity; one allows to death the limited rights which it still possesses. It is from beyond death that one expects the coming of the new man and of the new world, from the power by which death has been vanquished." (21)

For Dietrich Bonhoeffer, the decision for the resistance was inevitable. The one who knows the God who says "Yes" to human beings, who judges success and who promises new humanity, cannot ignore the despising of humankind, the glorification of success, the deification of death. It is not these perversions of humanity that give orientation, but "Christ, the Real," who shows (for Bonhoeffer, too) the direction. Because of this, his decision for the resistance is a decision for "Christ, the Real;" for the incarnated, crucified and resurrected Christ.

The conspiracy, however, was detected. Bonhoeffer was held in prison for two years prior to being executed on April 9, 1945 at the Flossenbürg concentration camp in Bavaria. In prison, he became acquainted with what he called the "view from below." From the perspective of the oppressed and beaten, he traced the shape of a new Christian life (*Gestalt des neuen Christseins*) and of a new Church. So, in the face of death, he made his third crucially important decision: the decision for the future. It found expression in the letters and poems which are collected in the book, *Wiederstand und Ergebung* (*Resistance and Submission*). This book appeared in English as *Letters and Papers from Prison*.

III. Christ, the One Who Shares the Suffering

For a person from the "upper class," what Bonhoeffer had to go through while in custody was a particularly humiliating experience. The cells of the Tegel prison in Berlin were small, narrow, and filthy. A companion from that time remembers: "The cells were rather narrow and not very clean (during the summer there were bedbugs inside). In the cell there was a tub for the necessaries... In the morning, when the food was served, at the same time the tubs were emptied, and the bread mostly was put on the cap." (22) Visitors, again and again, mentioned the nasty smell.

How did Bonhoeffer feel under these circumstances? To his parents he wrote: "I do want you to be quite sure that I'm all right." (23) How he really felt, a note from May 1943 indicates: He was isolated, completely alone; he was becoming indifferent, he longed for times past; he felt devastated. The desperation that had overwhelmed him is expressed in his words... "Suicide, not because of consciousness of guilt, but because basically I am already dead..." (24) Only the term "overcoming in prayer" indicated whence he always seemed to receive new strength.

In November 1943 Bonhoeffer mentioned those suicidal ideas in a letter to his friend Eberhard Bethge: "You are the only person who knows that this 'acedia-tristitia' (i.e. 'sadness-depression') with its menacing consequences, has lain in wait for me; and I feared at the time that you must be worrying about me on that account. But I told myself from the beginning that I was not going to oblige either man or devil in any such way – they can do what they like about it for themselves." (25)

What Bonhoeffer means by *acedia*, we can better understand if we listen carefully to what he said in his lecture on "Counseling" (*Seelsorge*) when he speaks about the different forms of temptation: "Another kind of known temptation is melancholy, *acedia*,... Through it a person falls to pieces. It drives him to complete isolation, so that he tells himself life is senseless and gratuitous. Darkness descends between God and the person, so that the person loses God. Melancholy does not stem too much from uncertainty about salvation as from doubt of God's presence (*Dasein*). The question of salvation never gets asked. The person who is tested by melancholy is a bouncing ball in the devil's hands, given to thoughts of suicide. At times nothing more is desired!" (26)

So *acedia* was the sad feeling of senselessness and emptiness, that reached down to desperation and suicide. Obviously, Bonhoeffer knew this sadness well, yet comforted his friend, Bethge, by saying that in prison he had resisted this longing for death "from the beginning". We know that he was not quite honest in the conversation with his friend. Nevertheless, this stage was truly overcome in November, 1943. Bonhoeffer, again, focused on new challenges to which he dedicated himself by writing.

As a response to the difficulties of faith and the "coming of age" (*"Mundigwerden"*) of the (secularized) "modern human being," he developed the vision of a secular, non-religious Christianity. If Christ is the one who "is totally present for the others" (*ganz für andere da*), then also the Church, in its actual form, only can be "present for others." Bonhoeffer thought in quite a radical way:

"To make a start, it should give away all its property to those in need. The clergy must live solely on the free-will offerings of their congregations, or possibly engage in some secular calling. The church must share in the secular problems of ordinary human life, not dominating, but helping and serving. It must tell men of every calling what it means to live in Christ, to exist for others." (27)

To this new understanding of being Christian, which consists of "praying and doing what is just among human beings (*"Beten und Tun des Gerechten"*), corresponds a non-religious interpretation of the Bible. Bonhoeffer always spoke directly of Jesus Christ, not of the great, inaccessible, far-away God, who lives in a world apart from ours. It is decisive to speak about how God has come into this world and reconciled it to Himself (Godself); to speak about God in our world, not about (a) god beyond our world.

Bonhoeffer did this now more often in a poetic form. For example, in his beautiful poem "Christians and Pagans", he gave account of what had lifted him out of his self-pity. His decision for the future was so fundamental that he once again came to know Christ anew. He had experienced that not only are one's own problems important. It is even more important to recognize that God has got one's problems, too. In "Christians and Pagans" Bonhoeffer wrote:

Men go to God when they are sore be stead,
Pray to him for succour, for his peace, for bread,
For mercy for them sick, sinning, or dead:
All men do so, Christian and unbelieving.

Men go God when he is sore bestead,
Find him poor and scorned, without shelter or bread,
Whelmed under weight of the wicked, the weak, the dead;
Christians stand by God in his hour of grieving.

God goes to every man when sore bestead,
Feeds body and spirit with his bread;
For Christians, pagans alike he hangs dead,
And both alike forgiving.

In the situation of the prison—in daily confrontation with those condemned to death, and in the face of the fear of bomb attacks—Bonhoeffer realized that both Christians and non-Christians in hopelessness and fear of death turn to God. This is nothing specifically Christian. What makes the difference is that Christians share the suffering of God in this world and because of this, companionship with others, who - guilty or innocent - are suffering. In the life and death of Jesus, God lives in solidarity with those who are "poor and scorned, without shelter or bread." As Jesus now is with those, his disciples cannot be somewhere else: "Christians stand by God in... God's suffering."

So Bonhoeffer's third crucial decision, the decision for the future, was a change in his position. Self-pity is replaced by real compassion, a commitment to God's suffering, once at the cross and today in the world. So Bonhoeffer became a martyr for Jesus. As he totally stood by the man from Golgatha, we find him hung and incinerated in the Flossenbürg concentration camp, side by side with the Jews gassed and incinerated in Auschwitz.

What does that mean today: Confessing Christ? According to the testimony and life of Dietrich Bonhoeffer, it means that word and deed are to be inseparably intertwined. We can only confess Jesus Christ as Lord if we are prepared to follow him today. We can only recognize Christ as "Real" if we are prepared to stand by him in his resistance to the depreciation of human beings, the glorification of success, and the deification of death. If we confess Christ as the One who shares the suffering, this suffering will not be spared us.

Notes

1. Bonhoeffer, Dietrich, *Letters and Papers from Prison*, [The Enlarged Edition, edited by Eberhard Bethge,] New York: (Collier Books, Macmillan, 1972 = LPP), 279.
2. Bonhoeffer, Dietrich, *The Cost of Discipleship*, [Paperback Edition], New York: (Macmillan, 1963), 343.
3. Bonhoeffer, Dietrich, *Ethics*, edited by Eberhard Bethge, New York: (Collier Books, Macmillan, 1986), 85.
4. Op. cit., 39.
5. Cf. Dietrich Bonhoeffer, *The Cost of Discipleship*, 250: "Discipleship never consists in this or that specific action: it is always a decision, either for or against Jesus Christ."
6. Bonhoeffer, Dietrich, *Jugend und Studium 1918-1927*, (*Dietrich Bonhoeffer-Werke = DBW* IV, ed. By H. Pfeiffer), München, 1986, 68.
7. Quoted from *A Testament to Freedom: The essential Writings of Dietrich Bonhoeffer*, ed. By G. B. Kelly and F. B. Nelson, San Francisco: (Harper, 1990), 364, 367f.
8. *Dietrich Bonhoeffer, Barcelona, Berlin, Amerika 1928-1931*, (*DBW* X, edited by R. Staats/H.C. v. Hase), München, 1991, 339.

9. Cf. H.E. Todt, "Dietrich Bonhoeffer's oekumenische Friedensethik," in: *Frieden: das unumgängliche Wagnis*," edited by H. Pfeiffer, München, 1982, 85-117, spec. 86-90.

10. Cf. G. Brakelmann, *Protestantische Kriegstheologie im 1 Weltkrieg, Reinhold Seeberg als Theologe des deutschen Imperialismus*, Bielefeld, 1974. As distinguished from Seeberg, you do not find any glorification of the state by Bonhoeffer, even when he was young.

11. Bonhoeffer, Dietrich, *Barcelona*, 576-581.

12. Bonhoeffer, Dietrich, "Illegale Theologenausbildung: Finkenwalde 1935-1937," (*DBW* XIV, edited by O. Dudzus/J. Henkys), Gütersloh, 1996, 112-114; cf. *A Testament to Freedom*, 447-448.

13. Bonhoeffer, Dietrich, *The Cost of Discipleship*, 62f.

14. Bonhoeffer, Dietrich, "London 1933-1935," (*DBW* XIII, edited by H. Goedking/M. Heimbucher/H.-W. Schleicher), Gütersloh, 1994, 303-304.

15. Quoted from *A Testament to Freedom*, 447.

16. Bonhoeffer, Dietrich, "Illegale Theologenausbildung: Sammelvikariate 1937-1940," (*DBW* XV, edited by D. Schulz), Gütersloh, 1998, 228.

17. Quoted from the report of G. Latmiral, who was also a prisoner in Tegel. See *Dietrich Bonhoeffer: Texte zum 80. Geburtstag*, (Dokumentationen 52/86), Ev. Bildungswerk Berlin, 99-101,100.

18. Bonhoeffer, Dietrich, *Ethics,* 114.

19. Op. cit. 77.

20. Cf. H.-J. Abromeit, *Das Geheimnis Christi: Dietrich Bonhoeffer's erfahrungsbezogene Christologie*, (NBST 8), Neukirchen-Vluyn, 1991, 247-252.

21. Bonhoeffer, Dietrich, *Ethics*, 75-77.

22. Ibid, 78-79.

23. G. Latmiral, quoted in Ch. Gremmels/H. Pfeiffer, *Theologie und Biographie*, München, 1983, 102.

24. Bonhoeffer, Dietrich, *LPP*, 21.

25. Ibid, 35.

26. Ibid, 129.

27. Bonhoeffer, Dietrich, *Spiritual Care*, translated and with an Introduction by Jay C. Rochelle, Philadelphia: (Fortress Press, 1985,) 52.

28. Bonhoeffer, Dietrich, *LPP*, 382f.

29. Op. cit. 348f.

(This essay was composed in 1998 and originally prepared for publication in *On The Way* later that year. The journal, however, did not appear.)

Dorothy C. Bass

Faith and Pluralism in the United States

When the planners of this colloquy on the church and civil religion first asked me to provide a historical perspective on this subject, the 1984 political campaign was just beginning. "We believe that this is a most timely topic given the current situation," one planner wrote to me, and as the months of this election year passed this assessment seemed to become more and more apt. In fact, discussion of the appropriate relationship between religion and politics was so widespread that I began to wonder what else could be said about it.

Prominently featured in this year's discussions of religion and politics were disputes in Catholic circles about the roles and duties of Catholic public officials in upholding the teaching of the ecclesiastical hierarchy; the apparent power of the new religious and political right in the circle around the President and among his grassroots supporters; and the religious dynamism of Jesse Jackson's preaching and practice. Less often covered, however, were the religious groups that have historically been in the habit of thinking of themselves as the most prominent and central members of the American public and its polity. Walter Mondale's declaration that he was the son of a Methodist minister and the son-in-law of a Presbyterian minister did not seem to stir many hearts.

The full practical implications of the current situation in the ongoing relationship between religion and politics in American culture are still unclear. Even so, my impressionistic reading of this year's events does discover one message: that of the diminished influence of the old "mainline" Protestant churches in American public life; the churches which were dominant therein from the time of European colonization until their final spurt of growth and self-confidence under the sympathetic reign of Dwight David Eisenhower. The disestablishment of these churches—not only in the legal sense that was accomplished long ago, but as institutions with extensive cultural authority—is beyond dispute.

In my discussion of the responses of Christian faith to civil religion, I intend to highlight the place of the groups often called "mainline." I have three basic reasons for doing this:

1) I assume—correct me if I am mistaken—that most of us in the United Church of Christ have at some point identified with this label. I have done so myself. The label, like all labels, has problems, I'll define "mainline" further in a moment - but its impact is important whether or not it adequately describes a social reality. If a church thinks of itself as "mainline," that is significant in shaping its self-image, its identity, and its approach to the rest of society, whether or not social reality would support the claim.

2) From the point of view of social and cultural history—quite apart from faith concerns or party interest—the changing place of the older, liberal, formerly established denominations marks a crucial alteration in the design of the American landscape. One sign of the change is numbers— and losses of membership by "mainline" denominations in the last two decades are seemingly related to other forms of eclipse. These losses, though causing some confusion and discomfort in mainline circles, are matters to be coolly analyzed as trends in American culture by some sociologists. As an example, here is a fairly typical analysis, pronounced in 1983 by the sociologist Wade Clark Roof of the University of Massachusetts:

> A major trend is the decline of liberal mainline religious institutions. Though less visible a trend than conservative growth, decline has nonetheless been very much a part of the American religious scene of the past two decades. During the seventies, many churches suffered from a widespread malaise brought on by a loss of institutional vitality and direction. As institutions, they were somewhat unprepared for the spiritual and ideological climate emerging at the time. Trends toward more experiential religion and absolutist belief left many liberal churches with shrinking appeal and support. As a consequence, a number of large, well-established Protestant denominations not only failed to grow, but actually reported significant membership losses in this period. Protestant traditions with long-standing records of sustained membership growth and prosperity, some dating back to Colonial times, experienced their first major downturn in membership. (1)

To this statistical evidence of "decline" we might add some impressionistic observations: the relative visibility of other groups; the shameless "Sixty Minutes" attack on the major ecumenical organizations;

and the intense interest of many mainline denominations in how to make their churches grow, which has created a major sub-industry in American religion.

3) To these personal and social reasons for highlighting the "mainline," I would add a theological one. We must ask whether our disestablishment is loss or gain, curse or blessing. What might our status as a minority church, if self-consciously appropriated, teach us about God's plan for our action in the world? I will conclude with reflections on these questions.

I

It is important to clarify the term "mainline" before proceeding further. ("Mainstream" is a frequently-used synonym.) Reflect for a moment on the images this term evokes; one thinks, for instance, of a central railway for which other "lines" are simply feeders or derivatives. Whatever is not "mainline" is consigned to marginality; whatever is "mainline" is at center stage. American Church History has been written and taught with this focus, and I should confess that it has been difficult for me as a historian to escape from the spell of this interpretation.

In one sense, the whole concept of "mainline" summarizes a massive historical and sociological fiction. Groups that are declared marginal by the term don't necessarily perceive themselves as marginal; their experience validates their own centrality. And numbers don't justify the claim that the liberal Protestant denominations are "mainline"; by 1850, the largest single denomination was already Roman Catholicism. Partly for these reasons, it is in some ways more appropriate to talk of a Protestant "Establishment" than a Protestant "mainline." Establishments stand over, not next to; they have power - social power, economic power, and cultural power. Of these, the cultural power or authority is often most subtle; it appears in places like Henry Luce's *Time/Life* empire, in leading educational institutions governed by quotas and certain ethnic habits, in the dominance of some groups in public office, as well as in many other subtle ways.

An Establishment doesn't have to defend its legitimacy: it has birthright membership in "the American Way." Sociologist Robert Ellwood's "temple religion" (though perhaps a bit overdrawn) catches the essence of this status: "Not far from where I live, a quiet shady street runs through a small suburban town. On one side of that street, as on hundreds of shady streets in as many American small towns, a large Methodist church complex rises. Over the landscaped grounds sprawl sanctuary, offices, auditoria, parking lots, and countless classrooms. The solidity and evident prosperity of this edifice proclaim that it is a local manifestation of the proper, legitimate, respectable religion of the land, akin in that sense to Canterbury Cathedral in England, or the Altar of Heaven of the old Chinese emperors in Peking." (2)

I think that smaller, less prosperous churches can also exude this aura of propriety, legitimacy, and respect; what is important in Ellwood's example is not its size but its comfort in its cultural setting.

Call it mainline, establishment, or temple, we are differentiating this kind of religion from others, and in doing so we implicitly point to the fact of pluralism in American life. The fact of diversity has been a central reality of American religious life since Europeans arrived on this continent; it must frame and inform all our discussions about religion and politics. Religious diversity is the kind of diversity that rises to mind when we take up a topic like that of today's colloquy, but in addressing this issue we should never forget the corrective offered by H. Richard Niebuhr in one of his early works almost fifty years ago: divisions in religion reflect and include divisions of race, ethnicity, class, and culture. Denominationalism (the American variety of religious pluralism) has social sources. (3)

The fact of pluralism affects the life of faith in so many ways, especially in the modern world. It challenges easy certainties and exerts social pressure for mutual respect among groups; it enriches our lives by introducing fresh options and opening minds. But it is also potentially troubling. Pluralism can undermine, perhaps even shatter, the common agreements that make social life possible. How deep can disagreement about fundamental issues go before it becomes impossible for us to share a society? In the absence of general consensus about ultimate concerns, about shared visions and values, how can a society be strong, or just, or even coherent enough to exist and function? Can a society make important decisions about using limited resources, protecting or taking life, and other difficult matters without some fundamental moral, and ultimately religious, agreement? In the view of many thoughtful critics, pluralism ushers in relativism and privatism; it becomes impossible to claim in the public realm that anything is really true, and private preference or individual self-interest become the ruling realities. In this situation, citizens are transformed into consumers; without a sense of the relation of morality and religion to hard public choices, there is little sense of accountability beyond the self, and justice falters.

However well this bleak assessment fits our current situation, the fact of pluralism and the problem of fundamental agreement have framed American thinking about the appropriate relationship between religion and politics for centuries. Religious pluralism already existed at the time of the nation's founding; in fact, when historians explain why the United States chose the unprecedented course of religious liberty, they concur that the fact of actual diversity was at least as important a motive as were ideals of religious liberty. But in the face of this diversity, even those Founders who supported religious liberty on philosophical grounds believed in the importance of having some fundamental agreements about religion. Thomas Jefferson, commenting on one colony's policy of religious liberty, stated that there "religion is well supported; of various kinds, indeed, but all good enough; all sufficient to preserve peace and order." (4)

Perhaps the leading model of how Americans have come to some unity of purpose (for good or ill) in the midst of pluralism is civil religion. This phenomenon has become a constant part of our discussions of religion and politics, as the title of today's colloquy shows. Given this fact, I shall spend a few minutes clarifying and assessing civil religion. Then I shall turn to the question of its importance for thinking about "mainline" Protestantism by exploring some aspects of the characteristic relationship between the two, before moving on to where we are now, as I see it.

II

An article by sociologist Robert Bellah in 1967 precipitated wide-ranging discussion of the issue of civil religion. (5) Although many students of American religion before him had commented on the religious tinge of national political life, Bellah named this phenomenon "civil religion" and described it in a way that other scholars found compelling enough to respond to. His ideas have also been widely discussed in non-academic circles, though not always with sufficient understanding of Bellah's original intentions and arguments.

According to Bellah, "there actually exists alongside of and rather clearly differentiated from the churches an elaborate and well-institutionalized civil religion in America." In his view, "the American civil religion is not the worship of the American nation but an understanding of the American experience in the light of ultimate and universal reality." This religion took the most formative events of American history - the Revolution, the Civil War - and interpreted them with reference to the ultimate concerns and moral aspirations of the people. It drew on biblical imagery, but it was not a biblical faith; therefore it ought not to threaten the churches, which it has not sought to displace. By setting the experience of the nation in a framework of ultimate and divine purpose, it gave transcendent grounding to certain moral commitments respecting liberty and justice; it also included the notion that this nation stands, at times, under God's judgment. (Here Bellah leans heavily on the words of Abraham Lincoln.) In Bellah's view, civil religion has never been lacking in prophetic voices; it fuelled many liberating struggles. Even so, Bellah grants its historic shortcomings: "Like all religions, it has suffered various deformations and demonic distortions. At its best, it has neither been so general that it has lacked incisive relevance to the American scene nor so particular that it has placed American society above universal human values. I am not at all convinced that the leaders of the churches have consistently represented a higher level of religious insight than the spokesmen of the civil religion."

Writing in 1967, Bellah intended to provide a basis for a morally vital consensus drawing upon what he saw as the enduring moral values of American history. In a time of change, he was offering a program of morally purposive unity. I would criticize this program and the view of American history upon which it was based in many ways; for instance, many groups were excluded from the consensus it traced. But it did make some sense as a call to reform and justice in 1967. Under Dr. Martin Luther King, Jr., the civil rights movement appealed to civil traditions as well as to Christian ones. And Bellah's final pages called for a new version of civil religion that would point towards internationalism and undo what Senator J. William Fulbright was then calling America's "arrogance of power." In that setting, the movement for peace and justice in which religious and secular groups worked together often appealed to some of the same ideals Bellah was advancing. But rarely has a publication been so ill-timed. The cultural context changed rapidly right as Bellah was writing and publishing, due to black nationalism, a more militant antiwar movement, and above all Nixon's apparently cynical use of civil religion in 1968 and beyond. "Civil religion" swiftly came to have a bad name, and before long Bellah also substantially revised his assessment of it, though he has retained his interest in the question of how American society can justly cohere in the midst of pluralism. (6)

Civil religion, in Bellah's definition, exists alongside of the churches; it need not displace or threaten them. So American Christians can presumably engage in both. The troubling issue of how to distinguish a person or group's exercise of Christianity from their exercise of civil religion then emerges. Is it really possible to say "God" in two religious systems and mean different gods? Which religion installed American flags in sanctuaries? Don't senses of belonging overlap? The possibilities of theological confusion (or worse) in this situation immediately startled some critics—and still do. Bellah's initial response, though not a complete answer, is worthy of some reflection on the part of concerned Christians: "Perhaps the real animus of the religious critics has been not so much against the civil religion in itself but against its pervasive and dominating influence within the sphere of church religion." (7)

III

Here we return to the mainline. Did civil religion and church religion overlap in the experience of the people? The answer would have to be: only in the experience of some people. Take, for example, the historical experience of the black community. This community could offer a strikingly different rendering of the transcendent dimensions of American history. The account might resemble that of civil religion in that both refer to an exodus from oppression, but in this telling George Washington would appear as Pharaoh, not Moses. And other "outsiders" to American civil religion would also find its claims distant and distorted. The idea that it could interpret the historical experience of native Americans is tragically absurd; Catholics have only recently come to claim it, and that not unanimously; Asian-Americans would reject its use during World War II. Most likely to recognize themselves in the account of history offered by civil religion are the groups of the Protestant mainline: the ethnic, cultural, social groups with the deepest long-term sense of belonging to the United States and with the greatest historic ease in identifying with its leaders.

For the denominations that constituted the Protestant Establishment in the nineteenth century (and here, I'll risk naming a few: Congregationalists, Presbyterians, Methodists, Episcopalians, and in certain regions Disciples of Christ and Baptists), church religion and civil religion were often conflated in a program for national unity and morality: the effort to build a "Christian America." Robert T. Handy's excellent book by that title shows how these church people came to think of Christian morality and "the American way of life" as virtually identical. Handy traces the development of this religious/cultural party from the colonial establishments of religion through its efforts to win the voluntary assent of the American people to its leadership in the context of religious liberty. In the process, the problem of double belonging that still confronts analysts of religion and politics in America emerged. "Most Protestants in the America of 1890 saw themselves as belonging both to a denominational tradition and to the national religion, a religion of civilization - and they experienced little or no tension between them." (8)

Sketching the many examples of actual overlap between these two religions would fill many books. The sketches would not be monochromatic, for the strong connection between mainline Protestant identity and national life left behind a complex legacy. At times it was a weapon for legitimating ethnic or national tyranny; for example, it was a tool against the full inclusion of Catholics in political life until 1960, and it fuelled numerous imperialist and militaristic ventures. At other times, however, the connection provided a means for calling both the churches and the nation to live up to their highest, supposedly shared, ideals; for example, abolitionists linked the moral traditions of the Constitution and the Bible effectively, as did the best representatives of the Social Gospel movement in the early part of the twentieth century. Sometimes prophetically, often oppressively, partly through accommodation, partly by ignoring or subjugating other voices, in the era of the informal Protestant establishment, mainline church leaders addressed public issues in the confident voices of insiders.

But by 1940, Handy believes, the "Protestant era" in American history had ended. Although almost no one recognized the fact at the time, almost every treatment of American Church History now concludes with this crucial shift. Why did this "second disestablishment" occur? The best and simplest reason is the advance of pluralism; other groups, growing in numbers for more than a century, formally got big enough and rich enough and assimilated enough to find their own voices and move into positions of cultural authority beyond their own communities. As Handy puts it, "the voluntary effort to mainline a Protestant America had failed." But his next sentence is the intriguing one: "For some, this seemed to mean the loss of religion itself; for others, it meant the freeing of religion from an alliance that was outdated and had become dysfunctional."

Among those who found this disestablishment freeing - and absolutely essential to faithfulness - were some theologians in touch with the European theological movement that provided the grounding for the Barmen Declaration of 1934. In the mid-1930s, Handy reports, "some conspicuous Protestant leaders were calling for the disentanglement of Protestantism and American civilization; they were asking for a reversal of what had long been axiomatically accepted. Instead of the church having Christianized civilization, they found that the civilization had captured the church." In 1935, Francis P. Miller, Wilhelm Pauck, and H. Richard Niebuhr published *The Church Against the World*, which explicitly sought to relate knowledge of the plight of the German churches in the 1930s to the American situation. The authors declared: "The plain fact is that the domestication of the Protestant community in the United States within the framework of the national culture has progressed as far as in any western land. The degradation of the American Protestant church is as complete as the degradation of any other national Protestant church. The process of degradation has been more subtle and inconspicuous, but equally devastating in its consequences for faith." (9)

IV

This ringing declaration from the 1930s summons us to reflect upon the theological implications of our topic for our own times. Is our disestablishment loss or gain, curse or blessing? What might our status as a minority church, if self-consciously appropriated, teach us about God's plan for our action in the world? This aspect of what it means to be church - which includes questions about appropriate relationships to the powerful and to the dispossessed and a weighing of the influence for good that seems attainable through establishment against the influence towards evil that seems to attend it - is a long-term issue in the life of the church. It may be a tension to be lived with amidst the ambiguities of a fallen world rather than a matter that possesses one right answer. If so, the positions Christians take must be shaped by their careful discernment of the needs of their own times.

I'd like to share a statement on this matter that shows how long American Christians have been reflecting on all of this. It was written in 1644 by Roger Williams, the New World's first sponsor of diversity in religion, and it refers back to events of the fourth century.

> The unknowing zeal of Constantine and other emperors did more hurt to Christ Jesus His crown and kingdom than the raging fury of the most bloody Neros. In the persecutions of the latter, Christians were sweet and fragrant, like spice pounded and beaten in mortars; but by those good emperors.. I say, by this means Christianity was eclipsed and the professors of it fell asleep. Babel or confusion was ushered in, and by degrees the garden of the churches of saints were turned into the wilderness of whole nations, until the whole world became Christian or Christendom.... When Christianity began to be choked, it was not when Christians lodged in cold prisons, but down-beds of ease. (10)

Williams' statement stands at an extreme of the tension I have described; he is calling the church to a radical sense of its distinctiveness from the world. Contrast an (admittedly stereotyped) account of American Christianity on its down-beds of ease, sociologist Ellwood's depiction of respectable mainline religion:

> If it is at all typical of the Middle American Protestantism the building suggests, the Sunday morning rite in the church across the street is not difficult to evoke. A moment's stillness, and one's mind echoes with hymns like "This Is My Father's World," with the sonorous words of scripture, the compassionate pastoral prayer, the announcement of youth group hayrack rides and basketball games, of committee meetings and pancake suppers. The sermon would be warm with the affirmation of honesty,

love, and understanding. Then, the coffee hour, the gathering-up of children from the far-flung reaches of the Sunday school, the ranch-wagons and sedans loaded again, long Sunday dinners in a hundred homes, and finally TVs turned to pro football. (11)

Let me be clear. I know that this is not a complete description of the old "mainline" churches as they exist today. I know that there are many churches out there that have very little in common with this fat one. I am not a seminary professor coming here to heap disdain on local churches. Rather, I am a Christian unsure of exactly how to proceed, yet conscious of some of what I have learned as a student of American culture as it manifests itself in dominant, popularized forms:

• Not everyone in America is rich, but American culture wants to tempt everyone into thinking that they might become so. It works against class-consciousness; it celebrates wealth; it lets us rest easy with our abundance.

• American culture is optimistic and promising about the new. It wants to sweep old wounds swiftly under the rug, and it calls those who name problems (like Walter Mondale) "gloomy."

• American culture seeks to ignore pain. It denies that there are starving people in this country, and it won't face up to the pain it inflicts around the world. While this may be a widespread human tendency, I think that it is particularly characteristic of this culture and this era. These are the signs of our times; if we are troubled, we are told that we ought to take up jogging, since pain is really an error.

It is in the context of these temptations and pressures from our culture —as well as the fact of our actual wealth in comparison to the rest of the world—that Roger Williams's words about down-beds of ease need to be heard by American Christians, and particularly by those who have been accustomed to thinking of themselves as "mainline." It is tempting at this juncture to point a finger at the members of the new religious and political right, whose growth demonstrates the vigor of the ideology of success in American culture, but I think that we will do better to get our own house in order.

Perhaps the second disestablishment is the gift of pluralism to the old mainline, shoving us from a position of pride and gracing us with an invitation to give up ruling and to begin following, as disciples of Christ. Since even as a self-consciously minority church we must be about serving the world and transforming culture, we must be about that with the aid of less of the world's power than we formerly possessed. This should, I hope, lead us to discover new partners in ministry among the disestablished and dispossessed.

As Roger Williams put it, "the most high and glorious God hath chosen the poor of the world; and the witnesses of truth are clothed in sackcloth, not in silk or satin, cloth of gold or tissue." Some current Catholic social teaching invites us to such partnership. In addition, perhaps international solidarity with the poor will become possible when we are less identified with national civilization. And it is intriguing to imagine some predominantly white mainline congregations having a relationship to the dominant culture that is something like the relationship black churches have had for generations.

Some of these alliances are already taking place. I believe that our "success" in transforming culture will depend, in this era of disestablishment, more on affirming connections like these than in seeking "success" as the world defines it, or as this wealth and pain-ignoring society defines it, or as Jerry Falwell and Robert Schuller define it. Whether or not we are "growing" as measured by the yardsticks of the dominant culture, our task is to be faithful.

Notes

1. Roof, Wade Clark, "America's Voluntary Establishment: Mainline Religion in Transition," in Mary Douglas and Steven M. Tipton (eds.), *Religion and America: Spirituality in a Secular Age*, Boston: (Beacon Press, 1983), 134.

2. Ellwood, Robert S., *Alternative Altars: Unconventional and Eastern Spirituality in America*, Chicago: (University of Chicago Press, 1979), 1.

3. Niebuhr, H. Richard, *The Social Sources of Denominationalism*, New York: (Henry Holt and Co., 1929).

4. Quoted in Sidney E. Mead, *The Living Experiment: The Shaping of Christianity in America*, Boston: (Harper and Row, 1963), 63.

5. Bellah, Robert N., "Civil Religion in America," first published in 1967, is published with several other articles on the topic in Russell E. Richey and Donald G. Jones (eds.), *American Civil Religion*, New York: (Harper and Row, 1974).

6. Bellah, Robert N., *The Broken Covenant: American Civil Religion in Time of Trial*, New York: (Harper and Row, 1975).

7. Bellah, *Civil Religion*, op. cit., 34.

8. Handy, Robert T., *A Christian America: Protestant Hopes and Historical Realities*, 2nd ed., New York: (Oxford University Press, 1984).

9. Ibid., 182-183.

10. Quoted in Perry Miller, *Roger Williams: His Contributions to the American Tradition*, Cleveland: (Bobbs-Merrill, 1963), 136-137.

11. Ellwood, *Alternative Altars*, 3-4.

(*On The Way*, Vol. 3, No. 1, Summer 1985)

Lee Barrett

What Should We Make of Non-Christian Religions?

I don't remember much about high school physics. But I still remember my high school physics teacher. Through countless, tiny ways, he managed to evoke in me and other unlikely specimens a love of research for its own sake. His name was Ibrahim Ahmed. He was a Moslem. Being a devout Baptist at the time, my heart was sorely troubled about his prospects for eternal salvation. So I summoned up my courage and asked my rather daunting pastor about Mr. Ahmed's probable destiny. Without hesitation he referred to the Gospel of John, reminding me that no one comes to the Father except through the Son. Evidently Mr. Ahmed was in serious trouble. But in my heart of hearts I couldn't quite believe that the God revealed by Jesus Christ would consign such a fine human being to eternal oblivion, or perhaps to something even worse.

A few years later in college another teacher, this time a religious studies professor, had a rather different impact on my attitudes concerning members of other religions. He magisterially explained to us poor unsophisticated sophomores that all religions are different paths up the same mountain, all aiming at the same state of ultimate bliss. I wondered about his contention about the "same" state of ultimate bliss. I immediately thought of my roommate who was a Buddhist, not one of the trendy variety, but a serious practitioner of the Mahayana school. Living with him, I knew that he was certainly on some sort of path, a path to nirvana. Accordingly, he was aiming to divest himself of all cravings, all particular attachments, and even to transcend self-consciousness. I was on a path too, but it seemed different from his. In my own faltering, anemic way I was striving to grow in faith, hope, and love. I couldn't imagine that however indefinitely extended these two paths might be, that they would ever converge. From long nights of desultory adolescent conversations about the meaning of life, we both knew that our respective faiths made us different from one another. The message of Religion 201 could not be entirely right.

By age twenty I had encountered two different teachings about the members of other religions that were presented to me as a disjunction: either Mr. Ahmed is going to hell or Christianity is not distinctive. Neither proposition in this disjunction satisfied me. In retrospect I realize that I was being torn by variations on the alternative positions known as "exclusivism" and "pluralism." "Exclusivists" believe that Christianity alone leads to a truly valuable state of blessedness, and, in its extreme form, that all other religions lead to a netherworld of spiritual darkness. "Pluralists," on the other hand, maintain that other religious traditions are equally valid paths to the same religious goal. As long as these remain the only alternatives, Christian attitudes toward other religions will remain hopelessly confused. My very tentative counter-suggestion will probably not endear me to much of anybody. Many liberals will not like me because I cannot affirm that devout non-Christians are headed for Christian heaven; many conservatives will not like me because I cannot affirm that they are headed for hell.

The multifaceted controversy about Christianity's relation to other world religions actually revolves around at least four logically distinguishable contentions: that Christianity is unique among world religions, that Christianity is preferable to other religions, that Christianity alone leads to any sort of truly valuable religious state, and that failure to attain this Christian goal is to be spiritually miserable. One-dimensional pluralists typically deny all four propositions, while extreme exclusivists typically affirm all four. I will argue for splitting the difference, siding with the exclusivists on the first two claims, but with the pluralists on the second two. At first glance, it may seem strange to even question the first proposition, that Christianity is unique. After all, Christianity typically makes certain theological and even historical claims that most other religions do not make. However, pluralists do indeed contest this conclusion. While admitting that the differences in belief systems among the world religions are striking, they maintain that this apparent divergence is only a surface phenomenon. They are quick to point out that religion is not primarily a matter of the head. Pluralists conclude that beneath the level of espoused beliefs lies a more foundational core of religiosity in the heart, in the believer's immediate experience. At this fundamental experiential level, pluralists maintain, the differences among the world religions are negligible to non-existent. To the pluralists, all religions, or at least all the "great" world religions, are variations on the common essence of religion-in-itself. Apparent differences are due to the fact that different cultures provide different, historically conditioned lenses through which the experience of the ultimate is conceptualized and articulated.

But let us take a closer look at the claim that all religions are in some relevant sense the "same" or at least variations on the same theme. The pluralist position suffers from a strange irony; an irony that should raise suspicions. Those most insistent in arguing for pluralism end up denying the existence of any significant religious diversity in the human family. Pluralism does not seem to involve any real plurality. Adherence to a religion is nothing more than a brand preference due to consumer choice, the historical accident of birth, or nostalgia. Some people like Chevrolets and some people like Buicks, but underneath the hood lays the same General Motors engine. Similarly, some people like their spirituality in Buddhist wrapping, and others like it in a Christian package, but inside it is the same reality.

There is a minor problem with this scenario: the contention about the essential unity of all religions may well be conceptually meaningless. Let us reflect for a moment about what sort of considerations might lead a person to assert, "These religions are the same." We could certainly do this if we could somehow peek behind the experience, to see if the same reality is causing it. Perhaps if we peered behind the curtains of Christianity and Hinduism we would find the very same wizard operating the machinery. But, of course, there is no evident way this side of the *eschaton* to check to see if the reality behind the experience is indeed the same. Or we would know that two experiences of "ultimate reality" are the same if we could directly examine and compare them, perhaps by sticking electrodes into the brains of a Christian and a Buddhist and connecting them to a spirituality meter. But, alas, no such procedure for directly comparing experiences exists.

Therefore, the only criteria for supposing that religious phenomena are the "same" would be observable similarities in the way that people manifest them. My claim that the world religions (or at least most of them) are so different that they cannot meaningfully be construed as variations on the same experiential theme can only be established through a comparison of the fundamental attitudes, emotions, passions (or *apathos*), valuations, and behavioral tendencies that they exhibit. A newer generation of philosophers of religion, having gotten their cues from philosophers like Ludwig Wittgenstein and anthropologists like Clifford Geertz, advocate taking a close look at what the practitioners of a religion actually do. (1) In order to understand a religious phenomena, including claims about its source or goal, we must engage in a "thick description" of the lives of the faithful. For example, to know what "grace" means in Christianity, one must know that the concept functions in the context of profound discontent with a person's own moral failings, and know that gratitude about being accepted in spite of these failings is the appropriate expression of trust in it. Anyone hoping to understand a religion must look carefully at how the practitioners of a religion express their basic hopes and fears, how their yearnings are enacted in their lives, and what behaviors they typically engage in. If the emotions, behaviors, and valuations associated with two concepts are different, then the concepts are different. If Buddhists do not exhibit the same behaviors, emotions, attitudes, and valuations when they talk about "enlightenment" that Christians do when they speak of "grace," then "enlightenment" and "grace" are not different names for the same thing. On a larger scale, the world religions are complex networks of recommended courses of inward and outward action, patterns of valuation, and desired emotional states. They are different if the courses of action, valuation, and emotions belonging to the patterns of life are different.

The "closer look" recommended by philosophers and anthropologists reveals that these patterns of life among the world religions are indeed exceedingly dissimilar. Christians, Moslems, Hindus and Buddhists actually say very different things about their most basic struggles, aspirations and fears. They follow different devotional and moral practices which inculcate different values and foster different sorts of emotion.

As a case study, let us consider Christianity and Buddhism. Most forms of Buddhism teach that one must follow the Eightfold Path in order to attain nirvana. Most forms of Christianity insist that one must grow in faith, hope and love in order to attain salvation. Are the pursuit of nirvana and the desire for Christian salvation different expressions of the same religious yearning? Consider that the First Noble Truth of Buddhism is that suffering is intrinsic to existence. Buddhism's Second Noble Truth is that suffering is due to the ego's attachment to anticipated goods. To eliminate attachments is to attain nirvana. In Theravada Buddhism the appreciation of one's own impermanence (*anatta*), the recognition that one's alleged "self" exists for no longer than a moment, is encouraged in order to eliminate concern for the individual's future satisfactions. This longing for liberation from attachments even leads Theravada Buddhists to regard the ethical life as merely provisional, for nirvana is beyond distinctions of good or evil.

But whereas Buddhists long to escape from attachments, most forms of Christianity embrace them, including the joys and sorrows that are their concomitants. For example, adherents of the Reformed tradition advocate glorifying God by accepting the blessings of this life with joy and gratitude. Christians typically celebrate the wisdom, power, and goodness of God manifested in the created order. Even George Fox, the abstemious Quaker, once smoked tobacco just in order to prove that he did not disparage the gifts of the Creator. Far from spurning all attachments, Jonathan Edwards, the champion of "disinterested benevolence," encouraged his flock to revel in Christ's beauty displayed throughout the natural world. This is a far cry from nirvana. While Buddhists cultivate the recognition of cosmic impermanence, Christians delight in God's permanence. While Christians pray for the final harmonization of all embodied beings, of Palestinians and Israelis and lions and lambs, all sharing the land flowing with milk and honey, Buddhists strive for release from embodied existence, including all land, milk, honey, lambs, and lions. The emotions, yearnings, behaviors, passions, and attitudes of Christianity and Buddhism simply do not match.

These considerations suggest that it is not meaningful to claim that a generic, raw "religious experience" underlies all these spiritualities. To say that the experience of justification is the "same" as the experience of absolute nothingness requires such colossal abstraction in order to remove all the disturbing differences that nothing is left of the original concepts. Asserting this would be like proposing that down deep affection for a golden retriever and anxiety about heights are the "same." It is not in the least bit clear what the word "same" might possibly mean in this context. One perceptive student once quipped that, if you subtract all the particularities from the various religions' descriptions of blessedness in order to arrive at some lowest common-denominator religious experience, the resulting description does not sound much different from falling asleep.

These considerations suggest, further, that the effort to homogenize all religions, rather then being a charitable extension of respect to other faiths, may actually be an act of ideological imperialism. The pluralist project attempts to twist and stretch other religions on the procrustean bed of our own convictions so that other people end up looking just like us. The Indian theologian M. M. Thomas has suggested that when pluralists intone that "we" humans religiously encounter ultimate reality in such-and-such a way, the "we" usually means the parochial "we" of western liberal academics. (2) In a way, the pluralist program is an offspring of the arrogance of the Enlightenment. Its meta-theory of the essence of religion is usually a not-so-very covert universalization of culturally specific values. The whole endeavor rests on the assumption that true mutuality and appreciation can only be founded on an underlying commonality. Pluralists implicitly assume that "I can accept you and deal with you because down deep you are really just like me." In spite of its noble intentions, this attitude actually makes encounters with true religious otherness impossible by dismissing that otherness as only superficial. All religions are regarded as antiquated in so far as they ascribe crucial importance to their particularity and take their distinguishing characteristics with utmost seriousness. The poor benighted devotees of traditional faiths are patted on the head and informed that they really do not understand the nature of their own convictions. This habit certainly does not make for a very interesting cross-religious conversation. Most frequently it eventuates in Christian religious liberals getting together with Islamic religious liberals and Hindu religious liberals, talking about liberalism, and calling it dialogue.

All these considerations add up to a cumulative case that if the world religions do look different, smell different, and taste different, they just might really be different. There is no reason to believe that they converge at the top, and very good reason to suspect that the claim that they do is unintelligible.

Several nagging questions still remain, including the second controversial proposition, the claim that Christianity is preferable to other religions. Many pluralists have concluded that the goals of the various religions are different but complementary. Perhaps Christian salvation and nirvana could both be pursued and somehow added together to augment the multidimensional richness of religious experience. Maybe even multiple religious goals could be actualizable by the same individuals, giving them well-rounded spiritual lives.

However, one feature of most world religions militates against this theory of complementarity. Even though the goals of the world religions are very, very different, most religions do share two things in common: the claim to be total orientations to life and to be so important that all other interests and pursuits should be subordinated to their goals. Most world religions make unconditional claims to provide the center around which all of life should be organized. For example, Theravada Buddhism is clear that the attainment of nirvana is to be ranked above all other goods. Similarly, in Reformed Christianity glorifying God is given priority over all other goals. Because these religions propose different conceptions of the highest good, their divergent visions cannot be simultaneously used to direct a person's life as a whole. So even if the goals of other religions per se do not contradict the goals of Christianity, and might be quite admirable in themselves, they do conflict in so far as they claim to be so important that they provide the orienting point for all of life. The ultimate goals of the world religions are not amenable to joint realization in a single life span. One must choose from among their rival claims to be of preeminent worth.

It is logically possible that the goal of one of these religions truly is so preeminently valuable that any other claim to be the basic, orienting goal of human life would have to be regarded as seriously misleading. Accordingly,

Christians have confessed that they cannot imagine Christian faith, hope, and love as anything other than the highest possible *telos* of human existence. Christianity, like most other world religions, does claim that the goals of other religions are only of subordinate worth. In the same way, if someone claimed that all of life should be structured around the game of golf, Christians would be obliged to respond, "Well, no, golf is fine in and of itself, and Christians can rejoice that there are golfers in the world, but it is not golf that should be the be-all and end-all of a human life."

Let us turn to the third claim that Christianity alone leads to any sort of truly valuable religious state. Many exclusivists contend that the religious alternatives to Christianity, far from being paths to lesser but still valuable goods, are devoid of even penultimate worth. This proposal warrants careful scrutiny. It is true that Christians would be obligated to critique any religion that promoted values, attitudes, or behaviors inimical to their vision of the goal of human life. The ancient Norse practice of cultivating hatred of enemies to the point of berserk rage probably does not mesh well with the exhortation to turn the other cheek. Such incompatibilities could only be discovered through a very careful empirical investigation.

However, this does not require Christianity to condemn other religions *in toto*, but only to critique those aspects that militate against the flourishing of the unique features of the gospel. Christians could still celebrate the assets of any religion that might actually contribute to the fostering of Christian virtues. Christians could even learn from them, being sensitized by them to discern novel dimensions in Christianity itself and inspired to elaborate motifs that had been latent or recessive. (3) For example, the Buddhist analysis of desire as compulsive clinging might help us to understand more deeply certain aspects of Augustine's critique of the sinful self as being *"curvatus in se."* We might even be able to view some of the other religions as containing preliminary values that could predispose their members to develop Christian virtues. Aspects of some world religions could be valued as preparations for Christianity, *"preparatio evangelica,"* in the way that Justin Martyr regarded Greco-Roman culture as serving a function similar to that of ancient Israel. In fact, in the Reformed tradition it is to be expected that other religions would possess some characteristics that could contribute to the Christian life. That hope is enshrined in the Reformed doctrine of "common grace."

With appropriate fear and trembling, let us turn to the fourth issue, the claim common among exclusivists that non-Christian traditions lead to spiritual misery. However, the themes of the uniqueness and preferability of Christianity do not necessarily entail this conclusion. It does not logically follow that, by failing to aim at the highest good, other religions fail to attain any good at all and are therefore highways to perdition. That conclusion would only be true if the absence of Christian satisfaction can lead to no other consequence than utter misery. If such an either/or of Christian blessedness or utter misery does obtain, it would have to be demonstrated on grounds other than the affirmation of Christianity's uniqueness and preferability.

Many Christians have felt the sweeping exclusion of all adherents of other religions from any form of religious satisfaction to be incompatible with the universal salvific will of God revealed in Jesus Christ. Exactly how the ultimate destinies of members of other religions should be envisioned varies among them. Throughout the centuries some "inclusivists," including Clement of Alexandria, John Wesley, and Karl Rahner, have maintained that many non-Christians have been "saved" by an inchoate trust in God or a diffuse compassion without explicitly confessing faith in Jesus Christ. Even Ulrich Zwingli suspected that some of the elect were to be found among the virtuous pagans. Pope Pious IX proposed that members of other religions might be saved through the cultivation of the best features of their own traditions. Other Christians, including George Lindbeck, have speculated about a kind of "moment of death" or post-mortem opportunity for non-Christians to respond to the gospel. Yet others, elaborating some hints from Karl Barth concerning God's sovereign will to redeem humanity, have articulated a hope that the reconciling work of Christ is not only offered to all people, but will eschatologically become efficacious for all people. (4) More recently Mark Heim has sketched a theory of plural salvations. Perhaps the devout practitioners of other spiritualities will attain the goal that they pursue. All these views share the hope that participation in a non-Christian religion is not ipso facto a one-way ticket to Inferno City. Which view is most adequate? Criteria for evaluating the validity of these various hunches are not readily available. Perhaps here we would do well to confess, with appropriate humility, that now we only see through a glass darkly.

So, a Christian can both hope for a blessed state for pious non-Christians and also affirm the irreducible particularity and preferability of Christianity. The acknowledgment of Christian distinctiveness need not be alarming news for people of good will who hope to avoid another round of religious wars. The differences among the world religions and their respective claims of preferability need not lead to mutual condemnation or hostility. After appreciating the distinctiveness of Christianity, we need not assume that the religious goals of Buddhists and Hindus are utterly worthless or that all non-Christians are doomed to hell. Therefore, when we come to the table with

Moslems, Hindus, Jews, and Buddhists, we can without hypocrisy look for aspects of the other religions that can be affirmed. Christians can do this without surrendering their own distinctive beliefs or expecting the other religions to surrender theirs in order to talk. Christians can admit in public that they do actually believe that a life of faith, hope, and love is preferable to other religious goals while at the same time they exhibit appreciation for the genuine virtues and admirable lives found in the other traditions. This is a logical possibility. May God grant us the grace to make it actual.

Notes

1. See S. Mark Heim, *Salvations: Truth and Difference in Religion*, New York: (Orbis Books, 1997), and Joseph DiNoia, *The Diversity of Religions: A Christian Perspective*, Washington, D.C. : Catholic University of America Press, 1992).
2. See M. M. Thomas, "A Christ-Centered Humanist Approach to Other Religions in the Indian Pluralistic Context," in *Christian Uniqueness Reconsidered*, ed. Gavin D'Costa, New York: (Orbis Press, 1990).
3. For an example of this, see Gerald McDermott, *Can Evangelicals Learn from World Religions?*, Downers Grove: (Intervarsity Press, 2000).
4. See Karl Barth, *Church Dogmatics*, Vol. 4/3/1, G. W. Bromiley, trans., Edinburgh: (T. & T. Clark, 1961), 477-478.

(An abridged manuscript of an address by Dr. Barrett given in 2003 at a theological colloquy held at the Mission House Center of Lakeland College with pastors and laity from the Evangelical Church of Westphalia and the Wisconsin Conference, UCC, as an expression of "Full Communion" ["*Kirchengemeinschaft*"] between the United Church of Christ and the Evangelical Church of the Union in Germany).

Richard L. Christensen

The Community That Glorifies God: John Calvin's Critique of Society

In this essay I would like to examine Calvin's theological understanding of human society, the Church's obligation toward the secular state, his critique of the relationships between people in society, and the ways he and his followers sought some sense of justice in society, particularly in economic matters.

In a nutshell, Calvin understood human society in this way: humanity's fall into sin has broken the original tie of love and equality among human beings, but in Christ God has begun the restoration of right relationships. And since the Church is the visible society of those united to one another in Christ, the Church must see to it that its own life demonstrates wholeness, justice and love. This is what lies behind Calvin's insistence on discipline in the Church: i.e., the Church's members must be held to a moral and spiritual discipline so that the Church could show the way to a society that conforms to God's will.

Now, what is the problem with human society? The trouble is that human beings spoil God's blessings that have been given to them. The result is that they take God's bounty, grab it for themselves, hoarding, monopolizing, speculating, so that the original order of nature is perverted. "Our Lord is mocked by those who want to have much profit," Calvin preached. "These people entomb the grace of God, as if they warred against his bounty and against the paternal love which he displays toward everyone."

The basic solidarity of humanity cannot be broken. But human greed goes a long way toward obscuring God's order. Along with its own internal discipline, the Church, in order to do its proper job in the civil order, has four tasks *vis-a-vis* the government:

1) The Church must pray for the political authorities, even though they will fall short of God's purposes in the exercise of their duties. Back in the 1980's, an American once visited a church in the German Democratic Republic (East Germany) to worship one Sunday. Surprised to hear the pastor pray for the mayor and the police chief (both

of whom were communists), the visitor inquired about it after the service. The pastor explained, "We pray for the them because Jesus has taught us to pray for our enemies. Besides, when I pray for the mayor, it reminds him that he's not God."

2) The Church must encourage the state to defend the poor and weak against the rich and powerful. Commenting on Psalm 82:3, Calvin wrote: "a just and well-regulated government will be distinguished for maintaining the rights of the poor and the afflicted." The preaching of the gospel is linked with the demand for social justice. For Calvin, it was the treatment of the weak in society that really determined the value of a political regime. "Those who are exposed an easy prey to the cruelty and wrongs of the rich have no less need of the assistance and protection of magistrates than the sick have of the need of the physician."

3) The Church must ensure its own status by calling on the political authorities for help in promoting true religion and even enforcing church discipline. The contemporary version of this might be to say that the Church should seek to maintain the principle of freedom of religion for everyone in the community.

4) The Church must warn the authorities when they are at fault. The ministers have the duty of speaking out sharply against all injustice, all neglect of duty, and all ungodliness in high places.

Now let's look at Calvin's thinking in regard to the matter of poverty and wealth. Like Christian thinkers of most eras, Calvin thought that material blessing was due to the bounty of God. But unlike some modern Christians, he never saw poverty and misfortune as evidence of God's disfavor of the afflicted person, nor did he regard prosperity as a sign of God's blessing for personal merit, nor as evidence of one's salvation. In fact, Calvin was much closer to Jesus' teaching about the impossibility of the rich getting into heaven than he was to any equation of prosperity with goodness. Listen to what he says:

It is an error which is by far too common among men, to look upon those who are oppressed with afflictions as condemned and reprobate... Most men, making judgments upon the favor of God from an uncertain and transitory state of prosperity, applaud the rich, and those upon whom, as they say, fortune smiles; so, on the other hand, they insult contemptuously the wretched and miserable, and foolishly imagine that God hates them... The error of which I speak... is one which has prevailed in all ages of the world (John Calvin, *Commentary on Genesis*, 1:28).

He also wrote once that prosperity is more of a danger than adversity, because those with possessions are likely to be proud and think themselves above others. Poverty is, in fact, the opportunity for people to do good to one another:

> God has joined and knitted us together that we might have a community... No one can say 'I will live for myself alone.' That would be to live worse than a beast. We should know that God has obligated us to one another to help each other... we should at least treat one another humanly. It is too great a cruelty on our part if we see a poor and afflicted man and turn away from him. All the blessings we have are entrusted to us by the Lord on this condition, that they should be dispensed for the good of our neighbors.

This is true gratitude, according to Calvin: not sitting back, enjoying what you have, and being grateful, but using what you have for the neighbor's good. Max Weber observed that Calvinists tended to find evidence of God's election in personal prosperity. Many Calvinists did that - but not Calvin. The great majority of the rich, Calvin said, refuse Christ and idolize their possessions:

> They entertain a firm and deep-seated conviction that the rich are happy, and that there is nothing better than to increase their wealth by every possible method, and to brood jealously over whatever they have acquired, rejecting as foolish paradoxes all the sayings of Christ which have a contrary tendency.

He spoke in a sermon of people who "are not content to have three times what they need," and he charged that such people delight in seeing the poor go hungry. Calvin had a concern that God's gifts not be misused. It was inexcusable in his eyes for some to have plenty and others to be in need. This was not a legalism, telling people they had to give a certain specified amount; it was simply that love for brothers and sisters in the community needed to be acted out. "No act of kindness, except when joined with compassion, is pleasing to God." You can give to others grudgingly and out of a sense of obligation, but that's not real charity for Calvin. So the organization of the diaconate was of prime importance for Calvin. The deacons were to handle money, to organize and supervise the hospital, and to aid the poor of the city. Ministers were to make quarterly visits to the hospital to see that the people there were given proper attention. The work of the deacons was funded in part by the allocation of money from the fines that people paid for breaking the laws of the city. Money from fines was divided so that one-third of the receipts went to the poor and another third to the deacons to help maintain the hospital.

None of this sharing on the part of the rich is based on or contingent upon the good will or gratitude of the poor. The poor are not immune from sin and self - centeredness, after all. "Although the poor acquit themselves badly of their duty," he preached, "and though having been helped they do not bless us, yet despite that we ought not to cease doing what God commands us." For a number of years, my parents in Baltimore, Maryland, have gone every Wednesday night to help cook and serve dinner for two hundred homeless people. One of the other women who had been helping said to my mother one evening, "I'm getting kind of tired of coming here every week. These people are not very grateful." To which my mother replied, "Well, go home then. These people are hungry whether you're tired or not." Work for others is not done in order to obtain thanks, but because people need it.

Calvin insisted that God's design provides for an equitable distribution of goods among human beings. He preached to the citizens and refugees in Geneva, saying,

> We must recognize that God has wanted to make us like members of a body. When we regard each other in this way, each will then conclude: 'I see my neighbor who has need of me and if I were in such extremity, I would wish to be helped; I must therefore do just that.' In short, this communication of which St. Paul speaks here is the fraternal affection which proceeds from the regard that we have when God has joined us together and united us in one body, because he wants each to employ himself for his neighbors, so that no one is addicted to his own person, but that we serve all in common. (see 1 Timothy 6:17—19)

Human solidarity is such that anything that contributes to the impoverishment of part of society is, in fact, evil. He accused some wheat dealers of gouging the public by letting people go hungry and refusing to sell wheat until the price went up considerably. In one sermon, he called such wheat-hoarders "murderers, savage beasts, biting and eating up the poor, sucking up their blood."

Understand, Calvin is a reformer, not a revolutionary, because he has a horror of social turmoil. He rejected the idea of finding theological support for open rebellion, convinced that persuasion of the magistrates by preaching and teaching was the way to bring change. He lashes out, though, at people who pay inadequate wages, or those who withhold wages from their workers, saying that such people "think that the rest of humanity exist only for their benefit." He also said, "We ought to notice that the cries of the poor come to the ears of God, so we may know that the wrong done to them shall not be unpunished." He supported the concept of private property and opposed the radical Anabaptists' emphasis on holding all things in common as in Acts.

But private property is meant to be used for the common good. Modern rugged individualists get no comfort at all from Calvin's harsh treatment of the greed of the wealthy, his belief that wealth is almost always built on the blood of the poor, and the economic regulation we see Calvin approving of in the marketplace of Geneva. What distinguishes Calvin's economic thought from the medieval theologians and from Luther is that he approved of commerce. For him, it was the natural way for people to commune with each other. He saw the exchange of goods as necessary for the spread of God's bounty throughout society. Both in Calvin's day and in ours, there has been a common attitude that commerce and business is grubby and sordid. Most medieval theologians reluctantly agreed that merchants were necessary to society, but they could not bring themselves to think of merchants as engaged in anything but a vile and disreputable business.

Luther had a great dislike for commerce, as over against agriculture. He wrote that "it would be much more pleasing to God if we increased agriculture and diminished commerce, and that they do much better who, according to the Scriptures, till the soil and seek their living from it." Sounds like Thomas Jefferson, or Emerson, or Thoreau!

For Calvin the real world was to be taken seriously, and for him the real world involved shoemakers, printers, and clockmakers, and cloth merchants, as well as farmers, scholars, and clergy. Calvin affirms the world and wants to deal with it. It's not that Calvin sees great altruism in commerce. Where Luther views with alarm the evidences of evil in the commerce he sees, Calvin assumes that all human enterprise is tainted with self-interest and evil - a safe assumption - and he sets about to make the gospel relevant to the city of commerce in which he lived and worked. True religion, for Calvin, not only visits the sick and takes care of widows and orphans, but it also tries to see the relevance of the gospel in the rest of the world that is. Calvin was more serious about this than the others of his day. Once he proposed a law to the Geneva city council requiring railings on second-story balconies. There had been several cases of small children being hurt by falling from such heights. Calvin's view was that all of life is under God's care, and the community ought to demonstrate that.

Work, for Calvin, was one of the good gifts of God, and one should make a choice of vocation on the basis of whether or not it serves the common good. That's the main criterion. Not to work meant to refuse to listen to God's word. This was not only true of those who were simply parasites on society - they put beggars to work in Geneva - but also true of those who holed up in monasteries and refused to live except on public charity. Calvin railed against those who go into monasteries, as into "pigsties well-garnished," where they "fatten themselves at the expense of others without working." Some monastics of his era spent up to eight hours a day in choir chanting the Psalms, but Calvin believed that it was far better to praise God by working for the common good.

Even more biting than his satire of the monks was his anger at those who prevented others from working. If one were to harvest another person's field, he wrote, everyone would say that's just robbery. But it is much worse "to deprive a poor man of the work of his hands." People should not be deprived of the opportunity to work. So when the city of Geneva was swollen to approximately twice its former size by the influx of refugees, the city provided public work for those in need. Often they put people like this to work on construction of the ramparts of the city. In the spring of 1554, about four hundred refugee families came at once, and they were put to work digging ditches, being paid by the work, not by the day. That way they could work as much or as little as they wanted each day, and they would still be paid a certain amount when they finished the task. When the means to pursue one's livelihood is taken away, then the individual and the common welfare suffer. Everything connected to labor must be an instrument of the common good and not an instrument of oppression. This means that human work must be conducted under proper conditions. Anything that makes work oppressive should be condemned. God wants human labor to be such that the worker can render thanks to God in the midst of his or her service. And the laborer should be paid a fair wage. Those who defraud the poor unmercifully will in the end find mercy denied to them. Calvin thunders against the employers in his congregation in a sermon, saying:

> When the poor whom you have employed at work, and who put their work, their sweat and their blood for you, have not been paid as is right, when you do not give them comfort and support; if they demand vengeance from God against you; who will be your lawyer, or your advocate, so that you will be able to escape? (on Deuteronomy 22: 1-4)

But Calvin is evenhanded; he recognizes that self - interest will lead employers and laborers to try to take advantage of one another. So in order to guarantee some sense of justice about wages and working conditions, he thought that legal contracts ought to be agreed to in advance, and that would help to prevent some inequalities and injustices.

Calvin's aim in all this was to have a society that was conformed to the will of God, one where people took their responsibilities seriously and where people were treated fairly. It was a purpose grounded in the conviction that all of life is under the sovereignty of God, that nothing is outside of it. In Geneva's social and economic policies, we see the impact of a monumental attempt to understand and apply the Word of God to human activity. The result, Calvin believed, would be a community that glorifies God by the way it lives.

(Monograph prepared for an issue of *On The Way* in the late 1990s. The issue was among several that were projected, but did not appear.)

Richard Stuckey Williams

Christian Worship and Witness in Our Times

In his book, "Cadences of Home: Preaching among Exiles," Walter Brueggemann offers us this arresting phrase: "...the church in the West must recover its baptismal nerve." (1)   Brueggemann advocates this need in the context of Douglas John Hall's proposal that the North American church must first disengage from the current culture in order to reengage with a fresh voice. (2) My view is that this pattern of disengagement and reengagement needs to take place simultaneously, not in any kind of chronological sequence. Further, I am convinced that in the context of our times God is calling us to undergo a reengagement that centers on the full recovery of trinitarian faith and that faith's creation of a "public" that is counter-cultural and supportive of consequential witness on behalf of ecelesial persons in community, whose hopes rest in the assurance of the coming of the Kingdom of God through the mediatorship of God's Son, Jesus Christ. In response to an essay I had written entitled "Kairos and September 11," John Burgess, Associate Professor of Theology at Pittsburgh Theological Seminary, wrote: "The church must indeed become a different kind of public that resists the current hegemony of the West, and... that can happen only as we recover a full trinitarian faith. (3)

Now, those of us in the North American "mainline" churches are immediately in rough territory. For most of us have grown up in a fairly "accommodationist" kind of church. Truth claims about the Trinity have not been high on our theological agenda. Baptism is often perfunctory and even corrupted by its familial social dimensions. And now the "graying" of "mainline" churches makes us anxious about the Church's future and thus open to a whole menu of techniques that can "bring people in," especially young people. Faithful pastors and lay-people are (if they are honest and perceptive) squeezed between discerning God's call to a deeper encounter with holiness and truth and a keenly felt need to "connect" with where people are culturally, using those idioms of music and production that "turn them on."

The way to proceed in faithfulness to God is no doubt to follow the pattern Douglas John Hall suggests of "disengagement-reengagement." The "disengagement" needs to center on the recovery of the full Trinitarian faith in worship and praxis. This can only take place in its proper fullness when there is a sense of the radical dimensions to the crisis facing both Church and culture in these beginning years of the twenty-first century. We are, indeed, in a post-modern age. And the whole Enlightenment project is being called into question. It is showing signs of near-fatal instability. In a curious way, "9/11" for the West heightened the realization of how frail is our Enlightenment underpinning while also lifting up the reality that a residual sense of community is achingly waiting to be energized. Horrible as was the event of "9/11" it is nonetheless true that even though the attackers zeroed in on the targets that constituted two of the deepest sources of meaning for the West, its consumerist-financial hegenomy and its military might, we in the West, and especially in the United States, were amazed at the strong evidences of community that appeared in the aftermath of the pulverization of the temples to our demi-gods. The "New York Times" collection of anecdotal biographies of the World Trade Center and the airplane disaster casualties introduced many of us to the flesh and gut realities of a multitudinous variety of mostly young persons, seeking in a potpouri of ways to bankroll aspirations for families and pleasures.

Even more touching is the material found in the first of the series, "American Ground: Unbuilding the World Trade Center," by William Langewiesche in the July-August 2002 *Atlantic Monthly*. Langewiesche's research discovered a unique kind of community among the workers at ground zero. In the face of unspeakable death and destruction those who worked there somehow were being fed food for the soul. It was amazing to see 250 pound construction "bosses" mingling with powerful business executives and renowned engineers all sitting on kindergarten chairs in the corner room of P. S. 29, the shelves of which were stacked with toys and Dr. Seuss books. This was the "inner sanctum" of the recovery effort. People there were not pulling rank on each other in regard to how they were dressed or any clues as to preferential status. There was no e-mail, none of the access to the technology of communication and information-gathering that are the marks of the "dot com" culture, only persons interacting according to their true value; if more information was needed one got up and walked down the street to the pile. Somehow that is almost a parable for the Church in our time—an inner sanctum (or "interior-holy") in which all are related one to another by the sacrament of lives offered up and all dedicated to going out into the world to clean up, to restore, to make possible new wholeness. The fact that the "inner-sanctum" is a kindergarten room is all the more on the mark—for surely only as we become as little children can we enter the Kingdom of Heaven.

But the nascent move toward community is only part of the post- "9/11" picture, for the political leadership in the West (and most of the people) seemingly embrace "the war on terrorism." It would be foolhardy not to admit that dimensions of the response to "9/11" and to the current challenge by Islamic fundamentalism must be of a military nature. But along with the direct challenge of the "9/11" attack we have all been aghast at the collapse of major corporations, the scandals involving the auditing profession, and the easy resort by governmental forces to the restriction of civil liberties. If the capitalist-consumerist-military show is the only real basis for meaning, we are again faced with that painful disease of late modernity- the disease of nihilism or nothingness. This specter of nihilism is what faced Karl Barth at the time of the Barmen Declaration in the Germany of the 1930's; the same specter faces us all in the West today—which means, in many ways, the situation for the entire globe. Our economic and political present is rooted in the Enlightenment projects of John Locke and Adam Smith. And our churches are still informed in regard to ethos and practice by the super-individualism and subjectivism wherein truth-claims have been abandoned in order to have a message thought to be understandable by faith's "cultured despisers."

In today's context, God's call to the Church is clear: to disengage from the surrounding culture and then to be open to a re-formation in the power of the Spirit to be the "public" which knows its very being as created, sustained, and sent on mission by our Trinitarian God.

The creation of such a Trinity-based "public" is surely the work of the Holy Spirit, calling forth faithfulness in worship and discipleship from the members of Christ's body. At the same time we, those summoned to be faithful, need to apply all the gifts of understanding, perception, and judgment that can be marshaled in order to enable this time of disengagement and recovery to answer the call to be Christ for our world in the twenty-first century. Two moves appear to be necessary: a move on the part of the faithful from being the people who shop, to being the people who live by a beatific vision; and a move from being a people depending on a thin culture for sustenance, to being a people depending on a thick culture...

First, what do I mean by the move from being the people who shop to being the people who live by a beatific vision? Stanley Hauerwas is quoted in a piece by Patrick O'Neill in the June 21, 2002 issue of the *National Catholic Reporter* as follows:

On September 11, (2001) Americans were confronted by people ready to die as an expression of their profound moral commitments... Their willingness to die stands in stark contrast to a politics that asks of its members in response to September 11 to shop 'American.' Christians simply lack the disciplines necessary to discover how being Christian might make them different... (4)

The term "beatific vision" is a term John Milbank uses in his work in the movement now labeled "Radical Orthodoxy." Milbank, (formerly at Cambridge but now at the University of Virginia), along with Catherine Pickstock and Graham Ward, is part of a movement in theology by that name. The focus of the movement, as I read it, is on a recovery of the insights and world-view of the triad: Augustine, Anselm, Aquinas - in which truth claims of an almost neo-Platonic nature are proclaimed in opposition to the nominalism deriving from Duns Scotus and coming down through Descartes and Kant. This "orthodoxy" is seen as the answer to the nihilism inherent in modernity and culminating in the despair of post-modernity. Understandably, the movement has been the target of considerable criticism, as, for example, in the book, *Radical Orthodoxy? A Catholic Enquiry*, edited by Laurence Paul Hemming. (5)

Some of the criticism is brutal. (However, it was John Milbank himself who, in an e-mail, directed me to this volume so that I might read his piece: "The Programme of Radical Orthodoxy.") One obvious and major criticism is that this movement comes under the heading: "nostalgia," which charge elicits strong counter-testimony from the "Big Three." On the other hand Methodist theologian, Stephen Long, in his work, *Divine Economy: Theology and the Market Place*, (6) while working from a confessed Radical Orthodox base, lines out Milbank's espousal of "socialism by grace." The whole ethic has a strongly aesthetic base. Long's chapter 14 is entitled: "The Beauty of Theology: Uniting the True and the Good, and Subordinating the Useful." Long points out that Urs von Balthaser reverses the order of Kant's critiques by "beginning with beauty, proceeding to the good, and ending with the true." (7) Such a radical move into a new and revivified orthodoxy makes possible the reception of the gift of the community in which truth dwells in humanity and energizes that work (*leiturgia*) which is co-creative with the work of God. As Jesuit theologian James Hanvey so concisely puts it:

In the case of Trinitarian orthodoxy, not only was a radically new conceptuality for speaking and thinking about God fashioned, but a new way of understanding humanity and the created order was forged. Theology knows that it can never be just talk about God, but must always be 'human talk' about God. This means that it must always be engaged upon the work of interpreting the human sphere in order that in and through that sphere it can speak rationally and truthfully of God... Theology is an always new event of speech, that must test its own truth by constantly offering to humanity an understanding of what it is to be human, an understanding that is more coherent and generative than anything humanity can devise for itself. (8)

Let us now look at the second move: the move from being a people depending on a thin culture for meaning and sustenance to a being a people depending on a thick culture. In his magisterial *Theology of the Old Testament*, Walter Brueggemann, in the chapter entitled "Mediating the Presence of Yahweh," has this to say in a sub-section headed: "Yahweh Generated in Communal Practice":

It is (Gary) Anderson's argument, informed by Clifford Geertz's notion of "thick description" and George Lindbeck's proposal for theological authority as "cultural-linguistic," that religious ideas are embedded in religious experience and practice, and that religious reality is constituted and generated by actual, sustained, concrete, communal practice. (9)

Brueggemann then announces that in succeeding chapters he will review the five prominent mediations in the Old Testament - Torah, kingship, prophecy, cult, and wisdom.

For a religious organization (or any group) to be blessed with a thick culture requires a rich and continuous amalgam of practices which form and support the community and its members. It is precisely at this point that, so far as churches in the North American Reformed tradition are concerned, "the rubber hits the road." For most of current worship and attendant church practices give evidence of a remarkably thin culture. What is the nature of this thinness? How can it be overcome? These are questions that are central to the "disengagement-reengagement" task facing the Church today.

To my mind the thinness is largely rooted in the collapse of the Biblical Theology movement and the demise of faithful, skillful, and biblically-centered preaching; conjoined with this are the realities of increasing biblical illiteracy, and the youth culture which finds meaning in the mall and in visceral music and attendant images. One obvious approach to bridging the gap between the traditional nature of the Church's proclamation and the cultural location of its younger prospects is to adopt the idioms of that culture. So one of the best exemplars of this may well be the "Willow Creek" church. Thomas

Long, in his "Beyond the Worship Wars" (10) suggests that the current options are the "Willow Creek" model and the "Hippolytus" model. Main-line churches have a way of looking covetously at the successes of churches such as Willow Creek. But at the heart of Willow Creek is ultimately a kind of "revivalism" decked out in suburban-niche clothing. When main-line churches try to imitate Willow Creek, the "practices" are lacking in the integrity that comes from rootage in a well-comprehended and articulated faith. There is a dissonance between the contemporary practices and a tradition still strongly present even if more in memory than in current reality.

On the other hand the Hippolytus model, so characteristic of the liturgical renewal proponents, has the burden of appearing "catholic" and "high-church," communicating a certain fustiness and excessive interiority as to the living out of the faith. But at least symbols and actions of ancient origin along with contemporary impact are strongly present in this option. The whole person is swept up in the embrace of baptism, of Eucharist, of being on life-support from the body of Christ. To be sure there are pitfalls in this Hippolytus path. The practices can become mechanisms of salvation; pious exercises devoid of prophetic power and criticism. The Reformation needs to continue to live! But there is an identifiable community that partakes of a thick culture for which the community members tender deep affection. (In the midst of all the troubles besetting American Roman Catholicism right now—the so-called "pedophile scandal"—one cannot but be impressed by the warmth of affection the laity have for the faith and life of the Church.)

As I have noted, "disengagement" and "reengagement" take place simultaneously. The recently retired Roman Catholic Archbishop of Milwaukee, Rembert Weakland, when asked by a non-Roman Catholic how to discover what it means to be a Roman Catholic responded: "Go faithfully to mass at the parish church and each week serve in the church-sponsored shelter for the homeless." The Craigville Colloquy in 2002 (an annual event on Cape Cod that has gathered pastors and laity each summer since 1984 for theological dialogue) surely had the topic stated correctly: "Worship and Witness in Our Times." Still, the "witness" in our times needs to be much more radical than what some of us knew as "the social gospel," or even more radical than in the hey-day of the Civil Rights Movement. For the "Enlightenment era" is in a Humpty-Dumpty mode, and only a radical orthodoxy can begin to provide the transformative work to establish meaning in the midst of nothingness; to affirm justice and generosity in the midst of rank injustice and avarice.

What is needed are communities of the faithful for which God's Word is central in the practices of preaching, Eucharist, baptism, and discipleship.

But such communities only become real as they find themselves graced with courage and love to speak to and embrace those being battered by the "ground zero" question-marks of our current suspension between the death of the modern and the coming of a new era, the outlines of which can now only be dimly perceived. At heart in such communities is mystery; the mystery of the active, involved, totally-giving trinitarian God, forming that "public" which challenges to its very depths the hegemony of a society that has nowhere to turn but to the worship of the golden calf of its own making.

Back in the 1930's the North American novelist, Edna Ferber, wrote a book about what it was like to grow up Jewish in the "Paper Valley" area of Wisconsin (roughly that area from Oshkosh north through Green Bay) Ms. Ferber titled her book, *A Peculiar People*. The sense of being "a peculiar people" surely must be part of what is involved in being a community of those faithful to Jesus Christ, especially at this hinge time of human history. An indispensable ingredient of the formation of the sense of being "a peculiar people" centers in the recovery of the fullness of "church practices." Reinhard Huetter, in an essay in a book edited by James Buckley and David Yeago entitled: *Knowing the Triune God: The Work of the Spirit in the Practices of the Church*, provides this list:

- Proclamation of God's word and its reception in faith, confession and deed
- Baptism
- Lord's Supper
- Office of the Keys (church discipline)
- Ordination/offices
- Prayer/doxology/catechesis
- Way of cross/discipleship

In the same essay Huetter notes further: "Pentecost initiated an eschatological, albeit very concrete, *"novus order seclorum."* A new public was created: the *ekklesia* of the eschatological polis was gathered. (12) In other words out of the Trinity-engendered *communio* which is the Church, flows the Church's witness to the life offered to the world through the cross, the death and resurrection of Jesus Christ and the continuing work of the Holy Spirit, all in a post-Constantinian epoch. Many of the issues that appear to be prominent on the plate of those planning worship - the kinds of music, using instruments other than the organ, and so forth - tend, to use Luther's phrase, to be *"adiaphora,"* of no lasting import. So a study quoted in the June 19-26, 2002 issue of *Christian Century*, asserts that growing churches in the West use electric guitars more frequently than "old-line" Protestant churches elsewhere (and also more frequently evidence "high involvement in social ministry!"). What really matters is the integrity of worship itself, integrity measured by faithfulness to the proclamation of the paschal mystery in Word and sacrament.

Finally, let us focus in a little more sharply on the "reengagement" dimension of this "disengagement- reengagement" dialectic. Kathryn Tanner has a piece in the Spring 2002 issue of the *Harvard Divinity Bulletin* entitled "What Does Grace Have to Do with Money? Theology Within a Comparative Economy." It is her thesis that "what is notable about Christianity as a field, what is unusual about it, is its attempt to institute a circulation of goods to be possessed by all in the same fullness of degree without diminution or loss, a distribution that in its prodigal promiscuity calls forth neither the pride of superior position nor rivalrous envy among its recipients." (13) This "generosity as to goods" has implications of the profoundest kind for the up-building of peace. Tanner recalls H. Richard Niebuhr's words from 1929:

> The values to which the modern world gives the greatest ven-
> eration and which it pursues with greatest abandon are values
> which inherently lead to strife and conflict. They are political
> and economic goods which cannot be shared without diminution
> and which arouse cupidity and strife rather than lead to coopera-
> tion and peace.

Thus, re-engagement rooted in radical orthodoxy subverts the consumerist-violence syndrome of the West; and it is in the eucharistically-centered community that the above-mentioned "prodigal promiscuity" finds both form and substance. (Always, of course, side by side the prophetic witness. As Archbishop Rowan Williams points out, the Reformed tradition keeps reminding us of the "peccability" of the Church; we can never let that go!) Stephen Long, in *Divine Economy,* echoing Milbank, maintains that "...we first think of economic exchanges in terms of the definitive social practice wherein the divine-human drama occurs—the Eucharist....The necessary daily exchange finds its nature in the *ought* of God's self-gift in Jesus, mediated to us in the church through its repetition in the Eucharist....We have no substance that exists separate and secure from the plenitude of this inexhaustible gift." (15)

Thus, faithful church practices in celebration of our trinitarian God provides the most profound critique of the nothingness of the materialistic-exchange economy and the loss of rootage in truth. At the same time such practices empower all with the beatific vision of that sunlight of grace and boundless love which offers abundant life to all now and eternally. And filled with that grace and vision we, the saints of the early twenty-first century, are empowered to be Christ's witnesses to all the world, in the name of the Father, and of the Son, and of the Holy Spirit.

Notes

1. Brueggemann, Walter, *Cadences of Hope: Preaching Among the Exiles*, Louisville: (Westminster,1997), 80.
2. Brueggemann's source is Douglas John Hall, "Ecclesia Crisis: The Theology of Christian Awkwardness," in *The Church Between Gospel and Culture: The Emerging Mission in North America*, ed. George R. Hunsberger and Chris Van Gelder, Grand Rapids: (Eerdmans, 1996), 198-213.
3. n a letter from John Burgess, dated February 20, 2002.
4. From "Online Archives" (*National Catholic Reporter*), June 21, 2002, in an article by Patrick O'Neill, entitiled "Theologian's feisty faith challenges status quo."
5. Hemming, Laurence Paul, editor, in *Radical Orthodoxy? A Catholic Equiry*, Aldershot: (Ashgate, 2000).
6. Long, D. Stephen, *Divine Economy: Theology and the Market*, London: (Routledge, 2000).
7. Ibid., 241
8. Hemming, op. cit., 153.
9. Brueggemann, Walter, *Theology of the Old Testament*, Minneapolis: (Fortress, 1997), 574. Reference is made to Gary A. Anderson, *A Time to Mourne and a Time to Dance: The Expression of Grief and Joy in Israelite Religion*, University Park: (Pennsylvania State University Press, 1991). Anderson's reference is to Clifford Geertz, "Religion in a Cultural System," in *The Interpretation of Cultures*, New York: (Basic Books, 1973) 87-125; and George A. Lindbeck, *The Nature of Doctrine, Religion and Theology in a Postliberal Age*, Philadelphia: (Westminster, 1984).
10. Long, Thomas G., *Beyond the Worship Wars: Building Vital and Faithful Worship*, Bethesda: (Alban, 2001).
11. Huetter, Reinhard, "The Church: The Knowledge of God: Practices, Doctrine, Theology" in James Buckley and David S. Yeago, editors, *Knowing the Triune God: The Work of the Spirit in the Practices of the Church*, Grand Rapids: (Eerdmans, 2001), 34f.
12. Ibid., 56.
13. From an essay presented as the Horace DeY. Lentz Lecture at the Harvard Divinity School, April 16, 2000. Dr. Tanner also is the author of *Jesus, Humanity, and the Trinity: A Brief Systematic Theology*, Minneapolis: (Fortress, 2001).
14. A response to a question by Stanley Hauerwas, quoted in *Christian Century*, June 5-12, 2002.
15. Long, op. cit., 268

(Unpublished monograph, dated 2003)

Louis H. Gunnemann

The Eucharist: Sacrament of Discipleship

If Baptism can be understood as the Sacrament of Vocation, or calling, the Lord's Supper (Eucharist) can be understood as the Sacrament of Discipleship. In this essay we shall explore how these two sacraments have a new and meaningful coherence or unity when viewed in this way.

For those acquainted with Reformation history, the mere mention of the Eucharist (Lord's Supper) brings to mind the heated debates over its meaning and the resultant divisions, many of which are not yet healed. On the other hand, North American Christians generally, who are unaware of these debates, often tend to be quite casual and indifferent about this sacrament. Even in those church bodies where the sacramental accent has been customary, there is alarming ignorance and misunderstanding concerning the Eucharist. On the popular level, regard for the sacrament ranges from pure superstition to cultural fad to complete neglect.

I

It is scarcely necessary to review the detailed history of this sacrament in the United Church of Christ as it relates to the Reformation roots in the teachings of Luther, Calvin and Zwingli. At the same time, it is important to recognize other strains of teaching that have fashioned the diverse understandings and attitudes among us today. That diversity is not new, of course. It was prevalent already in eighteenth-century England to the extent that William Pitt, Prime Minister in 1772, said on one occasion to the Parliament in exasperation: "We have a Calvinistic creed, a Popish liturgy, and an Arminian clergy."

The fact is that, although the Lutheran and Reformed differences over the Lord's Supper were firmly fixed on the continent of Europe, it was in England that the Puritan Reformation and the Wesleyan revivals of the eighteenth century introduced even more differences in the understanding of this sacrament. American Christianity inherited that strain of Anglo-Saxon diversity, and then added its own brands! We can identify three stages of development in the general attitude toward the Lord's Supper.

First, the place of the Supper in New England Puritanism: in Old England, the Reformation cry of "justification by faith only" had led to the Puritan rejection of all ritual marks of the Church. In place of these the Puritans insisted on individual, personal evidence of the spiritual regeneration that only the Word and Spirit could bring about. That evidence, a recounting of the experience of regeneration, had to satisfy the community of faith. Since most Puritans had been baptized as infants in the Church of England, that experience became the gateway to participation in the Lord's Supper.

As these Puritans migrated to New England, their insistence upon the evidence of regeneration was intensified, chiefly because many newcomers to Massachusetts Bay colony and other colonizing points were not all of that persuasion. They became members of the church by "owning the covenant" but they were barred from the Lord's Supper until acceptable evidence of regeneration was given. However, the experience of regeneration was often an elusive goal, and thus many were barred from the Table. The Supper became the private experience of the spiritually elite. The dilemma arose as the next generation was born. Could children be baptized who were born to parents who had owned the covenant but who had not been admitted to the Lord's Table? The response was to provide a way around a requirement that was self-defeating for the Church: the establishment of what came to be known as the "Half-way Covenant" which permitted the baptism of children of non-communing members of the Church.

There were years of agonizing debate over this, for the Puritans faced the classic dilemma of how to keep the Church pure at its innermost core while seeking to fulfill Christ's command to baptize and bring people into the Church. The result of the Half-Way Covenant was to have a majority of church members who never communed at the Lord's Table. This tended to undercut the very concern of those who sought to protect the Table: it led to a lessening of regard for the sacrament.

This experience of the New England Puritans illustrates the dangerous misuse of ecclesiastical authority, whether that authority is exercised by the clergy or by the laity. Again and again through Christian history, the Lord's Supper has been used to exclude persons from the fellowship of faith. Each effort of that kind had its beginning in times of social and moral deterioration. They were efforts to bring order out of chaos, but they often became the means of establishing human dominion in the Church and thus supplanting the Lordship of Christ. The history of eucharistic practice (or the practice of the Lord's Supper) in the past twenty centuries, is interwoven with this human error.

The second stage in the development of American Christian attitudes toward the Lord's Supper was in large part a reaction to the Puritan dilemma. A church filled with "half-way Christians" was bound to be filled with frustration, but even more, with unfilled spiritual need and hunger. This expressed itself in the First Great Awakening (1735-1750) in New England. At that time hundreds of church members for the first time had an experience of spiritual regeneration. Two results are to be noted here:

First, the authority of personal religious experience was validated for many people. Second, it convinced many persons that the sacraments, both Baptism and the Lord's Supper, were experientially important—not merely important ways for the Church to put its seal of approval upon a person's faith. Adult (or believer's) baptism became more acceptable and gave impetus to the spread of the Baptist movement in American churches. But equally important was the experiential emphasis in the Lord's Supper. No longer was it simply a seal of saving faith. Rather it became an experience of communion with the Lord. This inward emphasis was to have immense influence in all American churches, particularly of Anglo-Saxon background. And, it was accentuated in the Second Great Awakening as the nineteenth century dawned.

The third stage in the shifting attitudes of the American churches toward the Lord's Supper was marked by a slow but steady erosion of all substantive sacramental understanding of this Christian rite. The focus on individual experience was a major cause of the erosion. But another was the dominant accent on preaching as the central act in corporate worship. The late nineteenth century became the era of the "Pulpit Princes" in Protestant churches. The pulpit succeeded in eliminating the communion table. Generations of North American Christians grew up without any sense of sacramental life. The Lord's Supper became a relic of religious piety of little importance to those who thought of faith in terms of intellectual satisfaction.

An illustration of this trend may be seen in the Christian Church movement that became a part of the General Council of Congregational Christian Churches in 1931. Although portions of this movement originated in the revivalism of the Second Great Awakening at the end of the eighteenth and the beginning of the nineteenth century (which accentuated the experiential aspect of the sacrament), of equal significance are the roots of the Christian Church movement in the anti-ecclesiastical, anti-clerical attitudes of the Enlightenment. Christian churches, drawn from Methodist, Baptist and Presbyterian groups, represented the Enlightenment thought of John Locke who placed the authority of individual understanding as supreme in all of life, including faith. Rational belief was confidence in one's own interpretation of the faith and of its sources in the scriptures. Thus all ecclesiastical traditions were suspect: clergy, rituals, creeds, and sacraments. Preaching that reached out to the autonomous reason of human minds was the chief reason for the church.

Parallel to these developments, and at many points interwoven with them, were changing perceptions of the Lord's Supper among those denominations whose members had come from the continent of Europe; chiefly Lutheran and Reformed. Among them, in the latter half of the nineteenth century, were the German Evangelicals and a second wave of German Reformed people.

The early Lutheran and Reformed groups, arriving in the first decades of the eighteenth century long before the Revolution, were greatly affected by both of the Awakenings. In the resulting turmoil in the German Reformed churches, the Mercersburg Movement was born. That movement, under John Williamson Nevin and Philip Schaff, strongly resisted the reduction of the Lord's Supper to personal religious experience. The Mercersburg emphasis was upon the Lord's Supper as the corporate act of God's people in celebration of Christ's mystical presence at the Table. In that act, the Church shows itself as the extension of the incarnate Christ's presence in the world. The influence of this sacramental emphasis can be traced in the "Order for Holy Communion" in the old Evangelical and Reformed *Book of Worship* (1947), and in the UCC *Services of Word and Sacrament* (published in 1964, and again in 1967 and 1971).

Among the later immigration of German Reformed and German Evangelical people, the chief formative influence concerning the Lord's Supper was nineteenth-century German pietism, on the one hand, and German rationalism on the other hand. Pietism was a reaction to rationalistic tendencies; but the freedom of thought and independence of mind generated by rationalism gave impetus to pietism's independent spirit. This is particularly noticeable among the German Evangelical people who migrated to the Ohio valley and the Midwest in the 1840s and 1850s.

Although issuing from the government-sponsored union of Lutheran and Reformed churches in Prussia in 1817, the German Evangelicals in America tended to be more Lutheran than Reformed in thought and practice. This was largely due to the fact that the majority of German Evangelicals came from parts of Germany dominated by Lutheranism. At the same time, it was the pietistic thought and practice of the time that shaped their attitudes toward the Lord's Supper. The accent fell heavily (as Luther himself emphasized), upon the sacrament as a means of grace by which the forgiveness of sins was *effected* in the participant. It was not simply a sign and seal confirming forgiveness through faith, but an effecting of forgiveness in the believer. As an act of piety (devotion), participation in the Supper was obedience to the Lord, and in that obedience the forgiveness of sins was sealed. Thus it was a highly personal and individual matter, not primarily a corporate act. In this respect, it was somewhat akin to the experiential emphasis of the churches of Anglo-Saxon background, shaped in Puritan piety.

Because of this emphasis upon the Supper as a sacrament of forgiveness, both the German Reformed and the German Evangelicals of the late nineteenth century stressed the role of preparation for communion, either through a corporate preparatory service, or through corporate confession. Communion was therefore reserved for special occasions and became a very solemn experience in the life of a congregation.

When the Evangelical and Reformed Church was formed (in 1934), there was an attempt to bring together the diverse emphases resulting from the early and late German immigration periods, and from the North American religious experience. This was done in the publication of the Evangelical and Reformed *Book of Worship* in 1941 and again in 1947, as we have noted, in which the unifying accents were derived from the Mercersburg Movement of a century earlier. While the "Order for Holy Communion" therein was widely used, it is difficult to determine its influence on popular understandings of the sacrament.

While the foregoing historical survey gives some understanding of current attitudes toward the Lord's Supper, we can only admit that the range of belief and practice in United Church of Christ congregations today defies clear categorization. My own reading of this is that there is much ignorance, much misunderstanding—but also *much hunger for understanding.*

Experimental efforts to attract people to participate in the Lord's Supper have contributed to more misunderstanding. The churches themselves, not only the clergy, live under the illusion that if something is more attractive, or different, it will be "marketable." The "marketing" mentality has done immeasurable harm to the Church's proclamation of the faith. In general, the prevailing attitude toward the Supper is that it is one of the elective elements among the traditional activities of the Church. That attitude reflects almost total ignorance not only of the sacrament itself but also of what we mean by the word "Church." It is also ignorance of the Christian faith.

II

How, then, should the Church respond to the situation? I propose a two-step process. First, it is of the utmost importance to take into account what has happened in ecumenical studies and, second, it is equally important to develop the meaning of the perspective on the Lord's Supper suggested in the phrase: the "Sacrament of Discipleship."

It is unfortunate that many church members, and in this the clergy must accept responsibility, have very little awareness of the results of the ecumenical studies on the sacraments done since 1930 under the Faith and Order Commission of the World Council of Churches. I suspect that Protestants are more aware of changes in the liturgical life of the Roman Catholic Church since Vatican II, especially the shift from Latin to English in the liturgy. There is, we must admit, something ironic in that.

Ecumenical agreement about the Lord's Supper has actually been a monumental achievement, despite the tendency of the public media to highlight continuing differences. It is often overlooked that differences in particular accents and practices do not destroy the common agreement as to the central importance of this sacrament to the Christian faith. Common understandings grow from commitment to this crucial importance. Different practices are recognized as the products of different cultural and social conditions and are therefore not real barriers to Christian unity. The recent accord reached in the Lutheran-Reformed Dialogue illustrates this.

The common accord reached about the meaning of the Lord's Supper will do much to correct the erroneous understandings of popular religious piety. Some of them, because of the narrow and limited perspectives of our churches, will seem almost foreign and strange. But they are all rooted in the New Testament and in the mainstream of the Christian tradition. Let us note them:

First, the Supper is a eucharist, a service of thanksgiving. "Our Lord Jesus, on the night of his betrayal, took bread and gave thanks." In acting thus, Jesus did what his people had done from time immemorial when they gathered to eat. Thanksgiving to God was the mood at the table, even the reason for eating. Christians through the ages have understood the entire Supper itself as a thanksgiving to God, for it is always done in response to Christ's word: "This do in remembrance of me." Such obedient response is a thanksgiving to God. Unfortunately, this joyous eucharistic note has been lost in many of our churches. The solemnity of the forgiveness of sins seemed to leave little room for joy for those who were of the pietistic traditions. One would think quite to the contrary—that forgiveness express itself in joyous thanksgiving?

Second, the Supper is an act of the *community of memory*. It is not simply a time of quiet recollection, but of active representation of the story symbolized in the Supper. The Greek word here is *anamnesis*. It means "to recall" by participation in Christ's life, death, and resurrection. At the Eucharist, the Church is acting out its reality as a community of memory. In its rehearsal of the central point of the gospel, at the Eucharist, the community of memory continually corrects itself and refines its perceptions of the meaning of Christ's act for all humankind. It is thus accountable to the Christ and to all who are His.

Third, the Supper is *an invocation of the Spirit*. The Greek word is *epiklesis* (epiclesis). It is the prayer in which we call upon the Spirit for those gifts that enable us to live the life Christ calls us to share. The Supper is, according to Christian doctrine, dependent upon the gift of the Spirit for the effectual communication of God's grace, making possible our communion with Christ. To pray for the Spirit moves us out of self-concern and private seeking of blessings to a concern for others. Thus we know the "unity of the Spirit in the bonds of peace."

Fourth, the Supper is communion *with Christ*. It is the Lord's Table to which we come, not ours. He is the host; He has invited us, nay, commanded us. Communion, then, is not simply a matter of partaking the elements. It is responding to Christ's presence. Here is the real presence of Christ: in the promise to be with those who call upon Him. Such communion is of the very essence of life. Communion with one another is possible because of His communion with us as He has promised. The elements used in the Supper are important for this communion with Christ. For the Christ at the Table is not any Christ of our imaginations. He is the Christ whose body was broken for us, whose life was poured out for us, and who rose to live with us. And it is this Christ who by His presence assures us of forgiveness and new life.

Accentuating these meanings of the Supper is a first step in helping church members in our time know the sacramental nature of the Holy Communion. A second step, however, is necessary in order for the Church to be the Church in times like these.

The Supper must be understood as the *Sacrament of Discipleship*. Ecumenical studies have enabled Protestants worldwide to recover an understanding of the place of the Eucharist in the life of the Church. Only a few of the monastic orders have held tenaciously to the understanding that in the eucharistic celebration Christians know themselves as God's mission in the world. To recapture this sense is to understand anew the meaning of discipleship. It is at the Lord's Table that His disciples gather to know anew the dimensions of the relationship they have with Him, sharing His suffering and victory, knowing themselves as servants of His reconciling work among all people. The Faith and Order Commission document states it in this way:

> Reconciled in the Eucharist, the members of the body of Christ are called to be servants of reconciliation and witnesses of the joy of the resurrection. Their very presence in the world requires their solidarity with all people in their sufferings and hopes, to whom they can be signs of the love of Christ who sacrificed himself for all humankind on the Cross and gives himself in the Eucharist.

Although that statement does not employ the word "discipleship," it is the appropriate way to speak of the pattern of life required of "servants of reconciliation." This is certainly made clear in Paul's great discussion of our ministry in 2 Corinthians 4 and 5. (2) Discipleship is sharing the life of Christ; it is "joining him in his passion and victory." "Discipleship" consists of being *called* (baptism) and of being *sent*. Here again we are underlining a neglected aspect of the nature of the gathering for the Eucharist. Benefits, as Luther always emphasized, for the believer are important. But it is important also to know that our Lord gathered *His disciples* at the Last Supper, and so He does in all succeeding Suppers. It is the *disciples* of Christ who can give thanks for the opportunity to learn again what it is to follow Christ, and to be sent by Him.

The use of this accent on discipleship in the celebration of the Lord's Supper is long overdue. It is the essential corollary of Baptism as the Sacrament of Vocation. The call to discipleship needs to be impressed upon every heart; imbedded in the spirit of every Christian. Only in this way can the Church be pulled out of its persistent tendency to encourage only self-serving, exclusivistic religious activities among its members. Only then can those who hear the call turn around from their hopeless journeys to "seek first the Kingdom."

This accent has the potential of turning us again to some of the profound teachings of the Church concerning the real nature of repentance, conversion, and sanctification—all of which are essential to the recovery of a strong moral fiber in our personal and social existence. Words like repentance, conversion and sanctification have been lost from our vocabulary. It is striking that so many modern prayers of "confession" include no reference to repentance - sorrow for sin and a decision to "turn around." Discipleship is learning that obedience to Christ requires continual repentance, a turning from other lords, and thus a continual process of conversion. (3) Discipleship is thus a fulfilling of our sanctification - our cleansing under the power of the Holy Spirit. It is a turning again and again to our calling in our baptism. That is what the eucharistic celebration does: it returns us to our baptism and unites again with the Christ in obedience.

There is a repeated call for spiritual renewal among the churches. No one denies the importance of this. But spiritual renewal is not a goal to be achieved; it is a gift of the Spirit as we fulfill our baptism (calling)—first at the Table of our Lord in eucharistic celebration, and then in the service of reconciliation which He has demonstrated. It is in the Sacrament of Discipleship that spiritual renewal is defined and experienced.

Notes

1. Faith and Order Paper No. 73, World Council of Churches, Geneva, 1975, 23.
2. cf. 2 Corinthians 5:16-21 and Mark 8:34-37.
3. cf. David Steinmetz, "Reformation and Conversion," in *Theology Today*, 15:1, April 1978, 25-32.

(*On The Way*, Vol. 3, No. 2, Winter 1985-86)

Mark S. Burrows

A Contemporary Appropriation
of St. Benedict's Rule

We know this from observing the natural world, in the seasons' cycles and the changing weather patterns; we see this in the coming and going of generations, and in the shifting movements of history; we learn this in the flow and interruptions of our own lives: *the deepest reality of life, the only sure constant, is change.* Songwriter Pete Seeger, borrowing from the ancient lyrics of Ecclesiastes, etched this truth into our cultural memory when he wrote:

> To everything, turn, turn, turn, There is a season, turn, turn, turn,
> And a time for every purpose under heaven.

The modern prophet Bob Dylan tooled this theme in his own way, reminding us as if we had not noticed that, "The times, they are a-changin..."

In a poem written shortly before his death in 1993, the Oregon poet Bill Stafford turned to the same truth in a poem entitled "The Way It Is":

> There's a thread you follow.
> It goes among things that change.
> But it doesn't change.
> People wonder about what you are pursuing.
> You have to explain about the thread.
> But it is hard for others to see.
> While you hold it you can't get lost.
>
> Tragedies happen; people get hurt
> or die; and you suffer and get old.
> Nothing you do can stop time's unfolding.
> You don't ever let go of the thread. (1)

What is this "thread" we follow that "goes among things that change"? A thread which, if we hold onto it, assures us that we won't lose our way? What is the thread *you* hold onto, or grasp for when your life collides with tragedy? The thread that doesn't change—but which somehow is a part of change?

We live in a time of dramatic, sweeping, and often bewildering change, particularly compared with the pace of life a century ago. Our churches, as organisms within a wider cultural ecology, live within a shifting environment over which we can often exert only slight influence. And our best efforts at declaring our Christian witness often leave us in a seemingly insurmountable tangle of intra-ecclesial debates and arguments. The burdens of pluralism have "come home" to our own church communities, to be sure. The songwriter was right: "These times, they are a-changin."

But this has always been the case, and in fact change itself is not the profound and persisting problem we must address. Ours is rather the task of attending to our own ways of bearing witness, and, indeed, of living, in the midst of change. To do so, we must remember, first of all, that we are a people of faith whose journey always occurs in the deep river of tradition - which is, ironically, all about change, about currents that come to us from an origin we can at best dimly imagine and toward a destiny that is not within our sight. Swimming in these streams, we find ourselves carried by a memory inherited from a source rich with both a past and a hoped-for future—which is, in terms of the scriptural narrative, still beyond us. Within this river, our movement is always toward the shores of a vast sea—a destination that we know, in the strange irony of faith, to be but another place of beginning.

As we find ourselves midway on this journey of life, explorers not only by necessity but by choice, we do well to hear again the ancient psalmist's cry: "Is there anyone here who yearns for life?" (Psalm 34:12) Beneath this cry is the great existential question: Who are you? Who am I? Are we our own makers, creatures in a closed world without any transcending cause and no wider purpose than what we construct? Are we, as Luther posited, creatures who, left to ourselves, assume this to be so? Aew we those whose hearts, as Luther put it, are "turned back on themselves" *(cor curvum in se),* and thus find ourselves alienated from our own lives? Today, we turn our thoughts to the promise of Jesus' presence among us as the source of a continuity we discover in the midst of change; the great thread woven through the shifting tapestry of time and space. And, in the midst of this promise, we come to discover that change can be a gift, creating within us a deep longing: Who among us, weary and heavy-laden, yearns for life? What might happen if, with all the thinking and worrying and planning we devote in our churches to these "times (which) are a-changin," we grounded our common life in the depths of our desire for life—and life abundant? If we could remember that charting our way in the wide waters of our lives depends not only upon the stabilizing ballast of memory, but the lifting sails of hope? What is the texture of our hearts-longing? What desire for life forms the thread guiding us among things that change? Is this desire at once who we are, and who Christ is toward and with and in us?

In posing such questions, and suggesting the geography of desire as a starting point, we locate our way within an ancient and resilient tradition. Within the wide boundaries of the Church's long tradition, I'd like to consider with you how this question, how the "quest" of this question, functions within the ancient "Rule" of St. Benedict, written sometime in the middle of the sixth century C.E. (2) What we will discover is that the monastic tradition offers one particular image of how constancy and change mingle together in our lives, which is not to laud monasticism as a structural solution to the problems besetting us in these changing times, but to see within its ancient tradition a deep longing for Christ who is "the way" by which we might find a thread to follow through the obscure pattern of our journey.

First, a short word of historical orientation. Benedict (d. 547) was by no means the founder of the first monastic communities, nor was he the only craftsman of this way of life. But we know him to have been the architect who consolidated a pattern of monasticism that shaped the western church for the millennium leading up to the Protestant Reformation. But why Benedict, and not another? Primarily because his times, like ours, were "a-changin." He and his confreres lived in an uncertain boundary time; an unstable period marked by the collapse of the newly Christianized Roman Empire and the end of the short-lived synthesis of Christ and Caesar, church and state, that followed Constantine's conversion. The great eternal city of Rome had fallen to invading barbarian tribes from the north; the last Christian emperor had been deposed from power in 476. Warfare between invading peoples destroyed the revered *pax romana*; the Church's power and authority lay in shambles. No longer an institution boasting a proud place in the "public square," the Church found itself displaced from the center, living its witness at the margins of society.

Building his monastic model amid the ruins of antiquity, and in the vacuum of church leadership, Benedict was aware that his task had to deal with fundamental things. The church of his grandparents was no more, and pious nostalgia would do nothing to raise it from the dead. His reform vision grew out of the very currents of such change, and took for its building materials the practices of a disciplined, communal life that had flourished among holy men and women congregating in the deserts of North Africa and Syria, of urban Constantinople and rural Cappadocia. The shape of his "Rule" as a sort of manual for this building campaign voiced again the psalmist's familiar cry, which was to become the way of Jesus: "Is there anyone here who yearns for life?"

Far from envisioning change as the Church's defeat, Benedict saw this moment as a time of possibility. The monastic way invited his contemporaries into a particular "way" of Jesus – through forming a vigorous and intentional form of community; one grounded in what he called "stability of place," and shaped by a distinctive and defining "way of life." This way, an appropriately ambivalent word in English, is both a manner and a journey. The Latin word Benedict favored to express this "way," *conversatio*, captures something of this double meaning as well—it literally means a "turning around," but it can also suggest a "movement from one place to another," even a "revolution." And herein we already begin to see the genius of his ecclesial architecture: the Church should express stability in motion, identity in change, a way of finding one's identity "on the move," as a people on the way. He knew that we would find this needed stability of place in a particular way of relating to Christ and to one another; a rooting of our lives in God that was at the same time the sharing of a common journey. According to Benedict's design, our vocation had less to do with "holding on" than with "letting go": "To everything, turn, turn, turn..."

Now, this is not to suggest that ours is the task of launching an ambitious building program to construct new Protestant monasteries, though the idea of forming churches grounded in a more deliberately intentional form of communal life has crossed my mind on a regular basis. My interest is not in praising the external structure of monastic institutions, but in gazing through the lens of the "Rule" to discern how Christian community might come into clearer focus. What I would like us to reflect upon, in particular, is the expression of longing we find at the heart of this witness – and to test whether this might provide a guide for us, "a distant mirror" (to recall the title of Barbara Tuchman's vivid history of the fourteenth century) that might reflect something from this ancient experiment for our own quite different day. And here, let me be quite direct in saying that if we are to hear any echoing wisdom from the Benedictine way, it will probably be its founder's insistence that Christian life must have a certain shape, an incarnate form, but that this is only a means to the end of loving God—which is to say, that of living more faithfully, more courageously or "heartfully," more reverently in the world.

What is the "thread" of the monastic way, and what might we learn from this ancient *conversatio*, this "way of living"? The first monasteries shaped under Benedict's guiding hand were not fortresses secured against the threat of outside enemies. They were, rather, bearers of an older memory, rooted in the disciplined reading of scripture and singing of prayer. This way would be the "thread" woven within shifting cultural patterns and against the grain of political instability. These communities had a modest ambition, in other words: theirs was not the vocation of somehow saving the Church, but rather that of preserving a distinctive witness, a peculiar way of being in the world. In a word, the "way" of Jesus. This was to be an intentionally communal way, and a deliberately ordered way, a way marked by simplicity of life and the balanced rhythm of shared work and prayer. These communities found their particular shape in the slow and steady reading— one might rather say, to borrow one of their favorite words, the "ruminating" or chewing —of scripture. Their life consisted of spinning "webs" of prayer out across the vast and unknowable emptiness of the days and years.

Benedict understood that communities of faith needed for their structure and sustenance a shared "rule of life," a pattern by which they might live in bonds of mutual obedience—to an abbot, to one another, and, in all things, to God. The "Rule" he wrote is visionary, of course, but it is intensely practical and always shaped by a long view of life. It is unswervingly patient, never frantic or hasty. It is not designed for the sprint, but for the distance race; as such, Benedict nowhere offers a drastic program of retrieval, nor does he hold forth a flawless and inflexible ideal. He himself called it, in the final chapter, a "little rule... for beginners." Throughout its chapters, what the "Rule" offers is an invitation to discover faith in an experiential way of living. As he puts it in the opening pages of the prologue, "What, dear (friends), is more delightful than this voice of the Lord calling to us? See how the Lord in his love shows us the way of life."

What is this way of life? Among many emphases that emerge in the "Rule," three stand out with particular importance: first, the importance of indwelling our lives, which he referred to with the phrase "stability of place"; second, the significance of living attentively in the patience of waiting, in the midst of life's ordinary rhythms; and, third, the practice of hospitality as a way of listening to the heart's desire, which is to say, as a way of discovering what it means to follow Jesus. Perhaps we who live in what some have described as a "post-Christian" culture could do well to learn something from Benedict's commitment to stability, remembering as people on a pilgrimage that we are gathered not by strategic plans and programs but by mission; the mission of God's creative presence in our world and even in our midst, if we acquire "eyes to see."

I

First, let us consider the place of community that I shall consider under Benedict's peculiar notion of "stability of place." This theme is the very heart and soul of the communal witness Benedict envisioned in his "Rule." Now, such a notion seems strangely out of place in our day. Quaint. Inefficient. Perhaps even absurd. And perhaps this is finally true, because stability of life is not about a management technique. Nor is it about making the world somehow cooperate with our plans. Stability is about letting the world be, about relaxing in the given-ness of this world, and the "forgiveness" of our own lives. It is about giving up our need for control, about discovering – and choosing to live by – a different sort of agency than the aggressive, "muscular" sort we usually fall back upon. It is not, finally, about relevance, but about reverence. As we might say, paraphrasing Benedict's intent, "Don't just do something; stand there!" It is about a vulnerability to what is beautiful, even if often hidden under the dark sheets of pain. It is the finding together of a deliberate stability of life, or as he once callsof the central point of the gospel,ed it, "stability in the community" (*stabilitas in congregatione*; ch. 4, 78); a way of life that must be discovered over and over again in the midst of our human culture of violence and death.

And so we might well ask, indeed we must ask, what is finally "stable" in a world like ours "east of Eden," wracked as it is by irrational and unpredictable violence? With an economy whose global rhythms threaten to obliterate the local solvency of workplace, town, and city? With fiscal challenges that make it harder and harder for small businesses and farms to compete against conglomerates? When small towns can no longer hold the rhythms of their lives because of the steadily accelerating migrations toward the cities? Monasteries, despite their commitment to withdrawing from the world in order to live a life of prayer, offer a different "economy" of life that our hearts instinctively yearn to know about.

This is a crucial point: Benedict understood the monastery not simply as a gathering of people, but as a "family" able to provide for its own needs as far as possible and joined together by the concrete bonds of a genuinely shared economy (see particularly the "Rule," ch. 66, 6-7). One might even say that Benedict's is a "communitarian" way. Prayer was to be done together. The brothers shared their work, as well as the fruits of their work, in common. All the monastery's "tools and goods" were to be held as common property. Frugality was to be considered a blessing, since "whoever needs less should thank God and not be distressed, but whoever needs more should feel humble because of his weakness..." (ch. 34, 4). The brothers "should serve one another," not only in the great offices of leadership but in the most menial of tasks such as those of offering kitchen service (ch. 35). Particularly important is the care of the sick (ch. 36), and the concern for the welfare of the weak. The crucial foundation for all of this is the question of "economy": each monastery was to measure its strength in terms of the webs of interdependence by which its members found themselves yoked together, bound by a stability of relatedness. To revise the familiar Cartesian maxim, *Sumus ergo sum*, (We are, therefore I am.) The stability of the community, "*stabilitas in congregatione*," depended upon such concrete acts of commitment.

Stability of place also has to do with the sort of conversation cultivated there, and by this he meant not the kind of discussions one had but the texture of common life – the way of turning together, the way of Jesus, the revolution that creates deep relatedness with God and with one another. Benedict pointed to all sorts of ways to bolster this. I am less interested in the detail of this than in its underlying rationale, for even if we wanted to we could not and should not attempt to replicate the economy of scale he envisioned. But in our own culture, and in a time marked by mobility of life, transience of careers, rapidity of change, "instant messages" and the often overwhelming simultaneity of communication, Benedict's deeper commitment to stability suggests that simply setting ourselves adrift in the strong currents of a consumer-driven, ego-centered society will not sustain our sanity. Were he writing an updated edition of the "Rule" for us, he might remind us about the possibility of sharing property and what we might gain from such a practice, calling us to curb our ravenous and insatiable hunger for things, and particularly for inessential things. In a fragile global economy such as ours has become, our consumption and the mainspring of our wealth drives the grinding wheels of poverty elsewhere in the world. It is this concrete: our driving desire to be up to date, to have what is new, fuels social and economic problems in the wider global marketplace. This should be a wake-up call to affluent North Americans, whose frontier has become not a place but the world of things. In concrete ways, we must learn how to live more modestly than we do, that "less is more" and "simpler" is often not simply more efficient but morally better, and that such a "conversation" might bring us a greater sense of our relatedness to others and welcome a wider generosity given the abundance of our lives. This at least marks the vulnerability of Jesus toward the needy of his day, for he gave himself and shaped his own desires in relation to those whose needs were greatest. What might this mean for us? Perhaps that we should think about how we "indwell" our communities with a more public generosity than we sometimes do, how we find strength and vision to discern where we really are, who we really are, and how we might open ourselves to the legitimate claims of others upon us. Who are we? Are we what we have, or is our being a deeper mystery that moves us beyond the realm of things into a more intimately relational world - the Buberian world of "I/You" relations?

But this is to say that stability is not a way of closing ourselves down from engagement with others; securing ourselves against our neighbors' demands. It is, rather, a way of risking vulnerability, of imagining a common life as the very means by which we live in change, of finding our balance in locomotion and growth. And so the "Rule" opens, appropriately, with images of journeying, moving, going somewhere: as Benedict writes in the "Prologue," we are to "set out on this way, with the gospel as our guide…"; we are to "progress in this way of life and in faith," and "run on the path of God's commandments, our hearts overflowing with the inexpressible delight of love." Benedict describes our life as " a journey by heart," and as such one that is always a revolution—not by requiring us to change places but reminding us that we must often change direction in order to make progress. And thus we hear again the question we must ask over and over on this way: "Is there anyone among us who yearns for life?" How do we cultivate the desire for renewing life where we are, in a world whose dominant logic is that of throwing away and trading up? How do we measure the stability of our congregations as an expression of not staying put but of answering this most fundamental desire of our heart?

Benedict's notion of stability, grounded in an ethic of frugality, is revolutionary—terrifying in its threat to our consuming greed. It is counter-cultural in leading us toward a different image of identity than that marketed by the media. Because it calls us, as Jesus did, to the way of vulnerability to the "other"; in entering the waters of baptism (a "death" leading us toward "the new"!); to see the call to "let go" as holier than that of "holding on"; to acknowledge that the depths of our need are the "places" where community might take form – and so, the gifts most necessary for our growth. As the Revised English Bible correctly translates the first beatitude, "Blessed are you who are in need, for yours is the Kingdom of God" (Luke 6:20). This is the way of Jesus. And it is the basis for a religious and social revolution! What would this mean, that our individual needs are the places of our common blessing? If there is anything we learn about Jesus in the gospels and through the Church's long tradition, it is that community comes about primarily through our courage to live in authentic vulnerability with one another, by finding that our needs, our pain and suffering, our losses and our grief, are the very invitations by which we might find what is truly common in our lives. This requires that we come to know our suffering rather than our achievements, our courage in letting life be "what it is" rather than what we think it should be, as the sources that might finally bring us toward something that deserves to be called community. Jesus' way as we learn about it from the gospel accounts, his "conversation" with others in his world, had everything to do with his being available to others at the places of their need —touching and being touched at the places where others found themselves yearning for life. Because only there, in our despair, our own poverty, might our own hearts be "un-curved" (to recall Luther) so that we, too, might hear the gospel. Following this way for Jesus meant that he was willing to do the revolutionary thing, if need required it—opposing the very heart of Jewish law if this inhibited the higher principle of the human hunger for healing, setting the demands of love always above those of religion.

Benedict's use of stability, then, does not mean that we are to commit ourselves to an unchanging life. This would be an illusion of the highest order. It is rather a way of indwelling the life we have, of saying, "Come what will, we will remain committed to the way of Jesus, here and now." We will stay rooted here, in this place, so that we can begin to live in Jesus' Way. Artists know this, that it is in the long and patient view, the rooted-view that the world before us finally begins to come into focus. The painter, Vincent van Gogh, put it this way in a letter to his brother, Theo. Writing about his growing conviction that his move to the town of Arles in southern France was a help to his art, and that he knew he would have to come to know it slowly and patiently through staying still and learning to "see" the place, he concluded: "What I am sure of is that to stay here is to go forward. And to make a picture that will be really of the south, it's not enough to have a certain dexterity (of technique). It is looking at things for a long time that ripens you and gives you a deeper understanding... And that is why I see that I lose absolutely nothing by staying where I am and being content to watch things pass, as a spider waits in its web for the flies." (3) This is the asceticism of staying put, of indwelling, of learning to see where we really are and who we really are, that is so vital for our growth. For this way of life, this "looking at things for a long time," is the source of a stability that finally will "ripen" us.

II

"As a spider waits in its web": this is not a program of action, but a call to attentiveness, which brings us to the second insight in Benedict's way. We usually don't want to live with such ineffective planning – spinning webs into the air, and somehow hoping that a stray bug or two might fly by and become ensnared. We want to know about likely outcomes, and we organize our programs in order to plan for probable results. We strategize in order to maximize our investments of effort and work. Benedict's way is entirely irresponsible, judged by such standards of efficiency, The second vow Benedictines take, that of "fidelity to the way of life" (conversatio morum suorum), is finally about a form of attentiveness to what a common life is, and this means to discovering what is finally common in our lives. Benedict felt that this discovery, throughout our lives, called us into the landscape of silence. The Danish prophet of the nineteenth century, Soren Kierkegaard, put it this way:

> The present state of the world and the whole of life is diseased. If I were a doctor and were asked for my advice, I should reply: 'Create silence! Bring people to silence.' The word of God cannot be heard in the noisy world of today. And if it were blazoned forth with all the panoply of noise so that it could be heard in the midst of all the other noise, then it would no longer be the word of God. Therefore, create silence. (4)

Bonhoeffer echoes this conviction, when he insists that "to speak of Christ means to keep silent; to keep silent about Christ means to speak. When the church speaks rightly out of a proper silence, then Christ is proclaimed." (5)

We will not discover Jesus' way, this particular way of life, Benedict reasoned, without sufficient silence—because silence is the necessary condition for listening. It is the essential characteristic without which we cannot learn to pay attention, or see what is crucial about our lives in the midst of the clutter of distraction. Without silence we will be swept by the loudest and strongest "gospel" in the marketplace, and so fail to hear the Word inviting us to live! And this depends, to recall van Gogh's insight, less on dexterity or technique than it does on "the patience of place," an attentiveness not to what should be or might be but to what is. And what might this be? In Benedict's vocabulary, this "way of life," this thread of "turning together," is about a common search. Henri Nouwen once wrote in his *Genesee Diary* that "the basis of community is not primarily our ideas, feelings, and emotions about each other but our common search for God." (6) To share in the "common search" is to ground community in what is common to our humanity, recognizing together the Christ who still comes to touch us – at the places of our poverty and need; our brokenness, our struggle and failure, our public "uncleanness."

This means we must form what Dietrich Bonhoeffer called a "fellowship as the un-devout, as sinners." In one of his lectures to the young seminarians at Finkenwalde, Bonhoeffer argued against constructing the Church as "a pious fellowship" where "everybody must conceal his sin from himself and from the fellowship." Against such a false church, he insisted that the grace of the gospel—which is "hard for the pious to understand"—"confronts us with the truth and says: 'You are a sinner, a great, desperate sinner; now come, as the sinner that you are, to God who loves you. He wants you as you are; he does not want anything from you, a sacrifice, a work; he wants you alone.'" (7) The Church discovers the way of Jesus at the margins, not at the center, because the margin is the place where Jesus is. He does not say to us, as he did not say to his first followers, "Come to me all you who are worthy." No, he called the despairing, the depleted, the despised, the desperate. Those who "labor and are heavy-laden." This is the amazing thing about Jesus: in the fellowship of faith, we dare to come to him as we are: as the burdened, as sinners! And, if this is so, we must be bold in welcoming others at the places of their need. Herein lies the great vocation of our attentiveness—to Jesus, to ourselves, and to others. " Those who are well have no need of a physician…"

Benedict knew, as did Jesus apparently, that we come to know far more about ourselves, about our Maker, and about the precious if also precarious wonder of living in this world—and in our churches—not at those places where everything is well ordered, successful, and apparently permanent. No, but at the boundaries of uncertainty, the call to the exodus journey, when we find ourselves thrust out of the comfort of our home— and even the very life that enslaves us!—into an unknown wilderness where we can see no destination at the end of our wandering: a desert where our sense of the established order is most clearly threatened; a wilderness in which our desires and our fears seem to overwhelm our sense of propriety. In other words: those places in our hearts where we come to taste the fierce strength of our yearning for life, our longing for "sweet home;" (8) the wilderness through which we must pass, where we must gather courage to find in seeing that this stability is the very texture of change—and in our life, first of all. Ours is the vocation of discovering this beauty precisely in our "*conversatio*" together, where we come to know the revolution that our turning together with Jesus requires for us to embrace the agonies of our lives and in our world.

Perhaps this is the most fundamental definition of faith: the courage to enter the often parched landscape of life where need and the desire for life finally come to the same place. Our journeys through desert places, the intrusions and interruptions of our plans which force us toward those unwanted boundary crossings in our lives, are also the moments when we might be in the best position to answer the psalmist's plea, "Is there anyone here who yearns for life?" For it is in these places, and perhaps only here, that this ancient song rises again into voice – and seeks to discover us, when we are finally to let it come into its own peculiar melody. Because if the ancient biblical promise is true – that Jesus Christ is "the same yesterday, today, and forever" (Hebrews 13:8) – then we will discover this in the patient listening to our hearts in the midst of change, in the cavernous depths of our sin, in our yearning for life in the shadows of death, in our desire for light in the immense heart of our own darkness. The sanctity of our common life depends upon living in answer to this question – not only in times of bounty and blessing but in the wilderness seasons, in the grinding routines and tragedies alongside the occasionally shining moments of discovery. Following in Jesus' way means to live in the interruptions of our lives, to see in the patient rhythm of our work and our prayer, another simpler way of living in this impatient and hurried culture.

III

The third mark of Benedictine life I would like to consider is the call to hospitality, and this follows again the call to attentiveness. In the very first community Benedict established at Monte Cassino, we see his intention that the monastery be "set apart" but not isolated from society. It is to be more like a cell held together by a permeable membrane, and not a rigid container bound by a non-porous skin. As such, the boundary of this membrane does not serve to keep things rigidly separate, but creates the flow of an exchange based upon need and supply. The monastery functions as just such a "cell" by embodying Jesus' way of hospitality and living out its vocation as a place of home-coming for the homeless—not for those who might become suitable inhabitants, but for those who are in need of comfort, safety, and welcome. "Blessed are the poor…"

Indeed, Benedict adds to the "Rule" an important chapter on the porter's role (ch. 66) as the one who makes sure the door remains a place of welcome, and another on "the reception of guests" (ch. 53) where he reminds his brothers that, "All guests who present themselves are to be welcomed as Christ, for he himself will say: 'I was a stranger and you welcomed me…' By a bow of the head or by a complete prostration of the body, Christ is to be adored because he is indeed welcomed in them." What a strange and wonderful image this is—an honoring of the other not because of any attribute of theirs, but simply because they represent Jesus. To grasp this is to speak a word of revolution into our world, calling us to see the stranger as the anonymous Christ. This is the heart of the Benedictine way. To follow this path is to find Jesus in every guest, in each other. It is to worship God in each dimension of our lives, believing (as Benedict instructs us to do) that "the divine presence is everywhere" —and,… in everyone.

This commitment to hospitality is the consequence of the Benedictine emphasis upon listening. Indeed, the third vow Benedictines make when professing their lives to a monastery is that of obedience, which from its Latin root means to "listen." The command to listen comes in the very first word of the "Rule," when Benedict instructs his readers to "Listen carefully… to the master's instructions, and attend to them with the ear of your heart." To listen "with the ears of the heart": This is not just a physical act of audition. It is paying close attention, giving oneself over to the other. It is an expectant hearing, an attending that characterizes the monks' way of living with scripture; of listening for God's "voice" in the ordinary grit and grandeur of life; of attending to one another's needs, and to those of their guests. To listen to another is the deepest act of obedience; it is the most fundamental expression of hospitality.

Monks are also patient in the listening they do, and the hospitality they embody, in worship. They "live" scripture over and over again, in the endless chanting of the Psalter, in the unending liturgy of scripture and hymn, in the blending of their commitment to prayer and work. The monks have never forgotten the truth that the Christian way is a way of singing. But to sing together, more than vocal technique is important. "Auditory" and not simply vocal technique is finally essential. One must learn to listen to the others, to hear how they are carrying the melody, before one dares to bring one's voice to the choir. Benedictines have never produced any great soloists. Their life is about knowing that the greatest and most sacred music is that which we make together. It is about finding a choir for the community, but about seeing the community as the choir. And this means that our real work is in finding ways to invite each person, whatever their gift, to bring their voice into the common song.

Hospitality: I suspect that in our day, we will know the goodness and truthfulness and beauty of this hospitality by the amount of discomfort our invitations bring into our communities. For we discover Jesus not in doing the "right" thing, but in doing the revolutionary thing; which is to say, as Paul reminds us, that we discover who we are when we accept the call to "welcome one another as Christ welcomed (us)" (Romans 15:7), which is to say, as we are—strangers to God, beggars for mercy. The question we hope might be voiced toward us, "Is there anyone here who yearns for life?" is the very question we are to embody in our hospitality for others. Welcoming others is our answer to God's generous attentiveness to us.

What, finally, is the thread we are to follow that "doesn't change," and which, "while (we) hold it, (we) can't get lost" (Stafford)? It is the way of Jesus. And, as Benedict suggests, it is a way rooted in a stability of place that gives us the freedom to change and grow and accept and forgive. It is a way which is "the way it is" already among us; a way that calls us to a more attentive and reverent life. It is a way that invites us to extend to others the same generous hospitality God showed to us. And, in all these ways, it will often be a way that will cause others to "wonder about what (we) are pursuing." A way that might well be "hard for others to see." A way that will seem quaint, ineffective, un-dramatic. A way, as Bill Stafford reminds us, that "goes among things that change. But it doesn't change."

I'd like to close by telling a story; a modern variation of one of Jesus' parables:

There once was a great and wealthy and generous woman who invited all her friends to a banquet in honor of a new city she had built for them called simply "Home." For each she had designed a dwelling place suited to their basic needs, and more modest than the desires she knew they held —with some envy and even bitterness toward her because of her own wealth. She herself would live in the smallest of houses, without servants, and without any but the most necessary of things: a simple bed, a useful chair, a writing desk and, most conspicuously, an entry directly into a large banquet hall with a round table spacious enough so that everyone who wanted could find a place. There were no other buildings—no banks, no stores, no shopping malls, not a town hall, not even a church. All the other residents had the same single outside door as hers: an un-lockable front door — with a handle only on the outside—by which they might enter their homes, and a similar open entrance leading into the common banquet hall. Once the city had been constructed, the matron sent out invitations to each of her friends to come into an unknown but imaginable inheritance, with a promise that their real needs would never be ignored or denied. She included a sketch of each of their homes, none of which had kitchens or pantries or dining rooms, together with a general plan of the city. Each of her friends, receiving her invitation, thought this must be some bizarre joke. They could see there was no room for future expansions to their houses. And they did not appreciate the fact that their houses, once they entered through the front door, had only one exit—and that was an entrance into the great banquet hall. And so they finally decided to call a town meeting, without inviting their benefactor, to discuss what they should do and how they should respond to her offer.

In the heat of their debate, they could come to no agreement because none of them could understand her insistence that they would each find all their essential needs met in the new planned city. They finally formed several committees to discuss what should be done. A Space Allocations Committee to re-think how the same facilities could be arranged within the city's boundaries in order to avoid any common space, and to design separate dining rooms for each inhabitant. A Property Committee to determine how they could change the handles on the doors to open from the inside, and how they might add appropriate locks. A Human Resources Committee to determine how they might adjudicate future disputes about privileges and responsibilities. And, finally, a Long-Range Task Force to consider how they might keep out those who had not been invited to join this city. Before the meeting had ended, however, another messenger arrived from the benefactor with instructions for each committee. To the Space Allocations Committee, the response was brief: the gift required sharing of space only in the banqueting hall; any requirements for revisions to the plan to secure greater privacy and security would void the offer. To the Property Committee, the answer was equally succinct: no other handles were permissible since the community's life would happen in the banquet hall, and no locks were necessary. To the Human Resources Committee came an equally brief response: no such disputes would arise because property, such as it was, would materialize as needed and disappear when not used. And, finally, to the Long Range Planning Task Force, the answer was a single word: "No!" The messenger added a pronouncement for the entire gathering: they would need to come immediately to claim their homes or return to the lives they had left. The people gathered in the town meeting were outraged at such an inconsiderate response, for they knew their plans took into account conditions that were non-negotiable before they could accept this gift. And so it came to pass that they went back to their home and found them (and themselves) just as they had been when they left: not as they wanted, even though larger than their needs. And they were tired and anxious, and heavy-laden.

When the messenger returned to the generous matron, and she learned that all her friends had turned down her offer, she sent the messenger back to the towns and cities from which her friends had come with an invitation for all the others. The invitation was addressed with deliberate ambiguity as: 'Rest.' The messenger was to deliver this welcome to all those she found there 'who labored and were heavy-laden,' and she was to ask them but a single question: 'Is there anyone here who yearns for life?' Great was the crowd that came, and each found a place prepared just for them. And when their hunger drew them together into the great banquet hall, they found themselves gathered around a generously spread table; a place called simply: 'Thanksgiving.' And in the breaking of bread and in the sharing of the cup, their eyes were opened and each saw the face of Jesus in the other.

Notes

1. "The Way It Is" by William Stafford, in *The Way It Is: New and Selected Poems*, (St. Paul, MN, 1998), 42.
2. Many editions and translations of the "Rule" circulate. Throughout this piece I refer to Timothy Fry, OSB, editor of an edition published at Collegeville, Minnesota in 1981.
3. See Vincent van Gogh, *The Letters of Vincent van Gogh*, selected and edited by The Rule of St. Benedict, in Latin and English with NoMark Roskill, (New York, 1963), 293-294.
4. Cited without precise reference as the last word in Max Picard, *The World of Silence*, trans. Stanley Godman, (New York, 1948), 231.
5. See Dietrich Bonhoeffer, *Life Together*, translated with an introduction by John Doberstein, (New York, 1954), 77-81.
6. Nouwen, Henri, *The Genesee Diary: Report from a Trappist Monastery*, (New York, Garden City, 1981), 212-213.
7. Bonhoeffer, 110-111.
8. The phrase is found in Toni Morrison, *Beloved*, (New York, 1988), and is used by the old lay preacher, "Baby Suggs Holy," to describe the presence of grace as the deep yearning for peace.

(Monograph prepared by Professor Burrows to be printed in an edition of On The Way *that was not published)*

Carl J. Rasmussen

Wallace Stevens and the Death of Nature

"There is danger lest the *enchantments* of this world make them to forget *their errand into the wilderness.*" (Cotton Mather)
"The death of one god is the death of all." (Wallace Stevens)

Introduction

This paper is an appreciation of the poetry of Wallace Stevens. It concludes with a reading of his poem, "The Idea of Order at Key West." It is also a personal reflection, primarily inspired by a trip my wife, Cathy, and I took to Hartford, Connecticut, in April, 1996. Stevens has achieved a prominence not foreseeable when he died in 1955. Certainly his reputation is secure in the academy, in part because he explores the themes of post-modernism. In this regard, I commend to your attention the superb edition of Wallace Stevens, *Collected Poetry and Prose*, published by the Library of America in 1997.

I also consider another prominent citizen of Hartford, the founder of Hartford, the American Puritan Thomas Hooker and some other figures as well. As such the paper is best considered an idiosyncratic meditation and the opportunity to reflect, dear reader, on some captivating and alluring poetry.

Wallace Stevens lived from 1879 to 1955. In addition to being a major poet, he was also a lawyer, a vice president of the Hartford Accident and Indemnity Company in Connecticut. Raised in Reading, Pennsylvania, the son of a lawyer, Stevens attended Harvard, although he did not receive a degree. He graduated from New York University Law School in 1903, and settled into a career with "the Hartford."

The facade of the insurance executive was a mask. Behind the facade, Stevens lived a life of ecstatic states. One can see this in his poetry, but we derive a sense from his aphorisms: "(p)oetry must be irrational;" "(p)oetry is a means of redemption," and "(t)he final belief is to believe in a fiction, which you know to be a fiction, there being nothing else. The exquisite truth is to know that it is a fiction and that you believe in it willingly." As he perhaps put it best in a title to a poem, "reality is an activity of the most august imagination." These observations sound both idiosyncratic and oddly familiar. We find here in particularly elegant form the post-modern stance. Stevens is not at all out of place in contemporary discourse. What has occurred to me is that those views find their origins in the American tradition. They are in a certain way intrinsically American views. The thinking that informs Stevens' poetry did not originate with him. Rather, he punctuates the end of a line that begins with the Great Migration to Massachusetts Bay in the 1630's. Stevens completes the European spiritual errand into the wilderness.

Part One

The Snow Man (1923)
by Wallace Stevens

One must have a mind of winter
To regard the frost and the boughs
Of the pine-trees crusted with snow;

And to have been cold a long time
To behold the junipers shagged with ice,
The spruces rough in the distant glitter

Of the January sun; and not to think
Of any misery in the sound of the wind,
In the sound of a few leaves,

Which is the sound of the land
Full of the same wind
That is blowing in the same bare place
For the listener, who listens in the snow,
And, nothing himself, beholds
Nothing that is not there and the nothing that is.

Part Two

Along the Connecticut River
In April of 1996 my wife and I went to the Class of 2000 Family Weekend at Dartmouth College in Hanover, New Hampshire to visit our daughter Laura. As part of the proceedings we heard a lecture by Professor William W. Cook, "Reconsidering Robert Frost: 20th Century pastoral Poetry." I relieve Professor Cook of all responsibility for what follows. Frost

and Stevens were friends, and, while on the surface they are very different, they are both heirs of the New England Way. They both attended Harvard; they belonged to the literary elect, and they were assured in their election.

Professor Cook's theme was that Frost is a terrifying poet. Professor Cook drew on remarks made by Lionel Trilling at a celebration of Frost's eighty-fifth birthday in 1959. On that occasion, Trilling "outed" Frost as a poet of disturbing themes. We should not be taken in by Frost's persona as the wholesome voice of the rural New England sublime. For Frost, on the contrary, nature is quite indifferent. In nature human existence is a diminished and fortuitous experience. The best we can do in this circumstance is endure with dignity. Frost is a poet of the New England Way without God.

At the time, Trilling's observation touched a nerve, in part because we were deep into the "Cold War." Frost was thought to represent the old virtues and verities. Trilling pointed out that this was by no means true. It is not insignificant that as Frost's biographer, Jeffrey Meyers, has pointed out, Trilling had been chosen the speaker for that occasion only after Vice President Nixon was not chosen. It is also significant that Frost was chosen to read at President Kennedy's inaugural. It somehow is terrifying that America's chosen poetic voice is as nihilistic as any voice that came from behind the "Iron Curtain."

But the terror in Frost is something that deserves our close consideration now that after the Cold War is over. The terror in Frost lies in what I call the death of Nature. That issue requires a somewhat longer conversation. The idea of Nature is not a simple idea. It is a philosophical idea arising from the question of why our minds grasp things in the world that are other to us, like natural laws or the Good. According to the account of classical philosophical realism, for this correspondence to make sense, the world must have an order, and our minds must participate in this order. This philosophical idea of order has a name. It is Nature. In some accounts Nature as such is more than a principle. It is divine. For example, it is the goddess Natura, along with some unnamed god, that brings forth order from the primordial chaos in the beginning of Ovid's *Metamorphoses*. In Wordsworth's reflections above Tintern Abbey, Wordsworth apprehended this "presence" in Nature:

...And I have felt
a presence that disturbs me with the joy
Of elevated thoughts; a sense sublime
Of something far more deeply interfused,
Whose dwelling is the light of setting suns,
And the blue sky, and in the mind of man,

a motion and a spirit, that impels
All thinking things, all objects of thought,
And rolls through all things....

Since my meditation finds its inspiration in New England, we might
consider Emerson on Nature (1836):

> In the woods, we return to reason and faith. There I feel that
> nothing can befall me in life, - no disgrace, no calamity (leaving
> me my eyes), which nature cannot repair. Standing on the bare
> ground, - my head bathed by the blithe air and uplifted into infi-
> nite space, - all mean egotism vanishes. I become a transpar-
> ent eyeball; I am nothing; I see all; the currents of the Universal
> Being circulate through me; I am part or parcel of God.

What is most striking about these accounts is that they are archaic.
We are no longer taught to think about Nature this way. We no longer
believe it. For us Nature may have some objective status (although such
status is an interesting question), but it is no longer a presence, neither is it a
principle of order. If I may use a term from Stevens, Nature is "veritable,"
it exists only as some brute other. Although it occupies some qualified
status as object, that is all there is. There is nothing else there. There is no
there... there. Nature is dead.

The death of Nature has a number of important implications. It is a
theological development. It follows from the death of God. The death of
God, as Nietzsche understood, was a process that unfolds. The death of
Nature is part of this process. But we do not need to rely on Nietzsche.
The death of Nature is as American as apple pie. The death of Nature took
place in America apart from any invasion by unintelligible continental post-
modern cultural criticism. It took place before the emergence of a
counterculture in the 1960s. Indeed the counterculture is in part the result,
hardly the cause, of this development. The death of Nature is not attributable
to science. Science in itself has little to do with it, although the way science
is understood is implicated in it. If we consider Stevens from this point of
view, he embodies a dilemma. He does not resolve it. But he embodies it in
magnificent poetry.

Dartmouth lies along the Connecticut River. After parents' weekend,
we drove our rental car south to Hartford. Hartford, too, lies on the
Connecticut River. We followed Highway 91 south on the Vermont side,
with the Green Mountains at our right and the Connecticut River Valley at
our left. Our encounter with the New England sublime took place in a new
rental car on the interstate.

Part Three
Hartford: Thomas Hooker

Highway 91 heads straight into Hartford, Connecticut as we dropped south along the Connecticut River. However we had to look for the 384 tum-off that took us east to Storrs and Cathy's sister Laura Crow. We wanted to see Hartford, and we had particular sites in mind. We drove and walked around a number of sites: the Old State House, the State Capitol, the Mark Twain House and the Harriet Beecher Stowe House. I was primarily interested in two figures: Thomas Hooker and Wallace Stevens. Laura knew what I was interested in, and she was prepared. We drove into the middle of town, to what is now called the Center Church, the First Church of Christ, United Church of Christ, at Main and Gold Streets, whose foundation dates from the 1630's and in whose Ancient Burying Ground, in the churchyard, lie the saints at rest.

Thomas Hooker, the most prominent among them, is buried here, although no one seems to know precisely where. The church literature suggests that he lies beneath the current church structure. The granite and brownstone headstones, many dating from the seventeenth century, tell the affecting story of this colony. The original site of the church was near the Old State House, but it was moved to its fourth building in the old burying ground in 1807. This cemetery in downtown Hartford tells its explicit and implicit stories of the rigors endured by this small company of the faithful, the communion of saints. Here lies a direct connection between America and the European Reformation. Buried here are the visible saints of the New England Way, English Protestants who, as a condition of church membership, had undergone rigorous preparation and self-examination before making a confession and a public proclamation of their effectual calling and regeneration through grace.

Hooker (1586-1647) was born in Leicestershire, England and studied at Emmanuel College, Cambridge, the intellectual center of Puritanism. In 1633, after vicissitudes in England and the continent, he emigrated to Massachusetts Bay. He was the first minister of what became First Congregational Church in Cambridge, Massachusetts, the parish church of Harvard. He did not stay in Cambridge long. Indeed, he left while it was still called New Town. He led a splinter group west into the wilderness, to the Connecticut River, where in 1636 they founded Hartford. Hooker is associated with the Fundamental Orders of Connecticut (1639) that formed the governing framework for Connecticut colony. It is not precisely clear why Hooker and his followers undertook this arduous endeavor. Historians speculate that it involved the desire for land or a rivalry between Hooker and John Cotton of Boston, the other great theological leader of the great migration. Whatever the case, Hooker did not abandon his engagement with the original colony, and indeed, his influence was, if anything, enhanced by his participation in the antinomian controversy, through which his views came to be decisive for what we call "the New England Way."

Shortly after their arrival in Massachusetts Bay (and in Hooker's case parts west), the American Puritans erupted into a violent theological controversy, the antinomian controversy, which one historian has called the opening chapter in American intellectual history. Although all of the Congregationalist ministers of the 1630's agreed on the fundamental doctrines of natural depravity and regeneration by grace alone, small differences could and did emerge as major issues. In the words of Sydney Ahlstrom, a group in Boston led by Cotton , "stressed the unconditional nature of election and understood regeneration as a more arbitrary work of grace." Others, notably Hooker, developed "elaborate doctrines of preparation for grace until the process came to be regarded as an essential stage in the order of salvation." In the ensuing controversy Cotton was the loser. Hooker, who prevailed with his doctrine of preparationism, put the decisive stamp on this version of Protestantism we know as the New England Way. It is in the introspective preparationism of the New England Way that we find intimations of the role of ecstatic imagination in Wallace Stevens.

Preparationism turns us to Nature in the strict sense. The merits of the antinomian controversy aside (and it is a complicated debate), preparationism opened questions about the spiritual meaning of Nature. Nature had a deeply important place in the thought of the American Puritans. Primarily, they would consider Nature in contrast to grace. For the Puritans, Nature in this regard is secondary. They held to a Calvinist view of grace: Nature, and in particular human nature, is depraved and susceptible to rescue only by the entirely external act of God. But even so, among Orthodox Calvinists, the American Puritans held a special devotion to Nature. In Nature, the wisdom of God is manifest, as in a book, if we read it right.

As William Ames, the English Puritan who so deeply influenced the American Puritans, had written:

> Can we, when we behold the stately theater of heaven and earth,
> conclude other but that the finger, arms, and wisdom of God hath
> been here, although we see not him that is invisible, and although
> we know not the time when he began to build? Every creature
> in heaven and earth is a loud preacher of this truth. Who set
> those candles, those torches of heaven, on the table? Who hung

out those lanterns in heaven to enlighten a dark world?... Who taught the birds to build their nests, and the bees to set up and order their commonwealth? (William Ames, in Perry Miller I, 210.)

Thomas Hooker, himself, develops in striking natural imagery the relationships between regeneration and Nature. Hooker's imagery is particularly striking, for we will find very similar imagery put to very different purposes in Stevens' poem "The Idea of Order at Key West," with which I conclude this presentation. Here is Hooker:

> Looke as it is with the moone, the naturall Philosopher observes. . . now the sea ebs and flowes not from any principle in it selfe, but by vertue of the moone, being moved, it goes, being drawne, it comes; the moone casting her beames upon the waters, it moves the sea, and so drawes it selfe unto it selfe, and the sea with it; so the heart of a poore creature, is like the water, unable to move towards heaven, but the Spirit of the Lord doth bring in its beames, and leaves a supernaturall vertue by them upon the soule, and thereby drawes it to itselfe. (Thomas Hooker, in Perry Miller I, 218)

We spent some time in the ancient burial ground of Hartford. Then in my official capacity as a member of a national board of the United Church of Christ, I felt authorized to try the church door, but it was locked. I was neither called nor chosen. Like some anguished Cambridge undergraduate of the sixteenth century I might be among the vessels of wrath made for destruction. And so we went for a ride.

Part Four

Excursus: Ralph Waldo Emerson

Although it left a decisive mark on the American character and polity, the New England Way as practiced by Hooker and his congregation did not long endure. Why was this the case? I find this an interesting question. An important view was expressed by Cotton Mather: *"Religio peperit Divinitas, Filia devoravit Matrem; Religion* brought forth prosperity, and the daughter destroyed the *mother."* This view is oddly unsatisfactory, especially in a theologian like Mather. I suggest that much of the cause is really to be found in religion itself, in flaws or in-coherences within the New England Way. The most dramatic example is the Salem witch hysteria, where as Perry Miller points out, honest Christians who refused to lie were executed, while dissemblers who admitted what they had to in order save themselves survived. In the witch hysteria, New England encountered radical evil in which it was implicated and for which its theologians could not account.

This larger failure, the failure of the New England Way, has had consequences for our cultural life: despite our many august religious foundations, including great universities, despite the many awakenings, disputes and revivals, despite the ubiquitous religiosity, America, though it has produced much of value, has produced few significant theologians. Despite the apparent importance of religion in our traditions and in our public life we have little to show for it in our living native intellectual tradition that is either not vacuous or venal.

This has left a void that has had to be filled by other means. To find theologians in America, we must look to our poets.

If I were to hold to my Hartford theme, I might here discuss Horace Bushnell (1802-1876), a contemporary of Emerson, and a figure of enormous importance in leading Congregationalism to the liberal gospel of the twentieth century. Yet for all of his significance, Bushnell represents a dead end. To understand Wallace Stevens, we must remove ourselves from the conservative Connecticut River Valley to Massachusetts Bay where Ralph Waldo Emerson (1803-1882) was preparing a new way for the twentieth century.

Emerson plays a special and important role in this meditation. He is the key link between the New England Way and Wallace Stevens. Stevens was an Emersonian poet. He may not have been quite the American poet whom Emerson contemplated, but Stevens is the poet gestating between the lines of Emerson's great essays. In his essay Nature, from which I have already quoted, Emerson could find in Nature the God of his New England Calvinist predecessors. But in his idealism, Emerson also found in Nature the god of the human imagination alone. I quote:

> The sensual man conforms thoughts to things; the poet conforms things to his thoughts. The one esteems nature as rooted and fast; the other, as fluid, and impresses his being thereon. To him, the refractory world is ductile and flexible; he invests dust and stones with humanity, and makes them the words of the Reason. The imagination may be defined to be the use which the Reason makes of the material world.

And again, in conclusion Emerson speaking on behalf of his ideal poet:

> Nature is not fixed but fluid. Spirit alters, molds, makes it. The immobility or bruteness of nature is the absence of spirit; to pure spirit it is fluid, it is volatile, it is obedient. Every spirit builds itself a house, and beyond its house a world, and beyond its world a heaven.

This is American Idealism in its purest form. Emerson had to abandon the ancient Calvinist ordinances because they had become calcified into spiritless form in order to preserve the vitality of the religious impulse. But Emerson did so at the cost of God and of Nature.

Part Five

Hartford: Wallace Stevens

All my sister-in-law, Laura, could find about Wallace Stevens from the historical society was an address: 118 Westerly Terrace in Hartford. So we drove around, found the house and stopped. It was a private residence. An outgoing sort, my sister-in-law encouraged me to get out of the car and ring the doorbell. I did so. To my surprise, the door was opened by a man about my age in a clerical collar. I introduced myself, and asked if Wallace Stevens had lived in this house. The cleric said yes and asked if we would like a tour. I summoned Cathy and Laura, and we received the tour of the whole house; the upstairs study where Stevens wrote, and small features of the house from when Stevens lived there.

What was the meaning of the clerical collar? Our host is an Episcopal priest. The house is now an Episcopal rectory in Hartford. Before her death, Stevens' widow Elsie sold the house to the church, apparently out of spite. The Stevens' marriage was not a happy one. Elsie Stevens was known for her beauty: she was the model for the liberty head dollar and the liberty head dime. But she was reclusive, and she apparently had differences with Wallace. God does have a sense of humor.

Conclusion

The Idea of Order at Key West

"Idea of Order at Key West" is located in a place: Key West, Florida. Stevens is a poet very conscious of place, of the soil, of the climate, of the flora and fauna. His imagination seemed to take particular flight in tropical locations. Why Key West? The answer reveals something about Stevens the man. In his capacity as officer of the Hartford, Stevens needed lawyers around the country to litigate claims for the firm. One such lawyer was Judge Arthur Powell of Atlanta. Judge Powell was a distinguished regional lawyer with the firm of Little & Powell in Atlanta. He was Stevens' friend for thirty years. He was one of the few people who knew Stevens both as a businessman and as a poet.

It was Powell who introduced Stevens to his Georgia social set, a rather boisterous group who vacationed in the Florida Keys. From the early 1920s to 1940, Stevens went south on business for a few weeks each winter, where he spent time cutting loose with Judge Powell and his friends.

Despite the poem's high abstraction, the setting of the Idea of Order at Key West is elemental. It is set by the sea in Key West. The poet and a friend named Ramon Fernandez walk by the sea. They hear a woman singing in this majestic setting. We find a Stevens' triad of the natural world, art and beauty.

The general reader of poetry has encountered this woman or her analogue before. She is the figure of Nature personified who creates order, including intellectual order, from the primal chaos. This allusion is made express by the poet with the question that informs the poem. "Whose spirit is this?" the poet asks. This question is the foundation on which the poem is built, and it does not receive an immediate answer. Indeed, the poet suggests that this question ought in some respects to remain open. But it is open only so far. In the end, Nature is not a presence or entity. It is a human creation.

As the poem suggests, the singer consequently is the one who measures. She measures to the hour the solitude of the sky. (The referent in the poem is somewhat imprecise.) We recall the ancient dictum of the Sophist Protagoras: "Man is the measure of all things." Protagoras claimed that reality inheres in appearance alone: As things appear to a man so they are for him. Against this position, Protagoras' great opponent, Socrates, set himself. According to Socrates things are a certain way regardless of how we perceive them; we are not the measure of all things. But Stevens' singer reminds us that the realism of Socrates, which had been transmitted in America through the philosophical realism of the Western theological tradition, has met its end.

The singer is also the artist. The spirit at issue could be a presence in nature or it could be the human spirit, specifically the imagination, or some mystical union of the two. In any case, the question of art is involved in some fundamental way. Indeed, in the poem when the question receives an answer, it is in favor of the artist. The only presence in the landscape is the presence caused by the woman singing and the two men who observe her. The artist now occupies an elevated status because, insofar as there is a spirit here at all, it is the spirit of the artist. Nature has no spirit of its own.

For this reason, the singer is God. The poem makes this express in theological language: She is the single artificer of the world. She is the maker. She makes by perceiving in imagination and there is no other maker. Because of this, finally, the singer is everyone. By perceiving, we create whatever there is and there is nothing else. As Nietzsche suggested: If God is dead, then man must become a god.

As Stevens concludes the poem, the poet and his friend Ramon return toward the town, now in darkness. Now reflecting on the "blessed rage for order," Stevens turns his reflections from words of the sea alone to words of ourselves and of our origins. The spirit that informs nature is the same spirit that informs all human discourse, including history and science (the words of our origins). It is our spirit alone. There is no objectivity. All discourse, all thought, is a creation of the human imagination. This is the darkness that descends on the errand into the wilderness.

I conclude this essay with the words of Stevens' poem. I want to let Stevens have the last word. My thoughts are hardly final. My remarks are not intended to be reductive but suggestive. Despite issues I have raised, Stevens remains a great poet, beyond anything I can do to him. He deserves to be read. His poetry is worth more than volumes of bad theology. If I have an agenda it is only to encourage interest and discussion, including, in particular, interest in and discussion about the work of Wallace Stevens.

The Idea of Order at Key West (1936)
By Wallace Stevens

She sang beyond the genius of the sea.
The water never formed to mind or voice,
Like a body wholly body, fluttering
Its empty sleeves; and yet its mimic motion
Made constant cry, caused constantly a cry,
That was not ours although we understood,
Inhuman, of the veritable ocean.

The sea was not a mask. No more was she.
The song and water were not medleyed sound
Even if what she sang was what she heard,
Since what she sang was uttered word by word.
It may be that in all her phrases stirred
The grinding water and the gasping wind;
But it was she and not the sea we heard.

For she was the maker of the song she sang.
The ever-hooded, tragic-gestured sea
Was merely a place by which she walked to sing.
Whose spirit is this? we said, because we knew
It was the spirit that we sought and knew
That we should ask this often as she sang.

If it was only the dark voice of the sea
That rose, or even colored by many waves;

If it was only the outer voice of sky
And cloud, of the sunken coral water-walled,
However clear, it would have been deep air,
The heaving speech of air, a summer sound
Repeated in a summer without end
And sound alone. But it was more than that,
More even than her voice, and ours, among
The meaningless plungings of water and the wind,
Theatrical distances, bronze shadows heaped
On high horizons, mountainous atmospheres
Of sky and sea.

It was her voice that made
The sky acutest at its vanishing.
She measured to the hour its solitude.
She was the single artificer of the world
In which she sang. And when she sang, the sea,
Whatever self it had, became the self
That was her song, for she was the maker. Then we,
As we beheld her striding there alone,
Knew that there never was a world for her
Except the one she sang and, singing, made.

Ramon Fernandez, tell me, if you know,
Why, when the singing ended and we turned
Toward the town, tell why the glassy lights,
The lights in the fishing boats at anchor there,
As the night descended, tilting in the air,
Mastered the night and portioned out the sea,
Fixing emblazoned zones and fiery poles,
Arranging, deepening, enchanting night.

Oh! Blessed rage for order, pale Ramon,
The maker's rage to order words of the sea,
Words of the fragrant portals, dimly-starred,
And of ourselves and of our origins,
In ghostlier demarcations, keener sounds.

(An address given in the winter of 1999 in Madison, Wisconsin, and
prepared for the final issue of *On The Way*, which was planned for 2000.
But the journal did not appear).

Gabriel Fackre

Report to the Lutheran Bishops on *A Common Calling*

Perhaps you saw the wire service story about *A Common Calling* the day it was released to the public. The Associated Press rightly sensed the potential significance of this document. In examining its importance and supporting its proposals, I will draw on an article I was asked to write for the first issue of *Pro Ecclesia*, the "evangelical catholic" journal recently launched by Carl Braaten and Robert Jenson. Needless to say, a second viewpoint, one that opposes its theses, will also appear. Incidentally, we have a friendly debate going on about who owns the label "evangelical catholicity." The phrase was brought to this country in the nineteenthth century by the German Reformed theologian, Philip Schaff, the mentor (with John Nevin) of the "Mercersburg theology," a movement that contributed greatly to nineteenth and twentieth century ecumenism. For Schaff there were three types of church: "the Church of Paul"—the Reformation Churches, "the Church of Peter"—the Roman Catholic Church, and "the Church of John," the unity and catholicity (John 17:21) of a Church yet to be. Schaff argued that the way to "the Church of John" cannot be by the route of a sectarian Protestantism that wants to overleap the Church of Peter to get back to pure New Testament origins, nor by a sectarian Catholicism that wants to overleap the Reformation Church of Paul. What we are attempting in *A Common Calling* is the solidifying of the Reformation stage of the journey so we can move forward in strength to the wider ecumenism of "the Church of John."

The refrain of *A Common Calling* is close to Luther's theme of "mutual conversation and consolation." In the document we advocate a confessional hermeneutic of "mutual affirmation and mutual admonition." That means a firm commitment to the truths of *one's* own tradition. For Lutherans, for example, justification by grace alone through faith alone. And beyond that, to admonish others that the Gospel is not the Gospel unless these affirmations are integral to it. But it also means openness to learnings in other areas from other ecclesial traditions, a "Corinthian catholicity." So the word of Paul to the factions in Corinth: "The eye cannot say to the hand, 'I have no need of you...'" (1 Corinthians 12:21) The Church is a Body with many parts, each needing other organs to be whole and healthy. Or to put it another way: We may be right in what we *affirm* but wrong in what we *deny*. A hermeneutic of "mutual affirmation" among Reformation Churches —the participants in the Lutheran-Reformed Conversation—means a readiness for the Reformed to learn from Lutherans that something might be missing or muted in their own tradition, and for Lutherans to learn from the Reformed that something might be missing or muted in their own.

Many have wondered why thirty years of dialogue on this continent has yet to produce an agreement among the central Reformation traditions on church fellowship. In 1973, European Lutheran and Reformed Churches achieved their landmark Leuenberg Agreement. Again after protracted study, my own Church (with its Lutheran and Reformed roots) entered into *Kirchengemeinschaft* in 1981 with the Evangelical Church of the Union in Europe. But, perhaps a tough-minded confessional hermeneutic of "mutual affirmation *and* mutual admonition" was worth waiting for.

Let me illustrate the principle of mutuality by examining a familiar distinction between Lutheran and Reformed perspectives, and do so with special reference to topics that our Lutheran-Reformed team was asked to address—aspects of Christology, the Eucharist and predestination. Our respective histories and emphases can be characterized by two Latin phrases: the Lutheran *finitum capex infiniti* and the Reformed "*finitum non capex infiniti.*" That is, Lutheran theology and piety stress God's *solidarity* with us: in the doctrine of the Incarnation the high God comes among us unambiguously in the human nature of Jesus, with an intimate exchange of attributes (the "*communicatio idiomatum*"). Or, again, in eucharistic teaching, Christ is "in, with, and under" the elements and action. Dietrich Bonhoeffer called this recurring accent the "haveability" of Jesus Christ. And he extended it in his *Letters and Papers from Prison* beyond the Church to the secular sphere, speaking about the divine presence and pathos there. As Christ is in solidarity with us in the Incarnation, as Calvary's "crucified God," as eucharistic Real Presence, so he comes to us in the pain of the "other" and calls us to "participate in the sufferings of God" in the world.

The Reformed tradition, on the other hand, while sharing with the Lutheran tradition all the *solas* in the controversy with the Roman Catholic Church, had its own accent: God's *sovereignty over* us. Every doctrine reflected this emphasis on the divine majesty and mystery, from the stress on the distinction of the human and divine natures, Calvin's teaching on the Real Presence as ascent by the power of the Spirit to the Son on the right hand of the Father, the rule of Christ over the world, and thus the Calvinist impulse to change the secular systems and structures.

Using this taxonomy of Lutheran "solidarity" and Reformed "sovereignty," one can also see what happens when each tradition tends to sound only its own distinctive note. A Reformed reductionism ends up with a Nestorian Christology, separating the natures, and sometimes allows the divine to stray so far up into the clouds that the human becomes the predominant focus—so the Unitarianism that grew out of New England Congregationalism; or a Zwinglian sacramentology that so distances God from the elements and action that the Eucharist is reduced to a memorial service; or an ethics that so stresses obedience in the secular realm to the rule of Christ that a theocracy eventuates, or the Church is turned into only a social action movement. And a Lutheran reductionism has shown its own clay feet: a high doctrine of the Person of Christ turns into a Monophysite Christology; an "in, with and under" sacramentology disqualifies all other formulations of the Real Presence; a *pro me* soteriology and law/gospel ethic becomes the interiorizaion of piety and allows tyrannical social systems to go unchallenged.

The way toward the fullness of faith is to have the witness of our brothers and sisters at hand. For our common Reformation churches this means mutual affirmation and admonition and the goal of *complementarity*. We *need* each other in the struggle to resist our reductionisms. The outworking of the principle of complementarity in *A Common Calling* takes place in the examination of our assigned controverted questions. For example, on pages 40ff. we address in detail five Lutheran and five Reformed themes with respect to the Eucharist, each acknowledging the other's legitimate worries, and recognizing that the historic formulations were important to secure concerns about both the divine solidarity and the divine sovereignty. Let each tradition continue to witness to these accents in its theologies, liturgies and practice, and admonish the other to listen and learn.

Predestination has been another sticking point. Mutuality and complementarity are at work here, as well, in *A Common Calling*. Consonant with its emphasis upon the divine mystery and majesty, predestination took on a much higher profile in Reformed circles. Hyper-Calvinists still frame the doctrine in scholastic categories that question Lutheran fidelity. But Karl Barth's restatement of election, current Calvin scholarship (noting, for example, the relocation of the topic in the last edition of the *Institutes* [1559] from the section on providence to the later section on subjective soteriology), and the negative experiences over time of a speculative reading, have all had their effects on Reformed theology, resulting not in the abandonment of the doctrine but in its reformulation. As such, a rapprochement is possible in which Luther's understanding of predestination appears as companion to Calvin's purposes.

A moment of insight into Lutheran-Reformed complementarity came when a Reformed member of the Conversation brought a tape of the July 17, 1988 selections of St. Olaf's "Sing for Joy" program focused on the lectionary reading, Ephesians 1:3-14, with exegesis by host Alvin Reuter. The music, the text, and the interpretation expressed the believer's personal assurance of divine grace and thus the Lutheran *pro me* appropriation of election. At the same time, the music, the scripture and the exegesis celebrated the power of God, ultimately, to fulfill the cosmic purposes of God, a Calvinist refrain. Predestination/election has to do with both trust in the divine solidarity with us and hope in the divine sovereignty beyond our ken. "He destined us for adoption as his children through Jesus Christ...." and "he made known to us...a plan for the fullness of time, to gather up all things in him, things in heaven and things on earth." (Ephesians 1:5,8,10) Failure to understand predestination as the believer's testimony to the comforts of the gospel can turn it into an awful decree of an inscrutable despot. But without grasping it as the Yes of the One "who's got the whole world in his hands," a pious introspection can obscure its awesome scope. With this doctrine, as with the Eucharist, Lutheran and Reformed traditions will retain their respective formulations and accents. Both point in the right direction and each places "no trespassing signs" on either side of the trail, warning of treacherous ground.

Catholicity and complimentarity, mutual affirmation and mutual admonition, have implications for other controverted questions. One of them is the matter of confessional identity.

As *A Common Calling* notes, confessions function differently in the two traditions. For Lutherans, definitive doctrine is sedimented in classical and Reformation symbols. The Reformed tradition also is grounded in the ecumenical creeds and has its own Reformation texts. However, it holds it necessary to continue to articulate the gospel in fresh ways, and so adds new statements of faith to its corpus of teaching.

Once, again, the *finitum capex/finitum non capex* distinction appears to be at work. On the one hand is the Lutheran trust in the promises secured by durable tangibilities. On the other is the Reformed stress on God's freedom from our securities with its fighting word "*semper reformanda*." And their corresponding admonitions: Let the Reformed beware of captivity to every new circumstance and wind of doctrine! Let Lutherans be attentive to the fresh breezes of the sovereign Spirit!

The presence of the United Church of Christ in the conversation poses sharply both the problems and possibilities of the Reformed impulse. It is a case study in the determined commitment to the divine sovereignty with regard to the Lordship of Christ over the public arena and openness to the movement of the Spirit. Does the Reformed vision, here, finally lead to only a "social action church" with little theological substance, no common confessional identity, ever ready to accommodate to the *Zeitgeist*? The long footnote in *A Common Calling* on the UCC (by this author) challenges these caricatures, while acknowledging the susceptibility to reductionism in a Church shaped in its early years by the systemic challenges of the 1960s as well as by its pilgrim forebear John Robinson's counsel to attend to the "ever-new light and truth that breaks forth from God's holy Word." But UCC history and tradition have simply exposed it earlier than most North American denominations to the "culture wars" found now in the ranks of its Lutheran and Reformed companions, and beyond. As such, it has been a laboratory for learning how to live at the juncture of text and context. A result has been a remarkable theological ferment, one that includes re-entry of its confessional heritage and retrieval of its evangelical catholic (Nevin and Schaff) lineage. *Semper reformanda* is always under the sovereign Word, who ever and again calls it to re-form according to that Light alone.

We are at a critical juncture in ecumenical relations today. And as a systematic theologian, I would say the same is true in the "neo-tribalism' run strong - a zeal to retreat into one's own enclave, to keep company only with those of a like mind or like history. This can take the form of a hermeneutics of suspicion of any one who has a different social location than our own: only those with *this* epistemological privilege have access to the truth. Or tribalism can take a denominational or perspectival form. Many of the new systematics being written today—and there has been a great outpouring in this genre in the last several years—are Roman Catholic, Reformed, Lutheran, Nazarene, Methodist, charismatic, evangelical, liberation, and pluralist, with little conversation with other points of view. The return to denominational roots, the recovery of our theological memories after a period of amnesia is very salutary. But it can degenerate into a balkanizing of theology and the church, a retreat into our own tribes—all this with a striking resemblance to the political and social balkanization current in parts of Europe, and in North American society, as well.

The alternative to ecclesial tribalism is Paul's Corinthian catholicity. Faithfulness to one's own heritage does not require disdain of another's. With its hermeneutic of mutual affirmation and mutual admonition, *A Common Calling* advocates a kind *koinonia* that could make Lutheran-Reformed dialogue in our country a microcosm of larger ecumenical possibilities. In this proposal, "the Church of Paul" draws upon his Corinthian catholicity, one that honors the particularities yet welcomes mutual fructification (1 Corinthians 12-13), and so sets us on the path toward the more ultimate evangelical catholicity of "the Church of John."

(This "Report" to the bishops of the Evangelical Lutheran Church in America presents the author's reflections as one of several representatives from the United Church of Christ to the Lutheran-Reformed discussions that resulted in the historic "Formula of Agreement" between Lutheran and Reformed traditions in the United States as the twentieth century was drawing to a close).

Frederick R. Trost

Your Blessing, Please

The Porter of the Monastery

At the door of the monastery, place a sensible person who knows how to take a message and deliver a reply, and whose wisdom keeps them from roaming about. This porter will need a room near the entrance so that visitors will always find someone there to answer them. As soon as anyone knocks or a poor person calls out, the porter will reply, 'Thanks be to God' or 'Your blessing, please,' then, with all the gentleness that comes from reverence of God, provide a prompt answer with the warmth of love. Let the porter be given one of the younger members if help is needed. (Chapter 66 of *The Rule of Benedict*, devoted to "The Porter of the Monastery").

In her commentary this chapter, Joan Chittister has written:

Of all the questions to be asked about the nearly fifteen-hundred-year-old Rule of Benedict... one of the most pointed must surely be why one of the great spiritual documents of the Western world would have in it a chapter on how to answer the door. And one of the answers might be that answering the door is one of the arch-activities of Benedictine life. The way we answer doors is the way we deal with the world...

When the person knocks—whenever the person knocks—the porter is to say, 'Thanks be to God' or 'Your blessing, please,' to indicate the gift the guest is to the community... In the Rule of Benedict, there is no such thing as coming out of time to the monastery. Come in the middle of lunch; come in the middle of prayer; come and bother us with your blessings at any time. There is always someone waiting for you (Joan Chittister, *The Rule of Benedict: Insights for the Ages*, (169-170).

I learned something of this lesson years ago while serving as a pastor in the inner city of Chicago. In those days, we always opened the door to strangers. Many of our guests were strangers who would walk into the church from the street in search of bread or perhaps for an opportunity to take a shower. It was my discipline as a pastor in those days to attempt to study in the morning. Although the door to the church was open, I often kept the door to my study closed, believing in that way I could concentrate better on the book I was reading or the sermon I was writing. Invariably, however, there would be a knock at the door. I was frequently tempted not to answer the knock at the door, preferring instead to continue reading or writing. And yet, invariably I would open the door. Standing there, almost always, would be two ragged friends of mine, Jack and Don, "street people" who I got to know well over the years.

I was young and fresh out of seminary. Initially, I considered Jack and Don to be a nuisance. Were they not an intrusion on my daily discipline? Yet they would not be deterred. They kept knocking on the study door. And I kept opening the door. It took time, some months actually, but eventually I came to understand them and the other "street people" who followed them. I came to welcome them as among God's surprises. I did not ask them for their blessing and their visits did not elicit in me the words "Thanks be to God," but eventually I came to understand them as among God's gifts in my life and in the life of the congregation.

I remember how perturbed I was initially by the sound of a knock at the door. It was so annoying that I went to the members of the Church Council and complained, saying, "We've got to do something." One of the Council members, a distinguished looking German-speaking man, a house-painter who ever y year varnished the doors of the church as his gift to the congregation, said to me: "Have you ever considered, dear pastor, that the ones who are knocking at the door may be sent by God?" I had read the theology of Karl Barth. I had attended the lectures of Gerhard von Rad. I knew something of Reinhold Niebuhr. But the thought had not crossed my mind. "Have you ever considered, dear pastor, that the ones who are knocking at the door may be sent by God?"

Years later, after the congregation I was serving had helped begin a food program in our part of the city, I introduced Jack and Don in one of our worship services as the true founders of that project, which, it is said, during a period of about fifteen years, served over a million meals to "street people." It all began with a knock at the door.

"Welcome one another,..." St. Paul writes in Romans, "as Christ has welcomed you, for the glory of God." (Romans 15:7)

It impresses me that invariably among the brothers and sisters who live in accord with the Rule of Benedict, those of us who come and knock upon the door are welcomed. There is no "show" of hospitality. It does not seem to be contrived. It simply happens. We do not think of ourselves as a "blessing" or a "surprise" sent by God. Yet in this way we are received. I remember while still a pastor in Chicago going to a convent in our neighborhood to study. I would enter the vestibule and there, hanging from the wall, were written the words: "When a stranger comes, Christ comes."

"Your blessing, please." Like so much else in the Rule, those words turn the ways of the world upside down. To ask for a blessing from a stranger; to imagine that a stranger we do not know has a blessing to give; this is unusual in secular culture. But it is the way of Benedict. To ask for a blessing, to invite a blessing, to seek a blessing: is there not a gentleness here (and a humility) that reflects something of the way of Jesus? This is different than demanding a blessing, or requiring something before the door is opened to a stranger. There is an expectation here, and anticipation; faith that the knock at the door is related to the presence, providence and grace of God.

Perhaps you recall from the days when you were a child, seeing the famous painting by Holman Hunt that, at least among Protestants, hung in many Sunday School buildings. Do you remember it; a portrait of Jesus, knocking at the door of a humble cottage? (The original painting, incidentally, was donated to Keble College at Oxford by the widow of Thomas Combe, Printer to the University, on the understanding it would hang in the chapel. But the architect of the chapel made no provision for it in his design. So the painting originally hung not in the chapel, but in the library where it remained until 1892, when it was included in the side chapel by another architect, Thomas Micklethwaite. He had no misgivings about the painting, and made it part of his design. It is said that Holman Hunt, the painter< was so troubled by the treatment "Jesus knocking at the door" initially received at Oxford, that he painted a "duplicate" which hangs to this day in St. Paul's Cathedral in London. There, it has probably become better known than the original in Oxford.)

"Listen! I am standing at the door, knocking; if you hear my voice and open the door, I will come in to you and eat with you, and you with me." (cf. Revelation 3:20) If you were to take a close look at the famous painting by Holman Hunt, you would see there is no handle on the outside of the door. There is no possibility of a forced entry. The door is not opened from the outside. Such is the humble nature of the Creator of heaven and earth. The door can only be opened from the inside. May this reflect the fact that there is a sense, biblically, in which Jesus remains an outsider, an outcast,… a surprise to us, even in the resurrection narratives,… present in ordinary places, yet appearing too at the margins of life, coming to us from a place beyond ourselves... but daily knocking, seeking, asking,... accompanying us,... inviting our discipleship and welcome? "As soon as anyone knocks or a poor person calls out, the porter will reply, 'Thanks be to God' or 'Your blessing, please...'"

There is a story told about a humble man who lived amidst poverty. He had little to eat. His clothes were patched. The walls of his house were broken. One night, he had a dream about a fabulous treasure buried under a bridge in a far off place. Three times the dream occurred to him. At last, he set out to find the treasure. After several weeks on foot, he came to the bridge. It was guarded by soldiers. He did not approach the bridge, but each day he would look at the bridge from a distance. Finally, the captain of the guard came up to the poor man and asked what he was doing there. He told the captain the dream that had brought him from a far country.

When the captain heard the poor man's story, he laughed and said that he too had a dream. In his dream, a treasure was buried under the stove in the floor of the poor man's house. The poor man was bewildered. He hurried home and began to dig beneath the stove. To his amazement, he discovered that the treasure he had walked around the world to find was hidden under his nose.

I wonder sometimes if the truth buried in this story does not reflect the life of the Church, or at least parts of it in our time? I remember how impressed I was when two Benedictine sisters responded to an appeal to open the door of their little community to a family of refugees from the civil wars raging in Central America. There was welcome. The family was received and treated almost as if it was Jesus knocking at the door. The sisters brought the Church's words and deeds together. And as they did so, some of us gained a glimpse of the authenticity of the gospel. The simple gift of welcome, of open arms, opening the door from within the community of faith, making a place at the table for the stranger: surely this is an expression of the good news we hear about in sermons.

It has been my experience that the Church often struggles with the meaning of its life. We wonder how we might be authentically present in this world. We make big plans, we offer great speeches, we hint at bold truths. Some of us think how critical it is to keep up with other institutions, to be affirmed by the society in which God has placed us. We borrow from the world various schemes that ache for achievement or success. We beat loud drums. We turn on neon signs that blink off and on, telling of the "product" we have to offer. One is simply appalled by some of this, particularly when one catches a glimpse of it on television. The Church... attempting to say things that make it appear important or accommodating itself to what it believes is a road that may lead to recognition, attention, acceptance. But the Church's treasure is often buried deep within its own life; present but neglected or forgotten right there, in the kitchen, under the stove. The treasure is the basic, simple, plain gift of authenticity; offering hospitality and welcome as Christ has done to whoever may come knocking upon the door.

The mark of authentic congregational life is not the greatness of our preaching, the beauty of the stained glass, the brilliance of a pastor, the size of the parking lot, the height of the steeple, the number of people on the roles or their influence in the community. May authenticity not have something to do, rather, with the gift of being able to hear the knock upon the door? Or with the humility of someone in the community who whispers to the stranger... "Your blessing, please!"

Hospitality: Dietrich Bonhoeffer spoke of this in a lesson his students at the underground seminary at Finkenwalde could never forget. He taught that whether the Church that professes to be the Church of Jesus Christ is really the Church depends on how it answers the knock at the door. Its integrity, he believed in the midst of the 1930s, was dependent on its being present,... opening the door,... for the Jews. (cf. Larry Rasmussen, *Dietrich Bonhoeffer, Reality and Resistance*, 37) "The service of the Church has to be given to those who suffer violence and injustice," he wrote. "... the Church takes to itself all the sufferers, all the forsaken of every party and of every status... Here the decision will really be made whether we are still the Church of the present Christ. The Jewish question." (see, Bonhoeffer, "The Interpretation of the New Testament" in *No Rusty Swords*, 325, August, 1935).

Bonhoeffer, you may remember, was intrigued by monastic communities in England during his stay in London from 1933 to 1935. These communities influenced the shape of the daily spiritual exercises at Finkenwalde, including the morning and evening prayers that became an integral part of the training of pastors for the "Confessing Church." Bonhoeffer came to believe that Jesus is more than an historical figure, an inspiration that wondrously guides the life of a Christian. He affirmed the "real presence" of Christ. He spoke of the living Christ who is "encountered again and again at every juncture of personal and social life... In the compelling meeting with him, most often through other persons, one taps the source for the direction of action. Ethics is done in communion with Christ and one's neighbor." Bonhoeffer called this "*koinonia* ethics"—the fitting response to "the knock at the door." (Interestingly, Bonhoeffer worked on the outline, notes, and writing of what became his famous book called *Ethics* at the Benedictine monastery on the slopes at Ettal in Bavaria, where, it is said, he "was commended... to the care of Father Johannes,... (who) looked after everything necessary, (and) was aware of the underlying circumstances..." (see Eberhard Bethge, *Dietrich Bonhoeffer: A Biography*, Revised Edition, 701). By this time as he was welcomed at Ettal, Bonhoeffer had joined the conspiracy and was already being monitored by the Gestapo.

Bonhoeffer asked the question "Who is Christ for us today?" Who stands at the door and knocks? Who seeks entry into our lives? Who comes in search of hospitality and welcome? So the knock at the door to which the porter responds, or surely any one of us, invariably presents an opportunity to confess what it is that we believe. "The transcendental," Bonhoeffer wrote, "is not infinite and unattainable tasks, but the neighbor who is within reach in any given situation. God in human form,..." The Church, the body of Christ, is the community of those who "live for others." The Church is the Church, he wrote, "only when it is there for others." And so we are back to the knock at the door (see Bonhoeffer's "Outline for a Book" in *Letters and Papers from Prison*). For Dietrich Bonhoeffer, deeply influenced, I believe, by monastic thought, communion with God "is not a 'religious' relationship to the highest, most powerful, and best Being imaginable - that is not authentic transcendence - but our relation to God is a new life in 'existence for others,' through participation in the being of Jesus." (see Rasmussen, *Dietrich Bonhoeffer: Reality and Resistance*, 21).

In chapter 66 of *The Rule* we are given, in the person of the porter, an illustration of what it means to be present "for others." To care about the door, to listen for a knock at the door, to open the door, to utter words of welcome or a silent embrace of the one who stands at the door, is, while the most humble and simple of tasks, to experience transcendence. In opening the door to the stranger and welcoming him or her, the porter reflects transcendence; the very being of "the One for others." It is the vocation of the porter of the door in chapter 66 to conform to Christ in the act of welcoming the stranger and in so doing to participate in the very life of Christ. Thus, St. Paul can write to the Christian community in Rome: "Welcome one another, therefore, just as Christ has welcomed you, for the glory of God."

We are living in a time when we lock our doors. We guard our borders. We protect our way of life, often protecting or concealing what is most precious to us, lest "the stranger" come and take it away. We in the Church struggle with our circumstances, sometimes hiding from the world around us, afraid of who might seek entry into our life. We sometimes grow fearful of the knock at the door, and thus lose sight of our vocation and the costly joy of discipleship. There is a need in the Church in North America to think humbly and a little more consistently, less about our survival and more about offering welcome. Might we then become more willing, prayerfully, to take risks? May it be that the One who stands at the door and knocks today is the bearer of a message to the faithful… summoning us to a fresh life in which the idols of our time are challenged, the callousness of our time is softened, the despair of our time emptied? Were we to respond to that knock and open the door, might we be surprised to discover again that God is always seeking to challenge the soul of the Church to follow a radical Gospel of "presence" amidst "the troubles of the world?"

It is well that the Church reflects upon welcome, upon hospitality (or the absence thereof) in this world at this time. For at the moment, we are called to bear our faith amidst a society that is not particularly welcoming. We are witnesses to the dismantling of the courtesies of a civil community. We observe, ominously, the erosion of basic elements that contribute to a humane public life. There is a deepening anger towards "outsiders" that challenges and compromises not only the confession of the Church, but also the foundation of democracy in our country. *The Rule of Benedict* contradicts these dangers, opens doors, offers an alternative way for people of faith to be "present" in this world.

May people who dare to open the door to those who knock in search of bread or shelter or acceptance or welcome from storms that are raging beyond our sanctuaries have listened, at one time or another, with special care, to the teachings of Jesus, who touched the leper, welcomed the tax collector, conversed with the woman at the well? May the porter also know something, at least, of the prophets of old? Is it not true that, like the prophets, the porters and door keepers of our time are not strangers to the burdens people bear, the wounds people carry, the tears that flood the earth, the sorrows that separate the nations, the cruelties that accompany the sun on its course through each day of the year, or the crucifixion of the divine in daily life? May this not be a reason our hearts leap for joy when they appear in our midst?

According to the great biblical scholar, Abraham Joshua Heschel, "the frankincense of charity fails to sweeten cruelties" or the "secret obscenities of the sheer unfairness of life." The porter, as the prophet, by his very station near the door, is aware of this. He or she "perceives the silent sigh" that is so often present at our doorsteps. Who are they who can be heard knocking today and again tomorrow? May they include in our time the prisoners held in seclusion by our government in Cuba, stripped of the rights we say we wish to preserve in our many proud and glowing homilies about the glories of democracy? May they be the mothers who search desperately for their little children amidst the demolitions taking place at Rafah, in those scandalous variations on a theme repeated off and on in Palestinian refugee camps for nearly fifty years? "Your blessing, please!" Do the faithful consider for long the possibility that the gay couple seeking welcome at the Lord's Table without having to endure the scorn of the "people of God" may have a gift to bring to our sometimes proud, self-righteous communities? And what of those who bleed profusely and perish daily as a result of "the arrogance of power?"

A friend of mine asked me, as I was preparing this essay, if the temptation of Christians to ignore the knock at the door might stem from our resistance to the idea of "vulnerability" which, he pointed out, means a fear of being wounded for Christ's sake... May the suspicion of those who are unlike ourselves be a reflection of our own reluctance to risk receiving God's welcome, because it might mean having to give up our securities or at least to examine our prejudices and the self-righteous anger that sometimes scrapes against our pieties? Such are the impediments in church life that sometimes keep us from daring to risk the possibility of receiving a blessing as, according to "the Rule," the porter does each time he or she responds to the knock upon the door. Where are the porters today?

"We wish this rule to be read often," Joan Chittister observes of the Rule of Benedict, so that "the monastic never forgets that the role of committed Christians is always to grow richer themselves so that they can give richly to others." She goes on to tell a story told by Abba Cassian, a desert monastic, who said... "Once upon a time, we two monks visited an elder. Because he offered us hospitality we asked him, 'Why do you not keep the rule of fasting when you receive visiting brothers?' And the old monastic answered, 'Fasting is always at hand but you I cannot have with me always. Furthermore, fasting is certainly a useful and necessary thing, but it depends on our choice, while the law of God lays it upon us to do the works of charity. Thus, receiving Christ in you, I ought to serve you with all diligence, but when I have taken leave of you, I can resume the rule of fasting again.'" She concludes: "The person with a monastic heart knows that the Christ and salvation are not found in religious (disciplines) alone. They are in the other, our response to whom is infinitely more important than our religious exercises." (Chittister, *The Rule of Benedict: Insights for the Ages*, 171).

As Bonhoeffer would say... a life of prayer and the deed!

(An address given to the Ecumenical Board of the Sisters of St. Benedict, Madison, Wisconsin in 2004)